WALKING IN BRITAIN

WALKING IN BRITAIN

SUE SEDDON

WITH A FOREWORD BY
MIKE HARDING

WARD LOCK LIMITED · LONDON

• ACKNOWLEDGEMENTS •

The publishers are grateful to the following people and companies for kindly granting permission to include the following photographs: 'Britain on View' (ETA/BTA) (pages 53, 97, 156/7, 164, 165 (top), 175); John Heseltine (pages 49, 50/1, 54, 63, 64, 65, 117, 118/9, 121, 122, 185, 189, 190); Tim Hughes (pages 12, 14, 18/19, 21, 22/3, 26, 29, 30/1, 34, 35, 39, 40/1, 44, 46, 57, 61, 67, 68/9, 101, 105, 107, 111, 125, 129, 130/1, 143, 144, 148, 151, 161, 163, 165 (below), 169, 170, 172/3, 181); Landscape Only (113, 133, 135, 139, 141, 153, 178) and David Ward (pages 2/3, 8/9, 72/3, 74/5, 78, 80, 83, 85, 87, 88, 92/3, 95, 98/9).

All maps drawn by Peter Bull Art.
All line illustrations drawn by Ann Winterbotham, except the Youth Hostel illustrations which are reproduced with permission of the YHA.

The walks in this book were researched on behalf of the YHA by a number of people, and co-ordinated by John Richards.

First published in Great Britain in 1989
by Ward Lock Limited, 8 Clifford Street
London W1X 1RB, an Egmont Company

Designed by David Robinson
Text set in Linotron 202 Rockwell Light
by Fakenham Photosetting Limited,
Fakenham, Norfolk
Printed in Italy

British Library Cataloguing in Publication Data

Seddon, Sue
    YHA: walking in Britain
    1. Great Britain, – Visitor's guides
    I. Title
    914.1'04858

    ISBN 0–7063–6537–2

Previous page: *Pen-y-ghent from near Hull Pot.*

CONTENTS

FOREWORD

When I was a kid in the back streets of Manchester, 'holidays' were either a day trip to Blackpool or a day out walking on the moors above Oldham and Rochdale. Buses took us up onto the heights of Blackstone Edge, along the great cleft of Hardcastle Crags and over the wild moors above Howarth. I much preferred the moors to Blackpool and over the years grew to know and love them, so much in fact that I often played 'wag' from school just to walk on the seemingly boundless heights of the tops.

On one memorable occasion later in life I was standing at a bus stop on a summer morning waiting for a bus to take me to work in a mill where I was working as a fitter erecting storage shelves. It was a particularly beautiful morning, the early sun just warming the day from a cloudless sky and the red bricks of the streets glowing in the early light. In the far distance I could just see the Pennines – faint, hazy and purple – rolling away to infinity. When the bus came I let it go past, crossed the road and took the bus in the opposite direction into the hills and spent the day walking in the heather and lying by moorland streams listening to larks singing overhead. I got into trouble, of course, but it was worth it for a day of freedom. I'm afraid I have always had a feckless attitude to life and find it very difficult to take work and figures of authority seriously. There's a Brazilian proverb that goes 'If work is all that good, why haven't the rich kept it all to themselves?'

So what has all this to do with the YHA and walking? Well basically the YHA aided and abetted me in my many days of freedom. I travelled the Dales, the Peaks and the Lake District on my bike, staying at Hostels and walking on the hills and moors when I should have been doing more serious things like 'getting a proper job' and 'studying hard'. Youth really was far too precious to waste any of it.

Now there's a book on walking in Britain that will help you to escape from the stresses and strains of the daily grind. Not only will you find routes that will take you up onto the tops and along by the rivers, you will also hear the stories of the murdered lovers of Winnats Pass and be able to find your way to the Chapel of the mother of the patron saint of Wales. Not only is this book full of good routes, it also fleshes them out with the bits of gossip and tittle tattle that make walking all the more enjoyable. Enjoy the book but most of all enjoy your walking.

PS: If I can put in a plea for that much maligned man the hill farmer – please don't ever let your dog chase stock and always walk single file through a hay meadow. You wouldn't believe the number of idiots I have seen, cutting a swathe eight walkers' wide across a good hay meadow.

Mike Harding

Wassdale Head from Westmorland Cairn on Great Gable.

INTRODUCTION

Youth Hostels provide a truly unique base for walking and they buzz with social activity. Those featured in this book vary from a seventeenth-century manor house and a medieval castle, to a remote converted farmhouse. Each has its very own character and charm and all offer comfortable accommodation and the warmest of welcomes at the end of an action-packed day.

Walkers have been using Youth Hostels as a base from which to explore the countryside since the YHA was first established in 1930. Accommodation is offered at excellent value throughout England and Wales with a network of 270 Youth Hostels in towns, villages, National Parks, in remote countryside, at the seaside and on long distance footpaths. In fact the variety of location means that you can stay almost anywhere.

The YHA is a membership association, with over 280,000 members, and more than 2 million overnights are spent each year in the Hostels. There are similar organisations in more than 50 countries worldwide – between them, they run more than 5000 Youth Hostels, constituting the largest travel organisation in the world. If you are not a member of the YHA, the introductory guest pass available from Hostels means you can still take advantage of them. However, membership is cheap and incorporates travel and many other benefits, so it is a worthwhile investment if you plan to spend more than a couple of nights in Hostels. There is no upper age limit to using the Hostels in Britain, and young people can stay alone from the age of twelve, or from five if part of a group or family.

The YHA was begun 'to help all, especially young people of limited means, to a greater knowledge, love and care of the countryside, particularly by providing hostels or other simple accommodation for them in their travels; and thus promoting their health, rest and education.' The need for budget accommodation in the countryside is still just as great as it was in the 1930s, but today's image of the YHA is not the same as its original, somewhat spartan, one.

Each Youth Hostel has its own character and charm, and the facilities in Hostels vary too. They all provide accommodation in bunk beds within single sex dormitories or family rooms. Bedding is also provided, but you do need to hire or bring your own sheet sleeping bag, or two sheets and a pillowcase if you prefer. Communal washing facilities, showers and toilets are usually separate from sleeping accommodation. You can expect a good drying room at most Hostels, and at larger city

Stepping stones at Egdon bridge in North Yorkshire.

Hostels there may be laundry facilities.

All permanent Hostels provide self-catering facilities and usually have a shop selling basic necessities, so thankfully you do not have to carry heavy food with you. In all but the smallest and simplest of Hostels you can alternatively opt for meals prepared by the Warden, providing excellent value for money – there is normally a vegetarian option too. Many walkers on a tight budget decide to mix self-catering with one good meal a day; the packed lunch is also well worth taking if you plan to be far from civilisation in the middle of the day.

To keep costs down, guests are asked to help with light housekeeping tasks, such as washing up or sweeping the floor. Oddly enough this is a great way of meeting others using the Hostel as everyone mucks in together. Many a bit of vital route information, from a good pub along the way to a treacherous, lurking bog is exchanged over the washing up.

Most Hostels are closed for a period during the day, although wet weather shelter is often available. They also close their doors for the night between 11 pm and 7 am. Remember, too, that it is important to book Youth Hostels in advance, as they can get very busy, especially during the spring and summer and at weekends. Telephone or write to the Hostel(s) to make the reservations. Also book your meals in advance if needed and clearly state whether you require a male or female bed! If you want a family room it is essential to book these in advance where they are available as they are limited in number. Almost all Youth Hostels will take a credit card booking by telephone, but it might be difficult to get an answer between 10 am and 5 pm when the Hostels are closed.

Nearly all of the Hostels have car parking close by, if not actually at the Hostel, and many can accommodate your car while you enjoy the rest of the week on foot. It is advisable to check with the Warden when booking. Gone are the days when you had to leave the car a mile up the lane to arrive at the Youth Hostel on foot. Many of the routes featured here have been planned to bring you back to the starting point, and those that are linear rather than circular are mostly well served by public transport.

Although the YHA gives as much up-to-date information as possible on public transport, together with all other details about the Youth Hostels in England and Wales, in its annual *Guide*, you should always check services before setting out. (*The YHA Accommodation Guide* is sold through bookshops or given free when you join the YHA.) As far as the routes in this book are concerned, information for all the Hostels referred to in the text is given in the appendix at the back.

The routes have been carefully selected to introduce the walker to a range of different scenic areas in Britain, covering some of the most beautiful parts of the Lake District, Yorkshire Dales, Snowdonia, the south-west peninsula and the South Downs Way, to name but a few. They also include some of the most dramatically situated Youth Hostels in the British Isles such as Ravenstor Hostel backing onto the River Wye in the Peak District or Once Brewed close to Hadrian's Wall. There are many inter-Hostel walking routes in existence throughout the countryside and once you have walked some of the ones planned in this book perhaps you may be tempted to create your own inter-Hostel routes. All you need to do is arm yourself with a *YHA Accommodation Guide* and an Ordnance Survey map or two.

Although sections of each route can be walked as a day walk, they have been specifically planned to introduce the walker to the enjoyment of longer walks, over several days taking in overnight stops. They have also been planned to give you a feel for an area. For example the Devon Hills and Dartmoor week-long walk takes you across fields and moors, covering inland hills and coastal paths, with suggestions for visiting such sights as the Dart Valley Railway and Dartington Hall.

Both weekend and week-long routes are included. Novice walkers might consider allowing for a rest-day or pack-free excursion, suggestions for which are included in the longer routes. Within each route points of interest are also noted which might warrant extra time for investigation. The Lake District walk around Windermere and Ullswater is essentially a four-day walk but with the suggested pack-free days in Grasmere and Patterdale and taking in Townend House at Troutbeck, the walk becomes a delightful week-long discovery of the central Lake District.

The routes have been planned to appeal to a range of walking abilities, too. The weekends are particularly suitable for those with less experience. The distance and terrain covered is noted at the start of each walk. So, for instance, you can choose from a strenuous weekend in Llangollen covering 30½ miles (49km) of rugged terrain or a quieter 25-mile (40km) walk among the forests and marshes of Suffolk. Or how about tackling Yorkshire's three peaks (90 miles, 144km) in seven days, and 104 miles (167.5km) of the Pembrokeshire coastal path in six?

It is, of course, essential to always wear and take the right equipment when walking. Well worn-in walking boots with cleated composition soles and good ankle support are essential to your enjoyment of any walking tour. Smooth soled shoes without ankle support will be uncomfortable and should be avoided.

Because the British climate is unpredictable and temperatures can be radically affected by changes in altitude, you should always wear or carry clothing and equipment for the worst conditions you might expect to encounter. At the very least your clothing should include: a woollen sweater, a waterproof and windproof cagoul, a hood or woollen hat, gloves, a full change of clothing and light shoes for wearing indoors. When using Youth Hostels, you also need to remember to take a towel.

Maps and a compass are also essential to a hill walker. Take 1:50,000 or 1:25,000 Ordnance Survey maps for the area you intend to cover. Learn to read them and use your compass.

Naturally it is a big mistake to overload your rucksack. What seemed a good idea to take on day one can be a definite liability by day three. Use a framed rucksack that is comfortable, and take only the minimum you need. You should always carry a small emergency supply of high energy food, like dried fruit, mint cake or chocolate, in addition to your normal requirements for that day. A large plastic bin bag to keep clothes dry can double up as a survival bag in an emergency.

When walking in remote areas a proper survival bag should be carried, together with a whistle for summoning emergency help. The recognised emergency signal is six blasts repeated at minute intervals. A wise precaution is to always make sure someone knows your intended route and what to do if you do not arrive at your destination. (Full information on all these aspects of walking is included in the appendix at the end of the book.)

One final note. Footpaths do change from time to time and although to the best of our knowledge the directions for the walks in this book were accurate at the time of going to press, an up-to-date Ordnance Survey map should be used in conjunction with the routes described.

Happy walking!

• LAKE DISTRICT •

WINDERMERE TO AMBLESIDE

• VIA HAWKSHEAD, CONISTON AND HIGH CLOSE •

This walk is an excellent introduction to the Lake District and covers woodland, lakes and fells in one of the most picturesque areas to be found in Britain.
(26½ miles, 42.5km)

• DAY ONE •

Windermere to Hawkshead (10 miles, 16km)

This is the longest walk in terms of miles, but the going is comfortable and there is not much climbing by Lake District standards. The walk has a delightful start – you cross the lake by ferry from Bowness.

Turn R out of the Hostel and walk downhill to the Troutbeck Bridge. Turn L onto the A592 then R after ¼ mile (400m), and head for Bowness and the ferry across Windermere. The first mention of a ferry across the lake was in 1454. The earliest were rowing boats; today the ferries are mostly diesel.

Once you reach the other side of the lake continue on the road to the signpost for Sawrey, Hawkshead and Coniston. Turn R along the minor road which runs along the west shore of Winder-

mere. Continue along the road for about a mile (1.5km) and then enter the woods on your L over a cattle grid. Turn L onto a pleasant path which doubles back and ascends the woods diagonally. When you reach the top of the hill follow the path through a gate onto a lane. Stay on the lane until it turns sharp R (signposted to Hawkshead). Do not turn R but go straight ahead onto the footpath through the fields, signposted to Sawrey. A path descends to the B5285 at Far Sawrey. Turn R onto the road and walk to Near Sawrey.

You may think that this is a quiet Lakeland village, don't be fooled. Tom Kitten, Jemima Puddleduck, Pigling Bland and other such characters draw more than 70,000 visitors a year to the rather ordinary farmhouse where they were born. Hilltop was once the home of Beatrix Potter, the writer and illustrator of children's books.

Walk through the village and turn L down the hill, signposted Lakeside. Follow the road overlooking Esthwaite Lake and on to Hawkshead Youth Hostel, Esthwaite Lodge, which is on this road, about 1½ miles (2.5km) from Near Sawrey.

Previous page: *Windermere from the Bowness Ferry.*
Below: *Tarn Hows.*

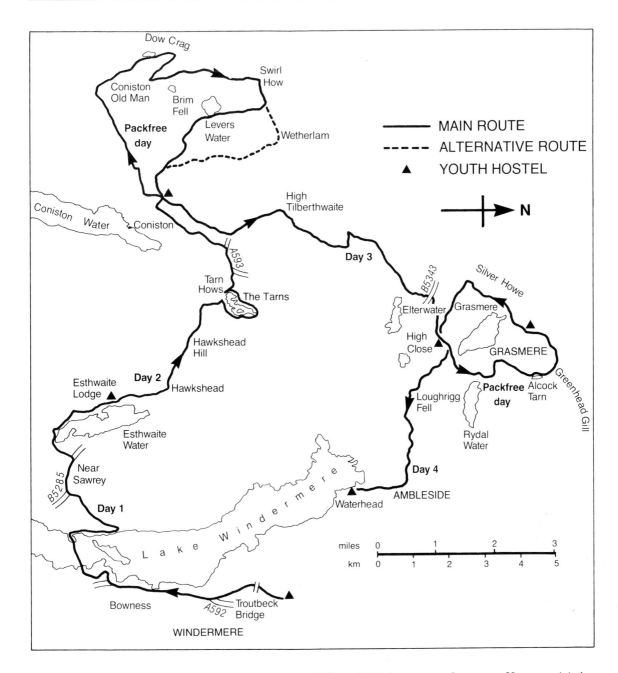

• DAY TWO •

Hawkshead to Coniston, (6½ miles, 10.5km)

Today's walk is mostly on minor roads and foot-paths, so it is an easy day.

Turn L on leaving the hostel and walk to Hawks-head. The village was Wordsworth's home from the age of 9 until he was 19 and still thrives on the tourism his name brings. It's a delightful example of a Lakeland village and it's well worth exploring

the cobbled streets and squares. You can visit the grammar school where Wordsworth was a pupil and see his very desk.

At the top of the second square, opposite the Red Lion, is an archway. Follow the road through this, past Ann Tyson's cottage where Wordsworth boarded and was lovingly cared for through his school and university days. Walk up the lane, then take a footpath on the R, signposted to Hawkshead Hill. Continue along the path to

Hawkshead Hill. Turn L onto the B5285 and then take the first R which goes to Tarn Hows. Then take the next L and then R on a minor road to Tarn Hows (The Tarns on OS maps).

Tarn Hows is one of the most famous beauty spots in the Lakes. It is very beautiful; the views are marvellous. It's almost too perfect to be real and in fact the tarn is man-made, created by damming a stream in the nineteenth century. It's hell during holiday periods when, to judge by the number of cars and visitors, you'd think it was the only open space for thousands of miles. True to the herding instinct of genuine tourists, few of them explore the many paths around the tarn, and the low hills to the north-west are often deserted, so take your time and you'll be well rewarded if you leave the main paths to the car drivers.

If you leave the tarn by the path to the R of the outflow it will take you down through pleasant woods to the A593. Turn L and after ½ mile (800m) turn L again onto a footpath through fields to Coniston. After crossing a bridge over a stream turn R to cross the main road to Coniston Holly How, the next Hostel.

• DAY THREE •

Coniston to High Close (6 miles, 9.5km)

Today is an easy day, walking on lanes all the way. Leave the Hostel and turn L onto the Ambleside road (A593). Walk along the road for about ¼ mile (400m) and then take the footpath through the woods on your L. The path runs parallel with the main road and avoids too much road walking. Return to the main road after about 1 mile (1.5km) and after a few yards turn L onto the minor road to Tilberthwaite.

Continue along the minor road until you reach High Tilberthwaite, about 1½ miles (2.5km) away. The Tilberthwaite area shows how well an old quarrying district can recover. The scars have been softened to an exciting and rather beautiful landscape. Where the road ends, at High Tilberthwaite, follow the footpath on the R through woods until you come to a stream with a ford and a footbridge. Do not cross the stream but turn L along a track beside it. After about 300 yards (250m) a stile gives access into a field on the R. Go over the stile and cross the field to the stream. A superb little bridge, known as Slater's

Bridge, spans the stream. Cross the stream by this perfect example of a slate bridge. The footpath continues up the field into a farm lane which joins a minor road. Turn L at the minor road and then R almost immediately into a small lane which leads to Elterwater. Continue past the Elterwater Youth Hostel and the Britannia Inn (although, if you have time, it is a nice old inn and worth a stop) until you reach the B5343 to Langdale. Cross this and turn L, then R into a minor road which leads to High Close Hostel.

• DAY FOUR •

High Close to Ambleside (4 miles, 6.5km)

The end is in sight. Turn R after leaving the hostel and walk to the road junction about 300 yards (250m) away. Go straight ahead through a gate into woodland. The path emerges from the wood onto open fellside of Loughrigg Terrace. Fork R almost immediately and continue along the path that climbs to the summit of the fell. This is a steep climb but you will be rewarded with a splendid view back over Grasmere – a marvellous excuse for lots of rests in which to take in the panorama. Keep resting and climbing until you reach the summit.

The view from the summit of Loughrigg is one of the best in the district. To the north the ridges of Fairfield are seen at their best and the western skyline is dominated by Crinkle Crags, Bowfell and the Langdale Pikes. If you turn to the south-west the gentle, wooded slopes around Windermere are in sharp contrast.

The walk continues over the summit on a path clearly marked by cairns. After about 1 mile (1.5km) it crosses a small stream and then rises very slightly to continue through fields to a lane. Go into the lane and follow it down a steep descent to a minor road. Turn R then L over a bridge onto a path through a park to Ambleside. The Hostel is at Waterhead, 1 mile (1.5km) south of the town centre.

Ambleside is principally a tourist centre but there are good shops for outdoor and climbing gear. There is history too. The Romans used Ambleside as a staging post on their road from Lancaster to Ravenglass. If you're feeling thirsty Ambleside has plenty of good pubs with real ale where you can celebrate the end of your walk.

The Hostel is at Waterhead, only a 1 mile (1.5km) stagger south of the town centre.

• PACK-FREE DAYS •

Coniston

If you need a rest (already!) a sail on the steam yacht 'Gondola' is a delightful way to give your feet a break. Superbly restored to its Victorian opulence by the National Trust, it provides an elegant tour of Coniston Water. Peel Island, one of three owned by the National Trust, appears in *Swallows and Amazons* as Wild Cat Island. Donald Campbell broke the world waterspeed record five times on Coniston but was killed here attempting 300mph (480km/h) in 1967.

A day's walk from Coniston (10 miles, 16km)

A walk on Coniston Fells is an excellent way to spend the day if you are still feeling energetic. If you climb all the Coniston peaks this will be your most strenuous day. The paths are good but rough in places. Set off early and take your time.

Turn R after leaving the Hostel and walk to the village. Cross the bridge by the Black Bull and turn R, keep R at the next junction. Go up a steep hill, this is Walna Scar Road. After about 1 mile (1.5km) it becomes a very pleasant path. After another ½ mile (800m) leave the track by a grassy path on the R. This path leads to Goat's Water. Follow the path to the tarn, which you will reach after about 1 mile (1.5km). Goat's Water is a splendid example of a mountain tarn, dominated by the impressive rock buttresses of Dow Crag.

Keep to the R bank of the tarn and follow the faint footpath to the col between Dow Crag and Coniston Old Man. If you turn R the path leads around to the R of the summit.

Coniston Old Man is a well-known view point. At 2633 feet (803m) you can see Blackpool on a clear day. But the view in the opposite direction is even better, across the Duddon Valley to the Scafells.

After pausing for the view, retrace your steps to the path, which swings round to the R and more or less follows the escarpment over the summit of Brim Fell and Swirl How. The path descends stonily to Swirl Hause (between Swirl How and Wetherlam). Turn R at Swirl Hause and descend to Levers Water and Copper Mines Valley, from where a broad track leads back to Coniston.

• LOCAL INTEREST •

The great lake

Windermere is the largest of the lakes. It is also the busiest. Steamers, pleasure boats, launches and sailing boats ply its ten-mile length and it is the only lake on which water skiing is allowed. Windermere Steamboat Museum near Bowness is worth a visit. Victorian craft, in working order, fill enthusiasts with nostalgia. Most of the islands on Windermere are owned by the National Trust, but the largest, Belle Island, is privately owned and has an eighteenth-century round house that is open to the public.

The woods

The woods around Windermere are mostly indigenous oak and silver birch. Until 50 or 60 years ago charcoal burners roamed them. The wood was also used for making oval baskets called swills and bobbins for the Lancashire cotton mills. In many places the native trees have given way to imports, including larch, which Wordsworth hated. In recent years plantations of conifers have proliferated, giving conservationists and environmentalists cause for concern because of the changes such plantations bring to the landscape.

Hill Top Farm

Now owned by the National Trust this robust, simple farmhouse attracts more than many of the Trust's much grander properties and is the most visited house in the Lake District. If you simply can't resist a visit while you are in Near Sawrey (the National Trust is trying to keep the numbers down) you will see a farmhouse, unchanged since Beatrix Potter's day, where Jemima Puddleduck lived and where Tom Kitten created mayhem.

Brantwood and John Ruskin

John Ruskin, art critic and writer, lived at Brantwood, a large house on the east side of the Coniston Water from 1871 to 1900. The house is open to the public and contains many items associated with the writer.

Rydal Water and Loughrigg Terrace.

The mines in Copper Mines Valley are now disused but they were probably in production before the Roman occupation and mining continued until about 1874, with only a short break during the Reformation. Quarrying Coniston green slate was continued until 1960 and huge underground chambers were formed. Today the mining and quarrying scars are reverting to nature in a pleasing way, which is more than can be said for their modern counterparts. Do not, for any reason, venture underground or climb the fences guarding the open shafts.

If you are an experienced and energetic walker there is an alternative route back to Coniston across the splendid ridge walk from Swirl Hause over Wetherlam. But the path back to Coniston via the broad south ridge is not particularly clear and great care and a compass are needed in misty conditions.

A day's walk from High Close (6 miles, 10km)

There is an excellent day's walk from High Close, so you can leave your pack behind and enjoy it to the full. It is quite a strenuous walk of 6 miles (10km), so set off early and allow plenty of time. The route from High Close crosses Loughrigg Terrace, with fine views over Grasmere, and takes you towards Alcock Tarn on the other side of the lake. A path zig-zags up the hill with extensive views at every corner. There are small pools with lone Scot's pine, the private domain of a discerning mallard last time I was there.

The path overlooks Grasmere sports field, where the famous Guides race is run. If the weather is fine the professional fell runners and other traditional sports can attract 10,000 spectators. If you feel tired after the climb, just imagine running up here on a hot August day. The best fell runners run up and down in under 15 minutes. If you so desire, you can shorten your walk by walking to and returning from Grasmere by road.

Turn R after leaving the Hostel and at the first road junction (300 yards, 250m) go through a gate onto a wide path, descending through the wood, to come out on Loughrigg Terrace, with fine views over Grasmere. Go along the edge of the terrace until you reach a stone wall where turn R, descending for a few yards, until a kissing gate gives access to the wood on the L. Go through the gate and follow a path that goes down through the wood to cross the River Rothay via a footbridge. Follow the path round to the R over another small bridge near public lavatories. Pass these on the R and cross the A591 and follow the footpath on the L of the wall in front of a cottage called The Old Coach House. Follow the path to a waterfall, where you take the R fork. Go up the stony lane and at the top take a footpath on the L. This path becomes a lane which passes a small pond on the R. Where the lane begins to descend take a footpath on the R, signposted Alcock Tarn.

Go forward until you come to a wall with a gate in it. Go through the gate into a wood on the L. The path rises gently through the wood and eventually comes out onto the open fell near some rocky outcrops. A well-engineered path now zig-zags up the hill and as you follow it up the views become more extensive with each turn. Eventually you will come to a small gate in a field overlooking Grassmere sports field. Go through the gate. The summit of Butter Crags is up to your left.

Continue to follow the path to the top of the crag and from there make for the obvious gap in the wall which runs behind the highest rocks. Go through the gap and follow a grassy path to the L to reach Alcock Tarn. Turn L along the edge of the tarn and go over the stile to descend steeply to Greenhead Gill, which is eventually crossed by a footbridge just above a wall. Turn sharp L through the gate into a lane which joins the A591. Turn L to cross the main road at The Swan Inn.

Go through Grasmere and turn R by the church onto the Langdale road. After ¼ mile (400m) turn R onto a footpath to Great Langdale. Follow this up a lane and through a field. On the far side of the field turn L and follow the wall on the L to its highest point. The wall runs downhill, but you should keep straight on, crossing a small stream. Continue to the top of the hill, which is marked by a large cairn. Turn L at this point along the broad, grassy ridge. Several paths cross the ridge but keep to the cairned path. When you reach the pine wood at the end of the ridge turn R on a grassy path. This path eventually reaches the road, where you turn L for the Hostel.

• LAKE DISTRICT •

WINDERMERE AND THE SHORES OF ULLSWATER

One of the loveliest low-level walks in the Lake District can be taken on this route. It follows the shore of Ullswater. There are also high fells to be walked, so the days spent in this area will give great contrast and changing scenery, as well as visiting some of the most popular tourist spots.

(33½ miles, 47.5km)

• DAY ONE •

Windermere to Grasmere (10 miles, 16km)

From Windermere Hostel turn L at the end of the hostel drive and walk up the road to Town End. At Town End, a National Trust house which is well worth a visit, turn sharp L on the road to Ambleside. After 300 yards (250m) turn R up a stony lane. Follow the path to the top of the hill. Where it meets another path, turn L and then L again on a path through fields signposted 'Jenkin Crag'. Follow this path, via High Skelghyll Farm, to Jenkin Crag itself. The crag is a marvellous viewpoint over the head of Windermere. From Jenkin Crag the path goes down and meets several other paths, all of which go to Ambleside. Take your pick and follow it into the town.

Go through Ambleside, past the much-photographed Bridge House, and after about ½ mile (800m) look for large iron gates on the R, signposted 'Footpath to Rydal Hall'. Turn R through the gates and follow the path. About a mile (1.5km) later it skirts the back of Rydal Hall, follow it round to the R. Immediately after Rydal Mount, which was Wordsworth's home from 1813 until his death in 1850, turn L. The path continues through woods and fields overlooking Rydal Water and eventually by White Moss Common.

After 1½ miles (2.5km) the path becomes a minor road which descends past a pond on the R to Grasmere village. You will pass Wordsworth's famous home, Dove Cottage, just before you reach the A591. Cross the main road and continue down the B5287 into Grasmere itself. Make for Butharlyp How, which is the Hostel, at the north end of the village. (There is another Hostel northwest of Grasmere.) Follow the road to Easedale for 150 yards (135m) and turn R down the drive to the Hostel.

• DAY TWO •

Grasmere to Patterdale (8 miles, 13km)

Turn R on leaving Butharlyp How and R again at the next junction. Go past the lane to Thorney How (the other Grasmere Youth Hostel) and after about ½ mile (800m) turn R over the bridge crossing the River Rothay. Cross the A591 and take the path signposted to Patterdale. There is a choice of paths up Tongue Gill but as they join up later near Grisedale Hause, you can choose the path you take. About 2 miles (3km) later the path reaches Grisedale Tarn. Turn R along the tarn and follow the path across the stream that flows out of the tarn. The rock scenery is awe inspiring here,

Above: *Field patterns above Grasmere.*
Previous page: *Lake Windermere.*

but even on a misty day the path remains clear as it descends Grisedale to reach Patterdale.

About 1 mile (1.5km) from the tarn you will pass a low building called Ruthwaite Lodge. The distance from here to Patterdale is about 3 miles (4.5km). A short while after Ruthwaite Lodge the path comes to a junction. Keep to the R and go down into Grisedale, with Grisedale Beck on your L. The path goes through patches of woodland and eventually becomes a tarmac road ending steeply to join the A592 at Patterdale. Turn R and the Hostel is ¼ mile (400m) south of Patterdale.

• DAY THREE •

Patterdale to Ambleside (11½ miles, 18.5km)

Turn R on leaving the Hostel and R again at the next junction. Cross the bridge over Goldrill Beck. At the end of this lane, past the first cottages, turn R on the lane signposted Hartsop. Follow this attractive footpath beneath the fell, near Goldrill Beck, for almost 2 miles (3km). Cross a stream by an attractive little waterfall and continue on the path down to Hartsop. This is a delightful hamlet, whose name means 'valley of the deer'. Several of the houses still have external spinning galleries under the eaves, where wool from the Herdwick sheep was spun.

Walk down through the village to the A592. Turn R onto the main road and follow it over the bridge across the river – it's still Goldrill Beck. Turn L immediately after the bridge and follow the lane beside the river on the L and woods on the R. The path continues along the eastern shore of Brothers Water (legend says that it was named after two brothers who were drowned here) and, after leaving the lake, reaches Hartsop Hall farm. From here to the summit of the pass is about 2 miles (3km). To reach it, go past the farm and then turn L through a gate in front of the farm building. The path is signposted Kirkstone Pass and Scandale Pass.

Follow the path through fields to where it forks L. The junction here is indistinct but there is a footbridge at the spot. Do not go over the footbridge, but keep R and go through a gate in a wall. Follow the path up Scandale Pass. The scenery along the approach to Scandale Pass is very fine. Ullswater is behind you and the mountains at its head are a splendid sight. The views up Dovedale, to your R, should not be missed either. Continue up the pass until you reach the summit.

The distance from the summit down to Ambleside is about 3 miles (4.5km). The path descends very steeply at first, so take care. The steep fellside on your R as you descend is High Pike, part of the Fairfield Range. As the path approaches woodland, beside Scandale Beck, you will pass an old packhorse bridge called High Sweden Bridge. It is an attractive reminder of the days when all goods were carried across the fells on horseback. You must have eaten your packed lunch by now, but if you haven't, or if you have

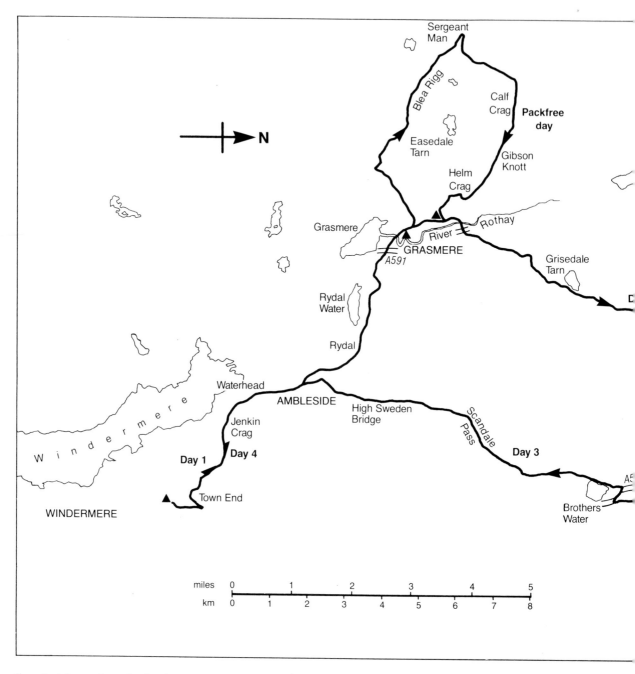

time to take a sit-and-take-in-the-scenery break, this is a lovely area.

After your break, continue on to the fleshpots of Ambleside, where tea and buns can be taken at one of the many teashops and cafes. The Hostel is a mile (1.5km) to the south of the town. It is on the A591, but it is also right on the shore of Windermere, at Waterhead, and has panoramic views of the lake and mountains.

• DAY FOUR •

Ambleside to Windermere (4 miles, 6.5km)

Today's walk is short and designed either to get you back to Windermere in time to get transport home or to give you time to explore the town before spending another night at the Windermere Hostel. Most of the walk is the reverse of the first day's outing.

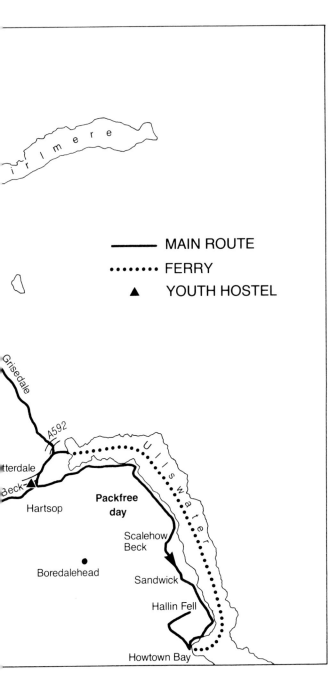

MAIN ROUTE

········· FERRY

▲ YOUTH HOSTEL

At the Post Office you have a choice: you can either turn R and walk 2 miles (3km) into Windermere and the end of your holiday, or you can turn L for essential refreshment at the Mortal Man Inn. You will find it by walking through Troutbeck for about ¾ mile (1km). It is on the L just before the junction with the A592. The Mortal Man is thought to have got its name from a verse:

O Mortal Man who lives by bread
What is it makes thy face so red?
Thow silly fool with face so pale
'Tis drinking Sally Birkett's ale!

Sally Birkett is no longer the landlady of the Mortal Man, but the ale still seems to have the same rosy effect on the complexion.

• PACK-FREE DAYS •

Grasmere

There is so much to see in Grasmere and the surrounding area that it is an excellent place to break your walk and spend a day, staying a second night at the Hostel. You may want to explore Grasmere and discover how Wordsworth lived. If you are feeling energetic you could take a day's walk in the Grasmere area.

A day's walk from Grasmere (9½ miles, 15km)

This walk takes you along Blea Rigg to Sergeant Man and returns to Grasmere by way of the ridge above Far Easedale. There are views of Langdale, the Langdale Pikes and Stickle Tarn.

Leave the Hostel and walk down Easedale Road to Grasmere village. Turn R and R again up a lane, just past the Heaton Cooper Studio. This lane eventually becomes a footpath through fields. The path passes a cottage on the R before climbing up the fellside to a grassy plateau where it joins the main footpath along Blea Rigg to Sergeant Man. It is a delightful path and weaves in and out of rocky outcrops so that the view alternates between Grasmere on the R and Langdale on the L. Looking down into Langdale early on you will see the Elterwater Slate Quarries where modern methods of quarrying have left scars on the landscape.

As you ascend the ridge the views open out and the Langdale Pikes dominate the middle

Turn R out of the Hostel and after 100 yards (90m) turn L onto a footpath going up through the woods to Jenkin Crag. Continue through the woods and come out into fields. Keep on the path past High Skelgyll Farm. Go downhill from the farm, crossing a bridge and turning L on a path through fields. The path eventually joins a lane. Ignore all the turnings on the R and the path will lead you down to Troutbeck Post Office.

Daffodils near Grasmere.

distance. Down to the L, below the cliff face of Pavey Ark is Stickle Tarn which once provided water for the gunpowder industry in Elterwater (the manufacturing site is now a timeshare development). Eventually, the path leads to the little peak of Sergeant Man. There are good views to the south here, right across Langdale to the Coniston Fells – given fair weather, of course.

Once you have done justice to the views retrace your steps for a few yards and then turn L in a north-easterly direction to pick up a path, faint at first, which descends to the head of Far Easedale. The head of the pass is marked by a gate, but the fence which it once went through has disappeared. Cross the pass and take the path that climbs up to the rocky little summit of Calf Crag. The path now becomes well-defined. Continue on it, over Gibson Knott to Helm Crag, a distance of about 2 miles (3km).

At Helm Crag there are superb views over the whole of the Vale of Grasmere. The summit of Helm Crag is a series of rocky pinnacles and it is one of the few Lakeland summits where you have to use your hands to reach the highest point, so take care. From the crag the path down to Grasmere is well-engineered. It has been renovated by the National Trust, using traditional methods of paving which were used to create the packhorse paths across the fells. When you reach the valley, turn L on a track through fields. This track eventually reaches the Easedale road where your day's walk began.

Patterdale

If you spend a second night at Butharlyp How, the Hostel in Patterdale, you can walk one of the loveliest low-level walks in the Lake District. It follows the shore of Ullswater to Howtown. Once there you can either walk back or catch the steamer at Howtown pier and travel back to Glenridding, just north of Patterdale, in the most delightful style.

A day's walk from Patterdale (5½ miles, 8km)

Turn R on leaving the Hostel and turn R again almost immediately on a minor road that crosses a stream. Follow the minor road round to the L, past the cottages, through a gate onto the fellside. Turn L. There is a choice of paths here, one higher up the fell than the other. Take whichever you prefer as they meet again in about a mile (1.5km). The views from this path are superb. Look west, across Ullswater, over Glenridding Pier to the Helvellyn range. The sharp, pointed beak of Catstye Cam can be seen very easily.

The two paths become one, which then enters birch and oak scrubland. The next mile of the path should be taken slowly and relished, as it is particularly delightful. The path rises and falls, sometimes close to the shore, sometimes climbing round little rocky outcrops above the lake. After about a mile (1.5km) the path swings away from the lake and crosses Scalehow Beck, just below Scalehow Force, a small waterfall. (If you want to walk back there is a side path just beyond the waterfall which can be used to get back to Patterdale via Place Fell.)

Continue along the main path to the little ham-

• LOCAL INTEREST •

Townend House
Townend House is at the southern end of Troutbeck. It was built in 1626 by a farmer called George Browne and the Browne family lived in the house until 1944. It is an excellent example of a Lake District farmhouse. The contents include the original carved furniture, family papers and other paraphernalia of a yeoman farmer's life. It has been owned by the National Trust since 1947.

Grasmere and Wordsworth
To Wordsworth, Grasmere was 'the loveliest spot that man hath ever found'. Today it is a tourist village, but still has many delightful features. Don't miss Sarah Nelson's Gingerbread, which is sold in a small cottage at the gates of the church. The cottage was once a schoolroom and Wordsworth taught there. The poet is buried in the churchyard, and St Oswald's has a fine interior and is worth a visit. Dove Cottage, where Wordsworth lived from 1799 to 1808, is a must, even if you are not interested in poetry, because the cottage is a superbly preserved example of life in the Lakes nearly two hundred years ago. The Grasmere and Wordsworth Museum, just behind Dove Cottage, is fascinating. Rydal Mount, where the poet lived at the height of his popularity, is open to the public. You can walk there through Dora's Field (after Dorothy, Wordsworth's sister). In the spring it is yellow with daffodils; a marvellous sight, even if you are unmoved by Wordsworth.

Not so silly sheep
The Herdwick sheep that you will see on the fells are hardy and shaggy fleeced. Lambs have black faces but this turns grey as they mature. There are many stories of their endurance but they also seem to have excellent memories, as their homing instinct shows. Lambs taken miles from the pasture of their infancy will often try to return to it the following spring. Perhaps this accounts for the solitary sheep which can be seen crossing remote fells with a sense of purpose. There are also stories of whole flocks sold to distant farms going AWOL and arriving back at the farm of their birth, miles away.

let of Sandwick. From Sandwick it passes through fields and reaches Sandwick Bay. Here it goes through woods, skirting the edge of the lake below Hallin Fell. Finally it turns R into Howtown Bay and the steamer pier. If you have some time to spare before the next steamer, it is worthwhile climbing to the top of Hallin Fell. Turn R on the minor road which zig-zags up a fairly steep hill. From the top a broad, grassy path on the R leads to the summit of Hallin Fell, from where there is an excellent view of Ullswater.

It is possible to walk back to Patterdale by continuing along the minor road down Boredale to Boredale Head, where a path climbs to Boredale Hause (hause is a local name for a pass between two hills). At Boredale Hause there are a confusing number of paths but if you descend in the direction of Ullswater you will reach the minor road by the gate from which you started out across the fell at the beginning of the walk.

For most people a delightful steamer trip along Ullswater is the best way to return to Patterdale. The boats have the added attraction of a bar on board, so you can sail back enjoying a beer.

NORTHERN LAKELAND

The Northern Lakeland walk starts and finishes at Keswick, staying in Buttermere, Longthwaite and on Derwent Water on the way. Most of the walk is on low or medium level footpaths but it also provides the opportunity to reach one or two of the most popular peaks.

(28 miles, 45km).

• DAY ONE •

Keswick to Buttermere (9½ miles, 15km)

Turn R on leaving the Keswick Hostel, and R again onto the main street through the town. Follow the road until you come to Greta Bridge, across the River Greta. Cross the bridge and turn L opposite the pencil factory onto a footpath through fields. Follow the footpath for about ¾ mile (1km), across the River Derwent to the village of Portinscale. Once across the bridge continue on the minor road, keeping L through the village, south towards Derwent Water. After about ½ mile (800m) take a footpath on the L signposted to Brandlehow. This public footpath leads through some beautiful woodland to Lingholm Gardens.

Take the footpath on the R of the entrance to the gardens. It crosses a field and another short section of woodland to join the path that goes down to the lake at Hawes End landing. Do not descend to the lake, but cross the track to a footpath through woods up to the road. Turn L uphill, then continue on, crossing the cattle grid on the lane to Skelgill Farm. Turn R into a lane. At the end of the lane go through a gate in front of the farmhouse, then turn L along a lane past two cottages. Go through a gate into a field. Take the R fork and go through two more gates, bearing R to join a minor road just before Ghyll Bank. Turn L onto the road and then R at a footpath signpost. Cross Newlands Beck by the footbridge and go up the field to a minor road. Turn L onto the road and continue along it. About ½ mile (800m) further on is a timber-built, purple-painted house which looks slightly incongruous in this setting. It is called Rigg Beck, after the stream beside it. Do not cross the bridge but turn R onto a footpath overlooking the beck on your L.

Previous page: *Looking towards Scarth Gap.*
Right: *Sunset at Buttermere.*

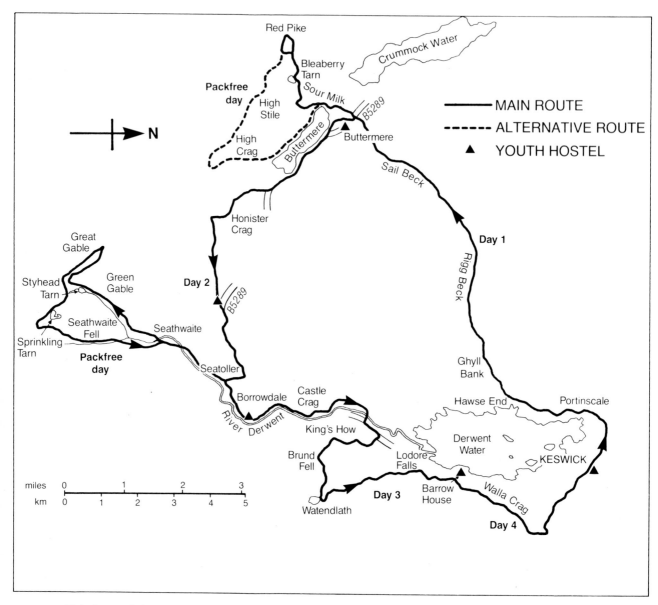

MAIN ROUTE ——
ALTERNATIVE ROUTE -----
▲ **YOUTH HOSTEL**

This footpath leads through the hills to Buttermere nearly 5 miles (8km) away. It is a delightful route which climbs to the top of the pass where Rigg Beck rises. The steep fell on your R is Causey Pike, which you may have seen from the lakeside at Keswick, as it is one of the most prominent pikes.

From the head of the pass the path descends to Buttermere. On the L is Sail Beck, and the path follows it all the way to the village. Near Buttermere the path reaches a small wood on the L. Go over the stile and follow the path through the wood to the minor road in Buttermere itself. Turn L onto the road and follow it to the Hostel. You can't miss it, as Buttermere is a small hamlet, but in addition to the Hostel it boasts a church, an hotel, a couple of guest houses and a Post Office.

Buttermere, with its grey fells and deep blue-green screes rising all round may seem remote, but it hit national headlines as early as 1802 when a local girl, called Mary Robinson, was tricked into marriage by a bigamist and forger. Not a wildly sensational story, you may think, but Mary Robinson was already a well-known beauty, made famous by travellers of the time and visited by many, including Wordsworth, Southey and De

Quincey. When the 'Beauty of Buttermere' married, it was reported in the local papers and her husband's deception was discovered. He was eventually captured and hung for his misdeeds a year later. Mary's sad story was the subject of newspaper and magazine articles, broadsheets, a play, and even a novel.

• DAY TWO •

Buttermere to Longthwaite (8½ miles, 13.5km)

Walk down into Buttermere village and take the first footpath on the L just past the church. This path leads down towards Buttermere itself, past farms and through fields to the shore, below the road to Keswick. It is thought that the lake got its name in the sixth or seventh century and means 'the lake with pastures that yield plenty of butter'. It could well have derived its name from 'beauty mere' as it is one of the loveliest of the Lakes. It is about 1½ miles (2.5km) long and surrounded by high fells. The walk along the shore of the lake is through bracken and trees and at one point it goes into a short tunnel through a rocky promontory. Eventually the path meets the B5289 on its way to climb Honister Pass.

Turn R along the road and follow it until it becomes unfenced, just past a clump of pine trees. Turn R here and walk along a pleasant, level, grassy path with a wall on its R. This gives easy walking for a good ½ mile (800m), until the path climbs across to the steep fellside on your L. This path gives a well-graded ascent as it was once the quarry road to Dubbs Quarry. After the initial climb the route veers L, keeping to the L of the beck. At this point the beck runs through a rocky gorge and over a waterfall before the path reaches the disused quarry.

From Dubbs Quarry the path becomes extremely straight because it follows the line of an old quarry tramway to Honister Pass. On your L is dramatic Honister Crag, its lower slopes broken by screes, topped by craggy rocks. The green rock is slate. If you look carefully at the face of Honister Crag as you approach Honister Pass, you should be able to see traces of the old galleries, ledges and entrances to a honeycomb of tunnels carved out by the quarrymen. They were quarrying for slate and used to get it down from

the crag on a sort of sledge. The sledges were dragged down by men, who ran down the steep scree slopes with the loaded sledges careering behind them. A feat which makes today's walk seem like a gentle stroll to fetch a newspaper.

When you reach the B5289 at Honister Pass, turn R and follow the road for about ½ mile (800m). Then take a footpath on the L, which is the original road over Honister and much more pleasant than walking on the tarmac road. The old road zig-zags back to the R to join the B road again at Seatoller. At Seatoller there is a resource centre in Seatoller Barn. It is run by the Lake District National Park and has information about the history, geography and geology of the beautiful valley of Borrowdale in which you are going to stay the night. A few yards down the road from the Barn is a car park on the L. From the car park a footpath leads through woods overlooking the River Derwent to Longthwaite Youth Hostel, about ¾ mile (1km) away.

• DAY THREE •

Longthwaite to Derwent Water (7 miles, 11.5km)

One expert on walking in the Lake District says that if he was only allowed one more walk in the Lakes ever, this is the one he would pick. It is a lovely stretch, the highest point is only just over 1300ft (396m) but for distant views and beautiful locations it is hard to beat.

The first part of the walk is through Borrowdale, justifiably famous for its beauty. Leave the Hostel by the car park, but do not go over the bridge, instead keep to the footpath on the L bank of the River Derwent. At first the path goes through fields and then through a delightful section of National Trust woodland below Castle Crag. The River Derwent is particularly attractive through here, with rocks and pools overhung by elegantly beautiful birch trees.

The footpath becomes a lane leading to the village of Grange, which got its name because it was once the Borrowdale granary of Furness Abbey. Cross the river by way of the elegant double-arched bridge and turn L along the B5289 towards Keswick. After about ¼ mile (400m) turn R onto a lane opposite Derwent View.

The lane leads to the secluded little valley of

Troutdale. The path keeps to the R of the stream and crosses a stone wall into a wood. It then zig-zags steeply, sometimes very steeply, up through a wood before levelling out and swinging round to the R to climb the open fell to the beautiful little summit of King's How. Below King's How, near the road, is the Bowder Stone. It is 62ft (19m) long and 32ft (10m) high and thought to be the largest boulder in the Lake District, weighing over 2000 tons. It was deposited here, seemingly balanced on one edge, in the Ice Age.

There is a path down to the road from the summit of King's How but do not take it. Descend on the opposite side to that of the ascent. The path crosses a shallow valley, then goes over a wall and climbs to the summit of Brund Fell, the highest point of the walk. From here you can look north to Derwent Water, east over Borrowdale

Left: *The Borrowdale fells.*
Below: *View from Dale Head.*

and south-east towards Scafell Pike. Brund Fell itself is a lovely spot, with miniature crags and small, rocky towers jutting out of the heather.

From the summit the path descends to the east to cross a wall and then continues to descend following another wall to remote and romantic Watendlath. Watendlath is a tiny hamlet on a tarn of dark water. If you stop and contemplate the scenery here it isn't long before your imagination runs riot. It is easy to see why Hugh Walpole, who lived in Borrowdale, set his novel, *Judith Paris*, in this place. Luckily, it will be preserved as it is because the buildings are owned by the National Trust. In the tourist season you can get tea at the farmhouse across the packhorse bridge.

After a break re-cross the bridge and turn R onto a footpath through fields. After about ½ mile (800m) the path keeps very close to Watendlath Beck. Follow it beside the beck for nearly a mile (1.5km), until you come to a crossroads of paths. You can quite easily miss the 'signpost' because it

is a circular stone at ground level. The route crosses the footbridge over the beck, then turns L through a gap in the wall onto a good path rising through woodland on the L. This eventually joins the minor road to Watendlath. Turn L when you reach it and walk along the road, but do take care as it is narrow and busy in the tourist season.

After about 200 yards (180m) turn off the road to the L for the marvellous Surprise View over Derwent Water and the mountains. It is a stunning view with Borrowdale, the lake and the River Derwent stretched out like a map beneath you. In your efforts to get the photograph that no-one else has achieved, take care! The view may give more of a shock than a surprise because the edge of the escarpment falls away very suddenly here. On Watendlath Beck, far below Surprise View and out of sight in the trees, is Lodore Falls, whose waters Robert Southey described in his poem for children, 'The Cataract of Lodore'.

'All at once and all o'er, with a mighty uproar,
And this way the Water comes down at Lodore.'

Return to the road and follow it for about ½ mile (800m) to Ashness Bridge, which must qualify as one of the most photographed bridges in the British Isles. Fame hasn't changed it, it is still an attractive little stone bridge with magnificent views over Derwent Water and the great peak of Skiddaw in the distance. After the bridge the road descends to the B5289. Turn sharp L and L again up the drive to Barrow House, the Hostel on Derwent Water.

• DAY FOUR •

Derwent Water to Keswick (3 miles, 5km)

This last stretch is short so that you can spend some time in Keswick or catch transport home, or both. Turn R out of the Hostel drive and R again, branching L up the road to Ashness Bridge. Just before you reach the bridge take a footpath on the L which climbs across the fellside behind the imposing, sheer rock face of Falcon Crag. The path crosses several small streams around the head of Cat Gill. To gain the summit of Walla Crag for some more spectacular views across Derwent Water climb over a ruined wall and continue up

to the summit of the crag. Once you have taken in the view, retrace your steps across the wall and follow the footpath. As it descends, it swings away to the R and joins a minor road at Rakefoot Farm. After 100 yards (90m) or so leave the road at L and follow a footpath. It crosses a stream and descends pleasantly through woods to join another minor road. Turn L and this road leads you to the centre of Keswick.

• PACK-FREE DAYS •

The pack-free days spent in Buttermere and Longthwaite are best spent walking. No apologies are offered because the walks are excellent and it would be a great shame to be in the area and not tackle them.

A day's walk from Buttermere (5 miles, 8km)
Red Pike, on the opposite side of the valley from the hostel, is today's goal. The total distance there and back is probably under 5 miles (8km), but part of the walk is a steep climb. Red Pike is 2477ft (755m) so don't underestimate the effort required. There are plenty of excellent views and a delightful mountain tarn to visit.

Pass the Fish Hotel in the centre of Buttermere village and take a turning on the L, which leads through fields, keeping L towards Buttermere. Don't be tempted to go R to Scale Bridge or Scale Force. Scale Force is the highest waterfall in the Lake District. But even though the water plunges 120ft (36m) between rocks, a visit isn't highly recommended because of its enclosed position, together with an extremely boggy approach.

Instead, cross the river flowing out of Buttermere by the bridge nearest to the lake and enter Burtness Wood. Cross the main track and continue on a path that climbs diagonally L, up through the trees. Once clear of the trees there are marvellous views, especially over Crummock Water. The two main peaks to be seen above Crummock Water are Grasmoor and Crag Hill. You can also see clearly the route taken yesterday through the hills to Buttermere.

The next part of the walk is particularly rough and stony. But after about ¼ mile (400m) the path turns to the R over less steep ground. Continue until you reach a beck. This is Sour Milk Gill, which at this point cascades downwards, falling about 1000ft (365m) in about ½ mile (800m). It is particularly spectacular seen from the opposite side of the valley after heavy rain. The main path crosses the head of the gill, but it is worthwhile keeping to the L of the stream to visit Bleaberry Tarn. It is a magnificent example of a tarn in a truly dramatic setting of mountains and surrounding imposing scenery.

Retrace your steps to the main path and cross the gill. The path now climbs diagonally up the fell side between Red Pike and Dodd. Dodd is a minor peak which is often mistaken for the real summit on the approach from Buttermere. Once you have reached the summit of Red Pike allow yourself plenty of time to take in one of the finest views in the area.

For the average walker the best way back is simply to return along the route of the ascent. For walkers more experienced in mountain walking there is a superb high-level walk back, which crosses the top of High Stile. Do not attempt this walk unless the weather is clear and set fine.

From the summit of Red Pike, head for High Stile, the next peak, about ¾ mile (1km) away, along the broad rocky ridge to the south east. After this there is about a mile (1.5km) of fairly level walking to the summit of High Crag. Along this section a line of old fence posts is a sure guide from one summit to the next. The fence posts also act as a guide to the descent from High Crag. Follow the posts L, down towards Buttermere. The descent for the first ¼ mile (400m) is unpleasantly steep and great care is needed.

The going levels off again but descends steeply to the head of Scarth Gap Pass. Here the path joins another, turn L and continue the descent to Buttermere. When you reach the valley do not cross the river but turn L along Buttermere, through Burtness Wood, keeping the lake close on your R. When you reach the river, which flows from Buttermere into Crummock Water, cross the bridge and retrace your route back to the Hostel.

A day's walk from Longthwaite (10½ miles, 17km)

The mountains at the head of Borrowdale are the northern guardians of England's highest peak, Scafell Pike. Today's walk climbs up Borrowdale to Sty Head, with an optional climb to the summit of Great Gable.

• LOCAL INTEREST •

Wildlife

Otters were once numerous in the Lake District but their numbers have dwindled and you will be extremely lucky to see one. Luckily there are many other forms of wildlife which make their home on the fells, by the lakes and in the woods.

The red squirrel can still be seen in lakeland woods and roe deer are found in almost every large stretch of woodland. Red deer keep to the southern Lake District.

Watch the skies above the fells and you will certainly see ravens. Buzzards are common too and many people mistake them for golden eagles. There are eagles in the Lake District, but you will have to have the luck of the gods to see one soaring majestically above the fells.

Bracken, the curse of all hill farms, grows profusely, but there are numerous other plants on the fells. These include rare saxifrages and many kinds of ferns. By the lakes, flags, meadowsweet and purple loosestrife colour the banks.

There are many species of fish in the lakes and rivers. Ullswater has its very own fish, the schelly, while another rare fish, the vendace, is found only in Derwentwater and Bassenthwaite Lake.

Keswick

Keswick is a tourist centre and bustles in the summer. But it has retained its individual character and is a thriving market town. It also has an unusual industry – pencil making. There are plumbago mines in Borrowdale, not far away, and the 'black lead' was brought to the town to be turned into pencils. At one time it was so valuable that workers in the pencil factory were searched before they left to make sure that they were not smuggling any of the precious material out of the building. If you have always wondered how the lead gets into a pencil, visit the Keswick Pencil Museum and find out.

From the Hostel walk back to Seatoller and then take the minor road and walk to Seathwaite, the hamlet at the top of Borrowdale. Seathwaite is the wettest inhabited place in England – a record of dubious merit. Where the road ends, Sour Milk Gill (a different one from that at Buttermere) comes tumbling down the fellside on the R. Half-way up, to the R of the gill, you can just make out the spoil heaps of the old plumbago mines which gave Keswick its pencil industry.

The road appears to end in a farmyard, but look for an arch in the buildings on the R and go through it. Cross the River Derwent by a foot-bridge and turn L immediately afterwards. Follow a path which keeps to the R bank of the river for about a mile (1.5½km).

The path becomes quite rocky as it rises, going through a small gate. At this point there is an excellent view of Taylorgill Force. The path continues through a little plantation of larches at the head of the force and joins the main path about ½ mile (800m) further on. At which point it runs between Seathwaite Fell on the L and Green Gable on the R. The path continues beside Sty-head Gill to Styhead Tarn and on to the top of Sty Head Pass itself, where many paths meet.

On the R of Sty Head is the bulk of Great Gable, one of the most famous mountains in the Lake District. The view from the summit is very fine, so if you want to see it, the ascent begins on the path on the R. It is steep, rough and stony, but the 1 mile (1.5km) climb is well marked with cairns.

Once there you are at 2950ft (899m) and on a clear day the long valley of Wasdale and the distant sea can be seen to the south-west. To the north-west Ennerdale and Pillar Mountain domin-ate the scene, while further north is the fine group of mountains surrounding Buttermere. Due south is Scafell Pike. On Remembrance Sunday hun-dreds of climbers and walkers gather on the summit of Great Gable for a service.

Retrace your steps to Sty Head to continue the walk. Follow the path which climbs away from Great Gable in an easterly direction, towards Sprinkling Tarn. Sprinkling Tarn is marvellous. It is a great mountain pool with little bays and rocky promontaries. The gully-riven face and buttres-ses of Great End tower over it. Continue on past the tarn, still climbing, until you come to Ruddy Gill, aptly named for its red sub-soil. Cross the gill just beyond the point where it turns R to descend to Borrowdale. Follow the stream, keeping to its R bank at first, but following the path across to its L bank after about a mile (1.5km). After ¾ mile (1km) the path reaches Stockley Bridge, another superb little packhorse bridge. Cross the bridge and follow the well-defined path back to Seath-waite and then down to Longthwaite.

• NORTHERN PENNINES •

HADRIAN'S WALL

I first walked Hadrian's Wall on a wild winter's day. The vistas are so vast from the Wall that you could see the snow showers whirling in before they hit you. Below, in the shelter of the great Wall I watched a lamb being born. It is a memorable and rugged landscape, whatever the weather. This walk begins in the northern Pennines and follows some of the most impressive sections of the Wall. Parts of the route are difficult but to compensate the daily mileage is fairly easy.
(54 miles, 86km)

• DAY ONE •

Alston to Ninebanks (8 miles, 13km)

Alston is one of the highest market towns in England and is on the Pennine Way. Before you set out remember that there are no meals provided at Ninebanks Hostel and no pubs or shops within easy reach so you will have to carry provisions for an evening meal, and tomorrow's breakfast and lunch with you.

From the Hostel go to the Market Place and take the lane by the Turk's Head, then turn R into Gossipgate gallery. A signpost marks the bridleway to Corby Gates Farm. The River Nent is on your L. Keep on the R hand side of the river and cross a stile onto a footpath. Continue along the river bank until you come to Nent High Force, a waterfall in a steep, wooded valley.

Continue out of the wood for ½ mile (800m) and come to a road bridge on the B6294. Turn L over the bridge and follow the road uphill until you come to a T-junction. Turn R and follow the road round a horseshoe bend, then take the first track on the L. As the track climbs there are good views back over Alston. At the next T-junction of tracks turn L and follow the track which climbs steadily past Foreshieldgrains Farm. Continue through a gate and follow the wall on your L until you come to another wall running at right angles to the track. The wall marks the boundary between Cumbria and Northumberland. If the visibility is good you can see the radar installation at Great Dun Fell, to the south. Cross Fell, the highest peak in the Pennines, is on the R.

Follow the county wall to the L for about ½ mile

Previous page: *Hadrian's Wall.*
Right: *Hadrian's Wall at Steel Rigg.*

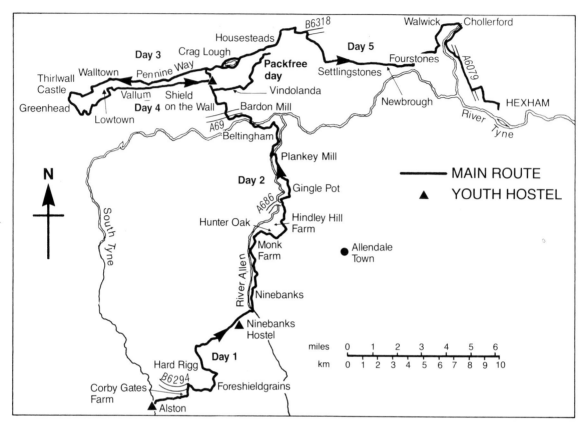

(800m) to the highest point, Hard Rigg. It is marked by a triangulation post. You are now walking over bleak and boggy moorland and the going is quite strenuous and needs some care. Do not stray from the line of the wall as there are few landmarks and if bad weather descends it is quite easy to become disorientated. So, keeping to the wall, continue forward and in just over ½ mile (800m) you will reach a conifer plantation. Follow the R hand edge of the wood until you come to a track on your R. Turn onto it and follow the track across the moor. There are many red grouse hereabouts and you may see curlews too. Follow the track for just over 2 miles (3km). It descends steeply to Allen Dale and reaches a minor road. Turn R and follow the road uphill for just under ½ mile (800m) to Ninebanks Hostel on the R.

• DAY TWO •

Ninebanks to Once Brewed (15 mile, 24km)

As this is one of the longest days an early start is a good idea. There are many scenic points so allow yourself plenty of time.

Turn L onto the road outside the Hostel and follow it in the direction of Ninebanks village. After 1½ miles (2.5km) you reach a bridge over the River West Allen. Turn L over the bridge and follow the road through Ninebanks village.

At the next road junction turn R along the road to Allendale Town and then shortly L onto a narrow road towards Gatehouse Farm. At the farm go through the gate onto the farm track, then through the next gate on the L into a field. Go downhill towards the river and join a path which goes down to the river bank. The track follows the course of the river, passing a caravan site and crosses the river twice by footbridges.

After a further mile (1.5km) the path joins a farm track at Monk Farm. This section of the route is very beautiful but it can get extremely muddy. The going is easier through the conifer wood which runs above the river path and can be joined just after Gate House Farm. The two routes meet at Monk Farm.

After Monk Farm continue along the track to the road. Turn R and walk along the road past

Hunter Oak. At the crossroads turn L towards Oakpool and then take the second track on the L to Hindley Hill Farm. The path from here to Wide Eals is not easy to make out but you can cut across the field to a footbridge which leads to Wide Eals Farm. Cross the bridge and follow the track to a hairpin bend on the A686. Keep R and follow the road up – be careful, the road is narrow and busy.

At the top of the hill a road signposted to High Staward leads off to the R. At this point a gate on the L leads onto a farm track. Follow this track past Gingle Pot, a ruined farmhouse. After about ½ mile (800m) the path enters woodland and runs along the top of a promontory with spectacular views of wooded valleys on either side. The path descends steeply into the L hand valley and runs along the R bank of the River Allen to Plankey Mill. This is a local beauty spot and there may well be many people visiting the area. Cross the river by the rope bridge and follow the path along the L bank. After 1½ miles (2.5km) the path reaches a car park with refreshments.

Turn L onto the road outside the car park and bear L at the next junction. You will come eventually to a path signposted 'Beltingham 1¼' (2km). Take this path to Beltingham which is a delightfully picturesque village. Follow the road past the church and past Beltingham Nature Reserve on the R. Cross the old wooden footbridge over the River South Tyne and go forward over the level crossing. Turn L through the station and then R outside it to the centre of Bardon Mill where you can enjoy a pint at the Bowes Hotel.

After your break follow the village street to the L (west). It eventually swings to the R and meets the A69. Cross the road, turn R and take the minor road to Henshaw. From here to the Hostel is about 2 miles (3km), but much of it is uphill. After a steep climb turn L onto the road signposted to 'Twice Brewed'. A few hundred yards later turn R towards Once Brewed. The road now leads straight to the Hostel and the last mile (1.5km) has excellent views looking back into South Tyne Valley and ahead towards Crag Lough.

• DAY THREE •

Once Brewed to Greenhead (8 miles, 13km)

This is a fairly easy day, although there is some gentle climbing. There are excellent views so give yourself time to stop and enjoy them. Most of the walk is along Hadrian's Wall and it is a good idea to look around the display at the nearby Tourist Information Centre before you set out. It explains how the Wall was constructed and used.

Cross the B6318 with care, the traffic moves fast along it. Take the minor road towards Steel Rigg. When you reach Steel Rigg car park cross the stile on the L hand side and follow the wall on the R. In a few hundred yards you will reach Hadrian's Wall. The path runs along the Wall, follow it west to the top of Whinshields Crag. It is marked by a triangulation post and is the highest point on the Wall (1200ft, 345m). On a clear day the views from here are superb. Ahead along the Wall the Solway Firth should be visible. To the north, beyond the vast expanse of Wark Forest is the massive bulk of the Cheviots. Behind you the Wall is seen at its most impressive as it straddles the hills and climbs over Hotbanks Crag.

1 mile (1.5km) further on, the path descends sharply and crosses a road before climbing the ridge again. Just before Cawfields you will reach the remains of Milecastle 42, the thick outer walls of which are well preserved. Beyond this the Wall has been destroyed by Cawfield Quarry. The quarry is now a picnic site. If you want to break your walk here you could turn L down the minor road and head for the Milecastle Inn which is popular with Wall walkers and serves good food.

Retrace your steps to the Wall and continue westwards past the derelict house on Great Chesters Farm. Not much of the Wall is visible on this section and the landscape is gentler than the wild moorland of Whinshield Crag. Just past the farmhouse are the remains of a fort.

After Great Chesters, the Wall gradually climbs again and the landscape becomes more rugged. There is a gap in the Wall before Walltown and you can see the remains of a turret. It was built as a signalling station before the main structure. At Walltown Crag the Wall is well preserved and on its north side several rare herbs have been found. It is thought that these were originally grown by the Romans who used them in medicinal potions.

Walltown Quarry interrupts the Wall here. Follow the path down to a minor road where you will find Carvoran Roman Army Museum which will give you an excellent idea of what life was like for the Roman soldier. If you have struggled along the Wall in bad weather it doesn't take much imagination to realise that life as a Legionary on the frontier was harsh and often regarded as a punishment. The museum has a coffee shop if you should be feeling in need of sustenance.

It is a mile (1.5km) from Carvoran to the Hostel at Greenhead. Turn L out of the museum, then take the path to the L a few hundred yards further on. The path leads down to Thirlwall Castle which was built by the Thirlwall family in 1346 as a fortification against the raiding Scots. From the castle the path leads L and follows the edge of a field towards the railway. The final section of the path runs between Tipalt Burn on the L and the railway on the R and emerges at Greenhead which was originally a mining village.

• DAY FOUR •

Greenhead to Once Brewed (7 miles, 11km)

The route back to Once Brewed follows the course of the Vallum at the foot of the crags. The Vallum was a great ditch and double bank built to the south of Hadrian's Wall. It is thought that this earthwork was constructed to create a safe zone for the military and their livestock and stores. There are crossings at each fort.

Turn L from the Hostel and go over the bridge. Take the footpath signposted on the R. This is an overgrown path but it will take you to a junction with a yellow arrow pointing to the correct route along the edge of a field. Do not go through the gate into the woods on the R, they are private.

Crag Lough.

Instead, pass behind the barn and the farmhouse on the R, then cross the stiles into the field. The path here is faint but if you aim for the farm ahead you cannot go wrong. At College Farm turn L onto the track which climbs the steep valley slope and eventually passes Wrytree Farm.

When the track meets the B6318 turn R along the road for ½ mile (800m), then turn L onto the signposted bridleway to Lowtown. The track goes round a farm and passes Peatsteel Crags on the R. At the derelict farm at Lowtown turn R onto a track and then R again at the next junction. The Vallum is ahead of you, a large embankment, relentlessly straight, with a path running on the R hand side. You will see Cawfields Quarry straight ahead. At the T-junction of paths go straight ahead through the gate and follow the Vallum through the fields for 1½ miles (2.5km).

The last field before Cawfields has been ploughed and the Vallum obliterated. At the minor road at Cawfields you can head R for the Milestone Inn, or if you want a change and a longer walk turn R and follow the path south by Haltwhistle Burn for a scenic river walk. At the village of Haltwhistle (2 miles, 3km) there are several pubs.

From Cawfields to Shield on the Wall the earthworks are very clear. The central ditch is bounded by banks on either side. The Vallum continues to run very straight but the ground is a little rougher than the previous section.

Beyond Shield on the Wall the ground is quite marshy in places and the Vallum is less well defined. Among the cows grazing in the fields there are one or two bulls, so proceed with caution. At Winshields Farm there is an old fort with arrow slits. This was a bastle, or fortified farm, built to protect the owners from marauding northern raiders in the Middle Ages.

At Winshields Farm turn R through the gate and then turn L onto the B6318 for the final few hundred yards to Once Brewed Hostel.

• DAY FIVE •

Once Brewed to Acomb (14 miles, 22km)

This is the longest stretch to be walked and there are several sections of road walking. There are

• LOCAL INTEREST •

Hadrian's Wall
Hadrian's Wall was begun in about AD 122 on the orders of the Roman Emperor, Hadrian. It was built by soldiers from three Legions based in Britain. The Wall is 80 Roman miles long (73 statute miles or 117km) and stretches across northern Britain from Wallsend outside Newcastle to Bowness-on-Solway.

The great fortification was built of limestone and whinstone on the line of a natural outcrop of rock called the Whin Sill. In the west it was a turf wall. It was constructed to protect the northwestern boundary of the Roman Empire, the boundary of the British province, and to control the movement of people and goods north and south of the frontier.

The Wall was originally to be 10ft (3m) wide, but for reasons of economy and speed this was reduced to 8ft (2.5m). There are Milecastles every Roman mile and two turrets, evenly spaced between each pair. There were forts every 7 miles (11km). The Wall was probably about 15ft high (4.5m) and topped with 6ft (2m) battlements. There is evidence that when it was rebuilt in AD 200 the Wall was limewashed. It must have been a stark reminder of Roman supremacy, visible for miles across the open country. The Wall was eventually abandoned in AD 383.

Once or Twice Brewed?
Although there are many strange place names throughout the British Isles, Twice Brewed must be one of the most intriguing. The name is said to date from the Middle Ages and has a Scottish connection. When James IV was king of Scotland his troops occupied the area. One of their complaints was that the local beer was far too weak and they ordered it to be fermented twice. The area was known from that time as Twice Brewed. In 1967, when the Hostel and information centre opened, it was called Once Brewed, referring not to beer, but to a nice pot of tea!

View from near Housesteads.

no pubs before Newbrough. However, you are not compelled to walk all the way as there is a summer bus service from Once Brewed to Chollerford which gives time to explore Chesters Fort, one of the most important Roman sites in Britain.

From the Hostel go up to Steel Rigg car park and take the path on the R towards Hotbank. There is a lot of excavation taking place here and you may have to follow signposted diversions. The climb to the top of Steel Rigg Craggs is steep. Continue along the Wall past Crag Lough towards Hotbank. There are marvellous views over the Lough and ahead.

From Hotbank Farm to Housesteads (1½ miles, 2.5km) the Wall continues its relentless sweep along the Whin Sill, the vein of rock which forms the spectacular foundation and the course of Hadrian's Wall. The landscape, cut by the Wall, is truly dramatic.

As you approach Sewingshields Crag (1 mile (1.5km) from Housesteads) there is an impressive view of the overhanging north face of the crag. Once at the top of the crag there are superb views to the north-east and the south. A little further on you will come to the remains of Milecastle 35 from which you can see the point where the Wall is engulfed in the B6318. The Wall was destroyed in the eighteenth century when a military road was built on its course, from here almost to Newcastle.

At Sewingshields Farm, which is in a small wood, follow the track down to the B6318. Turn L onto the road and then take the next turning on the R. Follow this road through a wood and across wet, open moor for approximately 1½ miles (2.5km) until a crossroads, where you turn L. This is the Stanegate, a Roman road. Continue along it for 2½ miles (4km) through Settlingstones to Newbrough. There is a pub in the village where you can take a break, or you can push on to Fourstones, where you will find the Railway Inn just off the main road near the railway.

From Fourstones follow the B6319 past Walwick Grange and on to the junction with the B6318. Just before the road enters Chollerford the entrance to Chesters Fort is on the R.

Chesters Fort is on the bank of the River North Tyne. It was the headquarters of a Roman cavalry garrison and contains the impressive remains of a Roman bath-house. The museum has a good collection of inscribed stones.

After looking round Chesters head for the bridge over the river – about ½ mile (800m).

Cross the bridge and turn R to join the footpath running alongside the disused railway line leading to the Roman bridge abutment. This impressive structure was built to carry the Wall across the river from the fort. This spot is a pleasant place to take a rest.

After a break follow the footpath back to the disused railway and cross the fence onto the track bed. This was the old Border Country's line from Hexham to Scotland and was closed in 1959. Continue to follow the line beside the course of the river downstream through a few farm gates. This part of the line can be overgrown but passes through a surprising variety of scenery from open fields to dark woodland. Be aware that bridges and other structures on disused railway lines may be unsafe, so exploration may not be a good idea.

The line emerges at Wall station, where you can still see the signal box and platform. A short track leads up to the A6079. Turn R and follow the road carefully – it is very busy – for about 1½ miles (2.5km) to the crossroads at Acomb. Turn L

and walk along the main street until you come to Acomb Hostel on the L hand side at the far end.

• DAY SIX •

Acomb to Hexham (2 miles, 3km)

It is possible to walk into Hexham along a bridleway which starts about 100yds (90m) from the Hostel on the L hand side of the High Street, or there are buses from Acomb Garage if you want to get a quick start. If you do not have to rush to catch a train then Hexham is well worth exploring. It has a very fine twelfth-century abbey and a market on Tuesdays.

• PACK-FREE DAYS •

Once Brewed to Housesteads and Vindolanda
A day free of your pack! Housesteads and Vindolanda were Roman forts and visiting the sites gives you an excellent insight into life on the Wall. There are spectacular views today as well.

Leave the Hostel and head for the car park at Steel Rigg. Continue for another 220 yards (200m) until you come to a path on the R signposted to Hotbank Farm. Follow the track which goes round the north end of Crag Lough. The lough is a legacy of the Ice Age, gouged from the rock by ice and originally filled with melt-waters, it has survived to be an important wintering ground for mute swans, whooper swans and tufted duck.

Once past the lough the track turns R to Hotbank Farm; follow it round and regain the line of the Wall walking along it eastwards. As you climb Hotbank Crags there is a marvellous view of Crag Lough and the Whin Sill. To the north you can see two more Ice Age lakes, Broomlee and Greenlee Loughs. The deep gap in the ridge through Wark Forest is where the Pennine Way carves north. Continue along the Wall and pass the well-preserved Milecastle 37. Housesteads Fort is ¼ mile (400m) further on.

Housesteads was known by the Romans as Vercovicium, which means 'hilly spot'. It certainly has one of the most dramatic settings of all the forts along the Wall – the views from it are stupendous. It was built in the second century and is in an excellent state of preservation. You will need to get an admission ticket from the museum. Housesteads looked after its men. Huge granaries with ventilation systems were incorporated into the design and remarkably the fort had a hospital complete with an operating theatre. It also had good drainage and a 24-seater latrine with a flushing tank. The headquarters building is still visible and there was a rather grand house built for the commanding officer. The whole site covers five acres, so there is plenty to explore.

Leave Housesteads on the track by the museum and follow it down to the B6318. Turn R on the road and follow it for about ¼ mile (400m) to a turning on the L signposted to Bardon Mill. Go down this road, passing the remains of Grindledykes lime kiln on the L. At the T-junction turn R and ½ mile later (800m) take the single track on the R marked 'Buses Prohibited'. Pass Chesterholme Farm and the entrance to Vindolanda is on the L.

Vindolanda was a Roman fort before the Wall was built. The site is quite extensive because, in addition to the military buildings, the surrounding civilian settlement has been excavated. There is a military bath house with a hot plunge-pool and hypocaust. There is also a good reconstruction of both stone and turf sections of the Wall. The museum has an outstanding collection of leather garments and some writing tablets giving details of day-to-day life. The audio-visual presentations help to give a realistic impression of life in the settlement.

Leave Vindolanda on the track heading west. At the T-junction turn R and continue straight ahead for Once Brewed.

THE NORTHERN WHITE PEAK

The gritstone moors of the Peak District wrap themselves in a horseshoe around the gentler limestone dales. It is glorious walking country and this route covers both peaks and dales, giving great variety of scenery and walking conditions. By staying two nights at Edale and Castleton, taking in some of the suggested sights, you will be able to see more of a beautiful and fascinating area.

(35½ miles, 56km)

• DAY ONE •

Hathersage to Edale (8 miles, 12.5km)

After staying at Hathersage Hostel overnight turn R and walk to the railway bridge. Take the footpath near the bridge. This goes across fields to a footbridge over the River Noe. Cross the bridge and go through the stile on the R. Follow the river upstream for about 2½ miles (4km) to Shatton Bridge. Turn R over the bridge and cross the main road (A625). Take the footpath under the railway bridge ahead of you. The path leads to Thornhill. Turn R when it meets the minor road in the village, then fork L and follow the road round for about ½ mile (800m). Take a footpath on the R which leads up to the summit of Win Hill. Climb to the summit and pause for breath while you take in the view over Ladybower Reservoir and Derwent Moors to the north and Castleton to the south-west.

From the summit take the track which follows the ridge and gives good views over the Edale Valley. Follow the ridge route for about 3 miles (5km). The last mile of this track is an old Roman road. When you are parallel with the end of the reservoir the track leaves the ridge to turn R. Do not follow it but turn L along a footpath which follows the contours below Nether Moor. It is a clear path which comes gently downhill and passes Clough Farm before arriving at the next Hostel, Rowland Cote, which is about 1½ miles (2.5km) from where you initially turned off the ridge.

• DAY TWO •

Edale to Castleton (8 miles, 12.5km)

Take the footpath in front of the Hostel which

leads across fields to Edale Village. There are several routes from Edale to Castleton but the best route is along Rushup Edge.

Turn R on reaching the minor road at Edale and walk up the village to Grindsbrook Booth. Take a footpath on the L signposted to Upper Booth about 1½ miles (2.5km) away. Follow the footpath to the village where it meets a lane. Cross the lane and then a footbridge. After the footbridge take the path that leads south to Highfield. The path continues over Cowburn Tunnel, which cuts through the mass at the base of Kinder Scout for 2 miles, 182 yards (3.5km), taking the railway line between Sheffield and Manchester.

The path continues straight up to Rushup Edge just under a mile (1.5km) away. On reaching the ridge turn L and walk along Rushup Edge. Near its highest point is Lord's Seat, a Bronze Age

Above: *Hathersage Moor*
Previous page: *The view from Win Hill*

burial mound. After ½ mile (800m) the route drops abruptly down to the Edale road at the foot of Mam Tor. Cross the road and take the footpath to the R which leads down from the ridge to the A625 below.

Cross the main road and take the path which leads L to Winnats Pass. The Pass may look innocuous enough on a fine day but it is an eerie place in bad weather and is said to be haunted. When high winds whine through it, the voices of two lovers murdered here by local miners in the eighteenth century are heard screaming for mercy above the storm.

At the bottom of the Pass a footpath on the R passes Speedwell Cavern, skirts Cow Low and comes out onto a lane. Follow the lane down into Castleton, where it emerges beside the Hostel.

• DAY THREE •

Castleton to Ravenstor (8½ miles, 13.5km)

From the Hostel cross the village green and take the road on the R which leads to Cave Dale. Climb up through Cave Dale past Peak Cavern and the imposing remains of the Norman keep of Peveril Castle above it.

At the top of the dale continue across the moor path for just over 1 mile (1.5km). It then joins a lane which leads to the village of Old Dam. From the centre of the village, follow the path which goes behind Dam Hall and cross the A623 at Peak Forest. Turn L and then take a path off the main road on the R (almost immediately). The path leads to Dam Dale. Follow the path through Dam Dale, Hay Dale, Peter Dale and into Monk's Dale, crossing a lane and two minor roads on the way. From Monk's Dale, where there is an important nature reserve on the opposite bank of the stream, continue until the path meets a minor road above cottages in Miller's Dale. The distance covered from the A623 to Miller's Dale is just under 5 miles (8km).

The dales walked on this stretch of the route are a contrast with the high moorland and peaks which you have already walked. They are easy to walk and are interesting for their geology and natural history. Miller's Dale is steep-sided, secluded and wooded and in the early morning you need to look to the top of the hills to see whether it is a sunny day.

Once you have reached the minor road at Miller's Dale walk down to the B6049. Turn sharp L and walk along the road underneath the double viaduct.

Continue along the road until it forks, just past the church. Here you can choose your route to Ravenstor Hostel which is about ½ mile (800m) away. You can either keep on the Tideswell road and enter the Hostel from it, or you can fork R and, after a drink at the Angler's, walk along a lane through a delightful stretch of Miller's Dale beneath rock faces beside the Wye. The back of Ravenstor Hostel is reached up a steep drive from the lane.

• DAY FOUR •

Ravenstor to Eyam (7 miles, 11km)

Drop down the steep path to the River Wye which runs behind and below the Hostel. Turn L along the lane to Litton Mill. The cotton mill was built in 1782 and had a black reputation for exploiting its young apprentices, some of whom did not survive the harsh treatment and were buried in Tideswell graveyard.

Go through the mill yard onto a track by the river. From here to Cresswell Mill a mile away (1.5km) the Wye twists through a delightful gorge hung with woods. It is a favourite haunt for rock climbers and botanists. Follow the path to Cresswell Mill.

The mill was built in 1815 and stands at the foot of Cressbrook Dale. Its first manager was the poet William Newton, who was also called 'The Derbyshire Minstrel'. Newton was a humane man and

Right: *Little John's grave in Hathersage graveyard.*

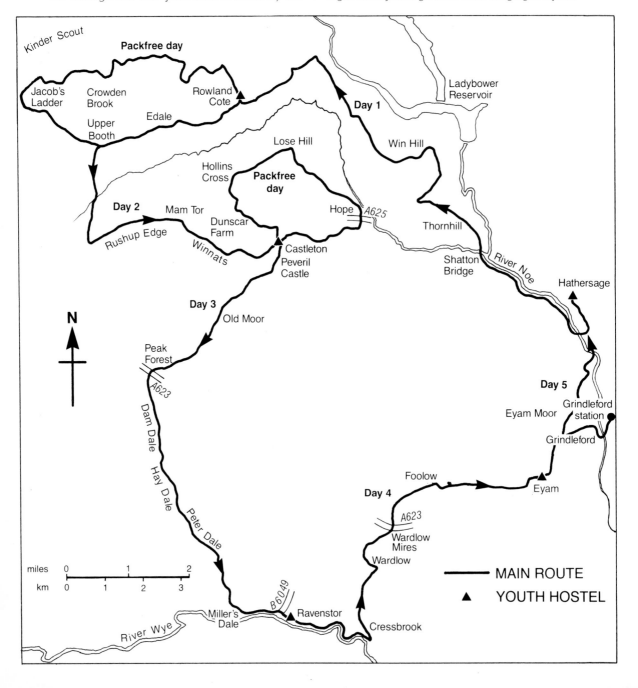

MAIN ROUTE
▲ YOUTH HOSTEL

cared for the apprentices who were in his charge who lived in a row of cottages opposite the mill.

At Cressbrook Mill turn L up the hill and continue along a minor road until it becomes a track. Follow the track up the dale past Ravendale Cottages. Less than a mile further on you have a choice of paths. You can either turn R on a track to the B6465 and then L along the road to Wardlow, or you can continue up the dale to Peters Stone, a block of limestone at the head of the dale, and so to the A623 at Wardlow Mires.

Cross the main road and take the footpath by the inn to Stanley House, about ½ mile (800m) away. Turn R and follow the path across fields to Foolow. Turn R in the village and then shortly afterwards take a footpath on the L across fields to Eyam. The Hostel is north of the village on the road to Grindleford.

Blackden Moor.

• DAY FIVE •

Eyam

There is an occasional bus to Sheffield or you can walk to Grindleford (3½ miles, 5.5km) or Hathersage (4 miles, 6.5km) over Eyam Moor where there are train services.

Before you leave Eyam take time to look around, it has a tragic history. During the Great Plague of 1665 a box of cloth from London was delivered to a house in Eyam. Within a few days people in the house had died. The box of fabric was infected – the plague had arrived in this isolated moorland village. The young rector, William Mompesson persuaded the people of Eyam to shut themselves off from the rest of the world to prevent the terrible disease from spreading to other settlements. If you turn R up the road from the Hostel and climb to the top of the hill you will see a small railed enclosure on the L. This is

Mompesson's Well where the stricken villagers left money in return for food brought to the well by people from the surrounding area.

The people of Eyam paid a high price for their heroism, whole families were wiped out and the graveyard was soon filled. People took to burying their dead in gardens and fields around the village. Riley's Graves south-east of the village are one example, now cared for by the National Trust.

• PACK-FREE DAYS •

Edale

Rowland Cote nestles into the side of the highest peak in the Peak District, Kinder Scout, so there are plenty of excellent day walks starting from the Hostel.

Kinder Scout cannot readily be called a 'peak' because it is actually a plateau rising to 2088 feet (640m). It covers 5 square miles (8km^2) and can be dangerous. It is boggy and featureless moorland, and finding routes across it can be very difficult. Even in summertime it can be a hazardous place for the inexperienced walker. If you venture onto it treat it with respect and if mist descends use your compass and get off it quickly. But Kinder Scout is also an exhilarating place and the sense of achievement at getting to grips with it is very rewarding. The walk described here takes you along its southern edge.

From the back of the Hostel a track leads up to the top of the plateau. Follow this path to the edge of the plateau where it turns L along the edge. Follow the path for about 2 miles (3km). As the edge path turns south above Edale village it is crossed by a path coming up Grinds Brook from Edale village. This path is the beginning of the great Pennine Way. Do not join it but continue along the edge admiring the views over Edale and the ridge of hills beyond. The route continues along the edge for another 2 miles (3km), crossing Crowden Brook. As the path turns north after Edale Head, leave it and turn L on another track which descends to Jacob's Ladder. This Jacob's Ladder (not to be confused with the one in Dovedale) is steps cut into a steep grassy slope by a tradesman in the eighteenth century who used it as a short cut while his packhorse went the long way round. You are now on another branch of the

• LOCAL INTEREST •

The Hollow Hills

The hills around Castleton are not as solid as they seem – the limestone is pierced with underground rivers, galleries, old mines and caverns. The most famous of these caverns are Peak Cavern, Blue John Cavern, Speedwell Cavern and Treak Cliff Cavern. The four are individually spectacular and well worth a visit. Peak Cavern is a vast cave 60 feet (18m) high and 100 foot (30m) wide, naturally formed by water erosion. It is open daily except during the winter months. Visitors to Blue John Cavern descend more than 300 feet (90m) below the surface down 240 steps to a cavern with stalagmites and stalagtites. It is open seven days a week, all year round, as long as the access road is not blocked by snow. Treak Cliff Cavern is also open daily and has many fine stalagmites and stalagtites. Speedwell Cavern at the foot of Winnats Pass is an old lead mine. After descending 104 steps you take a boat underground to view a huge cavern which drops away beneath the viewing platform and rises into blackness above you.

Legend and literature

Hathersage is a small village but has legendary and literary associations. In the churchyard is the grave of Little John, friend and lieutenant of Robin Hood. It is said that John Little was a nailmaker from Hathersage who fled to the forests after the Battle of Evesham, outlawed by being on the losing side.

Charlotte Brontë visited Hathersage in 1845 and stayed for about three weeks. She used the surrounding area as the setting for her novel *Jane Eyre* and many of the places she describes are easily recognisable. Her heroine was named after an old Hathersage family.

Stone walls and stiles

As you walk south the landscape is cut into a patchwork by dry stone walls. Each wall is a work of art and takes an expert builder. The skill is in finding the right shaped stone to fit each space. According to one expert waller it is a bit like doing a jigsaw on a giant scale, forever looking for the piece that fits. Look carefully at the walls as you pass them, this is limestone country and you should find fossils in the stones of the walls. Stiles are not the up and over wooden variety, they are usually wedge-shaped gaps in the wall, edged with two large upright stones. Sometimes large, flat stones are set into the wall as steps.

Pennine Way – it has two beginnings in Edale. Continue down to Upper Booth where you turn L onto the field path which will take you back beneath the peaks to Edale and Rowland Cote about 2½ miles (4km) away.

Castleton

Castleton is a large village and one of the most attractive in the Peak District. If you want to take a break from walking, you could explore the village, which has several excellent pubs, and visit some of the tourist attractions such as Peak Cavern, Blue John Cavern or Peveril Castle.

However, it would be a shame to miss the excellent walk over Hollins Cross to Lose Hill – and you can leave your pack at the Hostel.

From the Hostel cross the A625 and go into the village car park. Take the footpath to Hollins Cross, one of the peaks on the ridge north of Castleton. The path crosses fields and meets the lane to Dunscar Farm. Turn L down the lane for a short distance and then R onto the path across fields and straight up to Hollins Cross. As you walk, the crumbling mass of Mam Tor is on your L. It is known as 'Shivering Mountain' because it slips and moves, defeating all attempts to build a road round it. The A625 has made several brave attempts but is now a pitted and twisted wreck at the foot of its conqueror. It is closed to traffic, probably for all time.

Once you reach the summit of Hollins Cross turn R and continue along the well-defined path which follows the ridge. The wind howls up here, even on sunny days but the views are spectacular. To the south the Hope Valley begins pastorally, dotted with sheep and villages and ends scarred by quarries and bisected by a vast works chimney. To the north, Edale marks the beginning of the Pennine Way. Above it Kinder Scout stretches ancient, well-worn brown velvet to the horizon. Everything beyond it is truly the North of England.

Continue along the track towards the crags of Back Tor (take care on the approach to Back Tor, it is rocky and steep) and the final peak of Lose Hill. At times, walking this ridge gives the hallucinogenic feeling that you are tramping a whale's backbone, Mam Tor is the lashing tail, Back Tor the blow hole and Lose Hill the head rising out of green water.

From Lose Hill turn down a track towards the village of Hope, about 1½ miles (2.5km) to the south. Turn R down the village and cross the A625. Cross the river and turn R on a path beside it, following it upstream on the L bank until you reach Castleton.

• PEAK DISTRICT •

THE SOUTHERN WHITE PEAK

The route through the southern White Peak area rambles across the Derbyshire Dales and visits many of its famous beauty spots. Most of the walking is not arduous, so take your time and look around you. It is suggested that you spend two nights at Ilam and Youlgreave so that you can explore these areas more fully. (40½ miles, 65km)

• DAY ONE •

Ashbourne to Ilam (5½ miles, 9km)

The route begins in Ashbourne, which does not have a Hostel, but Ilam is only 5½ miles (9km) away and the walking is easy.

Go to the top of Ashbourne market place and take the road on the L in the direction of Mapleton. Follow it down the hill to the Peak Park car park. The Tissington Trail, along the disused railway line between Ashbourne and Buxton, begins here. Follow the trail as far as Thorpe Station where you leave it on the L and walk to the Dog and Partridge. From the pub walk down into Tissington village and at the public lavatories follow the sign to Dovedale. The path takes you through a gate, across a field and into Lin Dale. The conical hill on your L is Thorpe Cloud, a well-known land mark.

Continue along the Lin Dale track until you come to the Stepping Stones in famous Dovedale. You can cross these and walk downstream or, if you can bring yourself to resist the stones, continue downstream on the same side. When you come to a car park go through the field gate on the R and follow the field path behind the Izaak Walton Hotel (the contemplative angler fished here). The path takes you to Ilam. The Hostel is Ilam Hall in National Trust grounds.

• DAY TWO •

Ilam to Hartington (8½ miles, 13.5km)

The opening part of today's walk retraces the first day's walk to the Stepping Stones in Dovedale. There is a stile by the last house in the village which will take you onto the path to Dovedale. At

Previous page: *View from the Tissington Trail.*

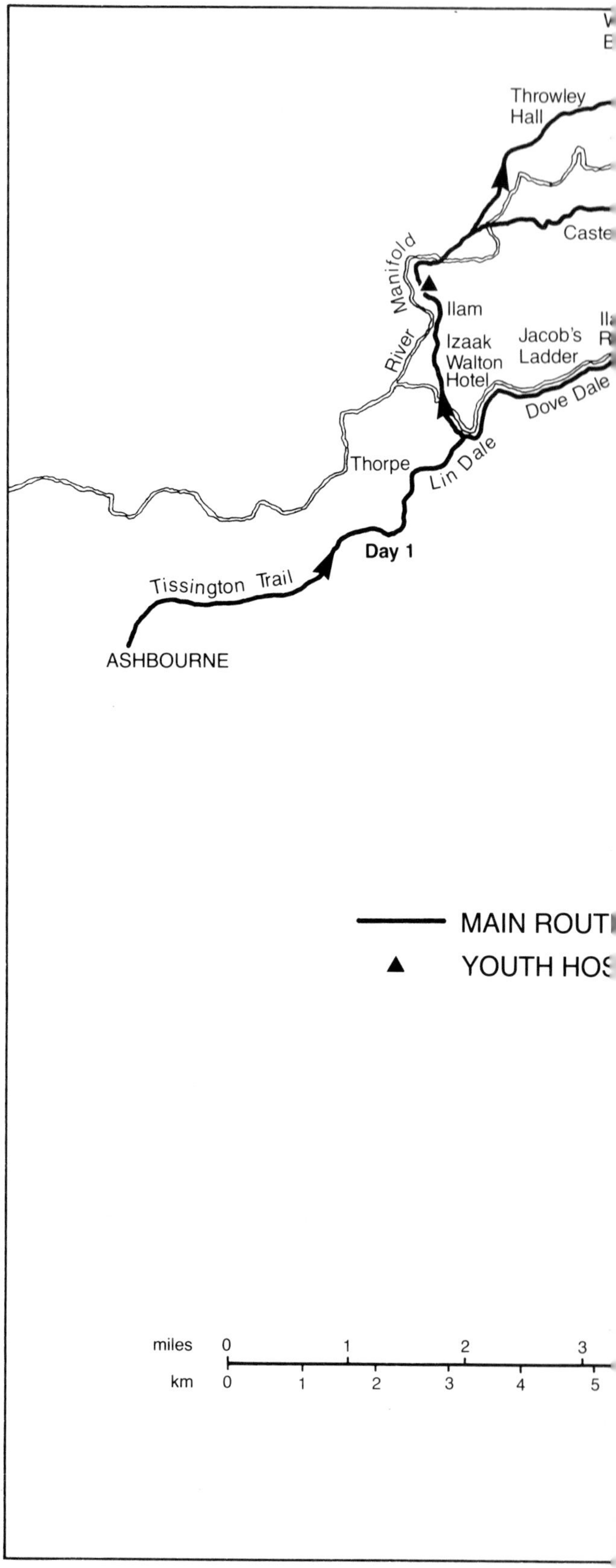

MAIN ROUT|

▲ YOUTH HOS

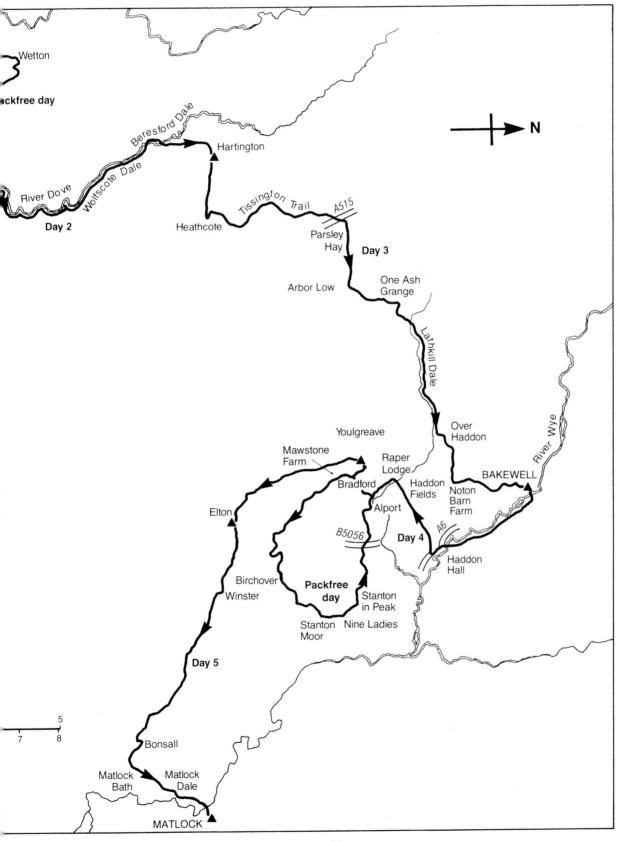

the Stepping Stones turn upstream and walk on the R bank of the river. The path through Dovedale is about 3 miles (5km) long, well defined and used by families for Sunday morning strolls.

Dovedale is a major tourist attraction and if you are walking it at a weekend or at holiday peak times you will not be alone. If you do not meet other walkers you will undoubtedly hear the instructions, commands and curses of rock climbers as they attempt the many rock faces in the dale. Their voices meet you before you see them, clinging to pillars of rock above the water.

The Dove is a picture book river. Clear, rushing, and extremely pretty it winds down the dale, flanked at the northern end by trees and reeds, long tresses of weed marking its flow. I always expect Ophelia to come floating round the next bend. Above it, rocks and hills rise steeply and complete its beauty. If you like open moorland you will find it all too chocolate boxy. On your way upstream you will pass some spectacular rock formations including Jacob's Ladder, the Twelve Apostles and Ilam Rock. There are also caves. Reynard's Cave is impressive, the Dove Holes less so.

Continue along the river until you come to Milldale. Here the path crosses a little packhorse bridge, made famous by Walton as Viators Bridge in *The Compleat Angler*. Cross the bridge and turn R into Milldale, where you can get a cup of tea even on a Sunday morning in peak season. Keep R and follow the road by the river to Lode Mill where, after crossing the river once more, you leave the road and take the river path upstream into Wolfscote Dale. Continue for about 3 miles (5km) until you cross the river again into Beresford Dale and then recross it by Pike Rock and Pool. After this the path swings away from the river and crosses fields all the way to Hartington, about 1 mile (1.5km) away. At Hartington turn L onto a minor road and then R, almost immediately at the next junction. The Hostel is Hartington Hall, up the hill beside a war memorial.

• DAY THREE •

Hartington to Bakewell (10 miles, 16km)

Turn L out of the Hostel gate and follow the road over the hill to the crossroads. Go straight across

to Heathcote. At the crossroads in the hamlet turn L and shortly afterwards turn R to follow the path to Hartington Station on the Tissington Trail. Follow the Tissington Trail for just under 2 miles (3km) to Parsley Hay. Turn R off the trail and walk to the A515. Cross the main road and go down the minor road to Youlgreave, turning R at the first junction. Just off the road to the R is Arbor Low, a prehistoric stone circle in a flat, windswept landscape. Perhaps that is why few tourists visit it, although it is an important site.

Follow the Youlgreave Road for 1 mile (1.5km) until you reach a footpath on the L leading to Cales Farm and One Ash Grange. Turn onto the path and continue past Cales Farm to One Ash. Turn R into the farm. It was once an old monastic holding and has an ice house and interesting architecture. The footpath to Cales Dale is marked by the side of the dutch barn. The path leads down a rocky gorge, keep R into Lathkill Dale.

Lathkill Dale is serene and beautiful, decorated with rocks and trees. Do not rush it. The Lathkill weaves over wiers and through trout pools and there is a nature reserve on the south bank of the river.

Enjoy the dale path until it meets a road, about 2 miles (3km) further on. Leave the dale and turn L up the road to Over Haddon where there is an inn. Turn R in the village and walk through until the road leaves it heading towards Bakewell. Keep R at the first junction and follow the minor road east to a T-junction at Noton Barn Farm. Turn L and pick up a path on the R going north to Bakewell. Follow the path into the town and head for the Hostel, which is close to the town centre.

• DAY FOUR •

Bakewell to Youlgreave (7½ miles, 12km)

This is an easy day and will allow you plenty of time to explore Bakewell or visit nearby Haddon Hall. Bakewell is a pleasant market town and has a fine church and Old House, a museum of past life in the Peak District. In the centre of town is a national park information centre where there are displays of the Peak District today.

To reach Youlgreave leave the Hostel and go

The Manifold Valley, near Ilam.

down to the old bridge. Turn R along the river bank and then cross the bridge near the cattle market. The footpath crosses meadows near the river and after 1½ miles (2.5km) reaches the A6 at Haddon Hall. Turn L along the main road for a few yards and then cross the road. Take the track which leads straight up the large fields known as Haddon Fields. The track leads across these fields for about 1 mile (1.5km) and meets the river at Lathkill Dale. Cross the river to Raper Lodge via the bridge and turn L downstream on the field path to Alport. At Alport the path meets a minor road and the River Bradford flows into the River Lathkill. Cross the road, leaving the River Lathkill and take the path beside the River Bradford. Follow it upstream into Bradford Dale for about ½ mile (800m). Any of the paths on the R goes uphill into Youlgreave.

• DAY FIVE •

Youlgreave to Matlock (9 miles, 14.5km)

Youlgreave was once a prosperous lead mining centre. It is now a comfortable village with a fine church and five wells which are dressed in June.

From the Hostel turn L up the village to the telephone box and then L by the public lavatories and the village hall. Follow the road to the bridge over the River Bradford. Cross the bridge and go straight forward through the stile into a field. Cross the field to a lane. Turn R and then turn L up the track to Mawstone Farm. Follow the track past the farm and keep to the path on top of the ridge until it drops down through the old quarries about 1½ miles (2.5km) from Mawstone Farm. Just after the quarry the path meets a minor road. Turn R down the road and after about ¼ mile (400m) take the footpath on the L up to Elton church. Turn L through Elton past the Youth Hostel and follow the road for about 1 mile (1.5km) to Winster.

Winster was once the centre of an important lead mining industry. The largest lead mine in the Peak District and one of the most productive lead mines in the world was nearby and gave employment to the men of Winster. After centuries of being worked, the mine was closed in 1938 when the price of lead fell. There is a small museum in the old Market Hall.

Turn up East Bank past The Bowling Green pub

Upper Lathkill Dale.

and the public lavatories. Take the L fork in the lane. Where the lane bends R go straight up the alley. This leads into fields and then climbs up the moor. There are several old mines on this moor, take care when near them as the shafts are often covered by a thin layer of rock. After about 1½ miles (2.5km) from Winster the path meets a lane. Turn L along the lane and follow it to Bonsall. At the cross go up Church Street and carry on through the gate along the track to the top of the quarries. Turn L through the stile. The track leads across fields into woods and care should be taken here too, as there are old mine workings throughout the area. Tracks through the woods lead down to Matlock Bath. The Hostel is at Matlock about 1 mile (1.5km) up river from Matlock Bath.

The spa at Matlock Bath was begun in 1698. It was based on the hot water springs which bubble out of the rock at a constant temperature of 68 °F (20 °C) and was extremely popular, particularly in the early nineteenth century. It must have been an exquisite spot, with houses clinging to the side of the limestone gorge above the Derwent. Now the main road and the railway squeeze into the gorge and much of the romance has gone.

• PACK-FREE DAYS •

Ilam and the Manifold Valley (8½ miles, 13.5km)
The River Manifold is erratic. Unless the weather has been very wet indeed it is a disappearing river. At Wetton Mill above Ilam it plunges underground and flows in the dark for 4 or 5 miles (6.5 or 7km). It eventually emerges at Ilam and continues on its way as if nothing unusual had happened. Today's walk gives you a chance to see the River Manifold and the beautiful valley which the river has created.

From the Hostel walk through the grounds down to the river. Turn upstream and follow the river path. You will come to the boil hole where the eccentric river bubbles up from its private underground life. Continue along Paradise Walk, which was named by Dr Johnson on one of his frequent visits to Ilam Hall, until you reach a footbridge. Cross the bridge and follow the path which goes diagonally across fields to the R to the lane at Musden Farm. When you reach the farm turn L away from the river and then almost im-

Above: *The River Dove near Dove Holes.*
Right: *Lathkill Dale.*

mediately R up a lane to Throwley Hall, about 1 mile (1.5km) away. At Throwley Hall farmyard look for a stile to the L. Go through it into a small belt of trees and cross a large field to another belt of trees on the skyline. Walk down the long grass slope to a lane. Look carefully as you go down the slope and you will see evidence of ancient strip farming.

Walk down the lane to Beeston Tor Farm, named after the limestone cliff across the river. Just past the farm there are stepping stones across the river. If they are not under water, use them and climb the track up the L side of the tor. If the river is up, follow the farm track by the river to Weags Bridge. Cross the bridge and follow the lane. The Beeston Tor track comes out onto this road. From the track cross the road and take the footpath uphill which cuts the corner of the minor road. Turn L when you come to the road again and stay on it for a short distance until you come to a stile onto a footpath on the L which leads to Wetton Village, where there are lavatories, a pub and refreshments.

The church and pub are on the main street. Go down the street and where it meets a crossroads on the edge of the village continue straight ahead on an unsigned lane. Follow this ridge lane over the crossroads to the clump of seven trees. Here you take the footpath to the R to Castern. Follow the track through the old mines, taking care of course, and pass through a stile. Turn L and follow the path, keeping to the contour. Go through a gate when you come to it. Below the path is a group of trees and a shed. Cut across the field, keeping slightly uphill, to join the cart track which comes in from the L. Go down the cart track to Castern Hall. Follow the track around the hall. At the sharp L hand bend take the path on the R. This crosses fields and meets the river bridge at Musden Farm. Cross the bridge and turn L across fields on the path you used this morning. It leads to the footbridge and the grounds of Ilam Hall.

A day's walk round Youlgreave (7 miles, 11.5km)
Harthill and Stanton moors can be included in a fine circular walk with several places of historical interest to see on the way. If you are not making

for Haddon Hall or the worldly delights of Matlock, the walk round these moors is an excellent way to spend the day.

Walk down through the village to the church, turn R downhill and cross the river. Follow the road for a short distance, then turn L through a stile into fields. Follow the path across the fields towards trees on a hillside and in the direction of Harthill Moor Farm which is about 1 mile (1.5km) distant. The green mound rising above the path is Castle Ring, an ancient camp.

After passing Harthill Moor Farm you will reach a minor road. Cross this and take the old track ahead of you. To the L is an ancient stone circle, ahead the path passes between the rocky outcrops of Robin Hood's Stride and Cratcliff Rocks, which climbers know well. A short way up Cratcliff is a cave once used by a fourteenth-century hermit. The path joins a track and then meets the B5056.

Turn L on the road for a short distance and then turn R up the path to Birchover village. Walk up through the village, which has a pub called the Druid Inn, and pass the sheds where stone from the quarries was dressed. Keep straight on for about ½ mile (800m), ignoring turnings to the L. There is a track on the L which leads across

Stanton Moor. Follow it onto the moor and it will give you panoramic views of the Derwent Valley and the moors behind.

Stanton Moor is littered with ancient barrows and must have been of significant importance to the people of the Bronze and Iron Ages. Most of the barrows have been excavated and the heather has grown back over them so that they are difficult to discern as man-made.

About a mile onto the moor you will reach a path which leads to the Nine Ladies stone circle, named after sinners who danced on the sabbath and were supposedly turned to stone. A nice story, but the circle probably dates from the Bronze Age. Nearby is a stone tower raised to Earl Grey's Parliamentary Reform Bill of 1832.

Return to the path and continue until you reach a road. Turn L and walk to Stanton in Peak. Continue through the village, ignoring roads to the L and R and reach the B5056 in about 1 mile (1.5km). Cross the road and pass through a stile, unmarked, and take the footpath uphill to the R. When the path reaches a road turn L along the road for a short distance and look for a stile on the R. The path leads down to Alport where you turn L and cross the bridge into Bradford Dale, following the river path and then turn R into Youlgreave.

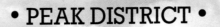

• PEAK DISTRICT •

THE DERBYSHIRE DALES

The beautiful Derbyshire Dales are superb walking country. This walk, from the fine town of Matlock to the tranquil village of Youlgreave and back, crosses moorland and dale, forests and fields. It passes through some delightful limestone villages, where ancient inns provide excellent ales for the weary walker. (21 miles, 34km)

• DAY ONE •

Matlock to Youlgreave (10½ miles, 17km)

Turn L outside the Hostel and walk into the town. Head for the bridge over the River Derwent and cross it, then turn R through the station car park. From the car park take the path which runs alongside the river to the R of the tarmac factory. Follow the path beside the river for about 1 mile (1.5km), then bear L on a path across the fields to a minor road at Snitterton. Turn L and walk into the village.

At Manor Farm follow a footpath on the R signposted to Wensley Dale. Continue along the path for about 1½ miles (2.5km) to the village of Wensley. Turn R along the B5057 to the attractive limestone village perched on a hillside. It has two pubs and a shop. Turn L onto a signposted path at the side of a cottage. The path leads through a belt of woodland and then turns L uphill on a wide track which was once part of an ancient salt way between Cheshire and Derbyshire. Fork R uphill through woodland and come to a road about 1 mile (1.5km) from Wensley. Turn L at the road and follow it for 1 mile (1.5km) to the T-junction with a minor road. Turn R and walk to Birchover.

Birchover is an interesting and attractive village with many old houses, some of which have been the homes of workers from the nearby gritstone quarry for many years. There are two old inns. Of these, the Red Lion is about 300 years old and has a well which is 30 feet (9m) deep, just inside the doorway.

Turn R through the village and R again at the road junction by Stanton Quarry. After ¼ mile (400m) turn L onto a footpath across Stanton Moor. The moor is a blaze of purple heather in the summer. It is scattered with prehistoric cairns

Previous page: *Peak landscape.*
Right: *Stone wall country near Throwley Hall.*

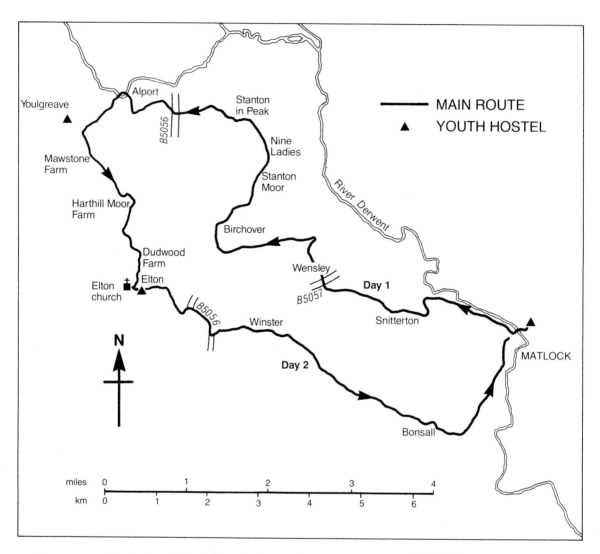

Alport
Youlgreave ▲
Stanton in Peak
B5056
Nine Ladies
Mawstone Farm
Stanton Moor
Harthill Moor Farm
River Derwent
Birchover
Dudwood Farm
Wensley
Elton church ✝ ▲ Elton
Day 1
B5057
Snitterton
B5056
Winster
▲
N
Day 2
MATLOCK
Bonsall

—— MAIN ROUTE
▲ YOUTH HOSTEL

miles 0   1   2   3   4
km 0   1   2   3   4   5   6

and barrows and just to the right of the path, about ¾ mile (1km) onto the moor, is a stone circle known as the Nine Ladies (see page 66). Continue across the moor to a minor road. Turn L and walk into Stanton in Peak.

Walk through the village along the long main street. (You could make a late lunch stop at The Flying Childers pub.) Continue on the road to a T-junction. Turn R on the B5056, then L along the minor road to Alport, about 1½ miles (2.5km) from Stanton in Peak.

At Alport, cross the river, turn L, cross the River Lathkill and immediately take a path on the L which follows the River Bradford through Alport Dale. After ½ mile (800m), turn R up a minor road into Youlgreave. Turn L at the church to the Hostel which is along the main street on the L.

• DAY TWO •

Youlgreave to Matlock (10½ miles, 17km)

Turn L along the main street for 150 yards (140m) then L down a side lane towards the river. Cross the river and go forward along a path which leads south to Mawstone Farm, about 1 mile (1.5km).

From the farm continue along a path which skirts a wood on your R and passes Bleakley Plantation on your L. Continue south-east on the path across fields for about 1½ miles (2.5km) until the path meets a minor road. Turn R on the road and after ¼ mile (400m), turn L on a path to Elton church. After the church turn L through the village and walk along the road until you are about 200 yards (180m) past the last house in Elton. Opposite a narrow metalled lane on your L, turn R down a cart track. The track is part of the Portway prehistoric track which can be traced from Belper to Mam Tor near Castleton.

Follow the track to a minor road. Turn L along it for a short distance to the B5056, where turn R. Very shortly afterwards leave the road on a track which goes L and runs east, above Winster. This is part of the Limestone Way and is waymarked with Derby Ram signs. The Limestone Way connects Matlock with Castleton by waymarked paths across the White Peak District. Continue to follow the Limestone Way waymarks for 3 miles (5km) along linking paths into Bonsall.

Bonsall is a delightful hillside village of limestone houses. There is an unusual medieval stone cross set on a dais of 13 steep steps. It is just opposite the King's Head. Climb the walled track above the pub and follow the Derby Ram signs across Masson Hill. Continue downhill past Masson Lees Farm and so into Matlock.

• LOCAL INTEREST •

Youlgreave
A tour of Youlgreave might begin with the Hostel itself, a handsome three storey building, built for the Cooperative Society in 1887. Seen from one direction the perpendicular tower of Youlgreave church with its eight pinnacles, appears to block the street. Beside it a lane leads down to the river which may be crossed by one of three bridges. The five wells which are dressed here annually (see page 62) are fine examples of this traditional art.

Matlock
In the eighteenth century, eight individual settlements merged together to form the spa resort of Matlock. Thermal waters, discovered at Matlock Bath in 1698, had led to increasing popularity as a health resort. Above the town, 750 feet (225m) up, stand the Heights of Abraham which can be reached by cable car. Their name is said to come from the similarity they bear to the heights climbed by General Wolfe's forces at the capture of Quebec.

Bonsall
This hillside village rises to 850 feet (260m) above sea level. A couple of workshops still remain to remind us of the stocking making industry which existed here. The Via Gellia, the road which leads to Cromford, was built by Phillip Gell to ease the transport of lead from his mines. The Viyella factory took its famous brand name from this eighteenth-century roadway.

THE COAST AND NORTH YORK MOORS

On the rock-strewn coastline of North Yorkshire the towns and villages cling tenaciously in clefts in the crumbling cliffs. The area abounds in stories of heroic sea rescues and the sea and the weather need respect. Sweeping eastwards towards the coast the summer-purple moors are fine walking country, they too demand respect and careful navigation. This walk includes the coast and the moors and is an enticing introduction to a glorious landscape. (52½ miles, 84.5km)

· DAY ONE ·

Scarborough to Boggle Hole (11 miles, 17.5km)

Scarborough is a seaside resort with all the fun of the fair, but it is also a fishing port and a town of historical interest. The Cleveland Way, a designated long distance path, runs through it and the walk follows it along the cliffs. If you reach Scarborough early you can start the walk to Boggle Hole but if you arrive after midday you should stay at Scarborough Hostel and begin the walk the next morning. It is not a long walk, but it is deceptively strenuous.

From the Hostel at Scalby Mills turn L up the steepest part of Burniston Road. Keep to the R hand side until a footpath sign directs you R along the edge of fields to the cliff path. Once on the path navigation is simple – the sea on your R and farmland on your L. There are valleys to negotiate at Cloughton Wyke, Hayburn Wyke and Stoupe Beck.

The wooded valley of Hayburn Wyke can cause confusion because several paths meet. Follow the waymarks carefully. Where Hayburn Beck drops to the beach over a little waterfall is an ideal picnic spot. If you turn inland the Hayburn Wyke Hotel has bar snacks.

Under no circumstances be tempted to continue the walk along the beach from Hayburn Wyke. Continue along the Cleveland Way for 2½ miles (4km) to Ravenscar. Here the path ends on a road which you follow to Raven Hall Hotel gates. In the summer the hotel has an outside bar open to non-residents. About 200yds (180m) up the

Previous page: *Whitby harbour.*
Right: *Robin Hood's Bay.*

road leading away from the gate is a cafe, at Crag Hill House. From the hotel gates walk down a track past the National Trust Information Centre. Follow the track downhill, then across fields and back to the cliff top. Take care that you do not confuse the nature trail signs with the Cleveland Way and 'acorn' signs, which you should follow.

At Stoupe Beck the Way meets a road which peters out in a muddy track, dropping steeply to the beach. It is paved on one side but can be slippery when wet. If the tide is well out you could walk the last ½ mile (800m) to Boggle Hole along the beach, but be warned, if a strong tide is running in you could find the sea right up to the cliffs at Boggle Hole. If in doubt, cross the bridge at Stoupe Beck and follow the path to the Hostel.

· DAY TWO ·

Boggle Hole to Whitby (6 miles, 10km)

A short walk to Whitby along the Cleveland Way will give you time to explore Robin Hood's Bay or Whitby. If the weather is fine you may wish to spend a second night at the Hostel and use the spare day to explore the area.

If the tide is out it is possible to walk to Robin Hood's Bay along the beach (beware of the Boggle, it lives in Boggle Hole Cave on the R as you reach the beach). If the tide is in, use the cliff path on the L as you go through the Hostel gates. Once in the village climb the steep main road. At the top of the hill walk along the Whitby road past the Post Office. Where the road swings L there is a Cleveland Way sign pointing R along Mount Pleasant North. At the end is a broad, grassy path which leads onto the cliff. Continue along the path to Whitby, where the path ends, follow the road to the R of the Abbey. The Hostel is down the cobbled Church Lane, through an arch on the L.

Warning: Do not be tempted to walk along the beach from Robin Hood's Bay to Whitby; many have tried and had to be rescued.

· DAY THREE ·

Whitby to Wheeldale Lodge (12½ miles, 20km)

Whitby is an intriguing town and you may wish to stay a second night so that you can explore it.

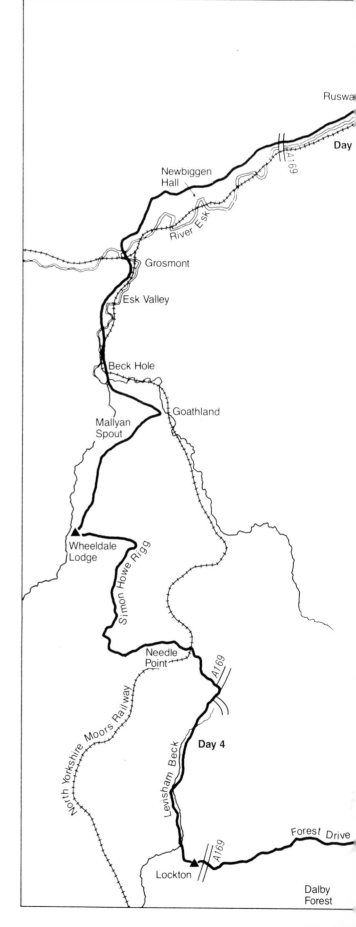

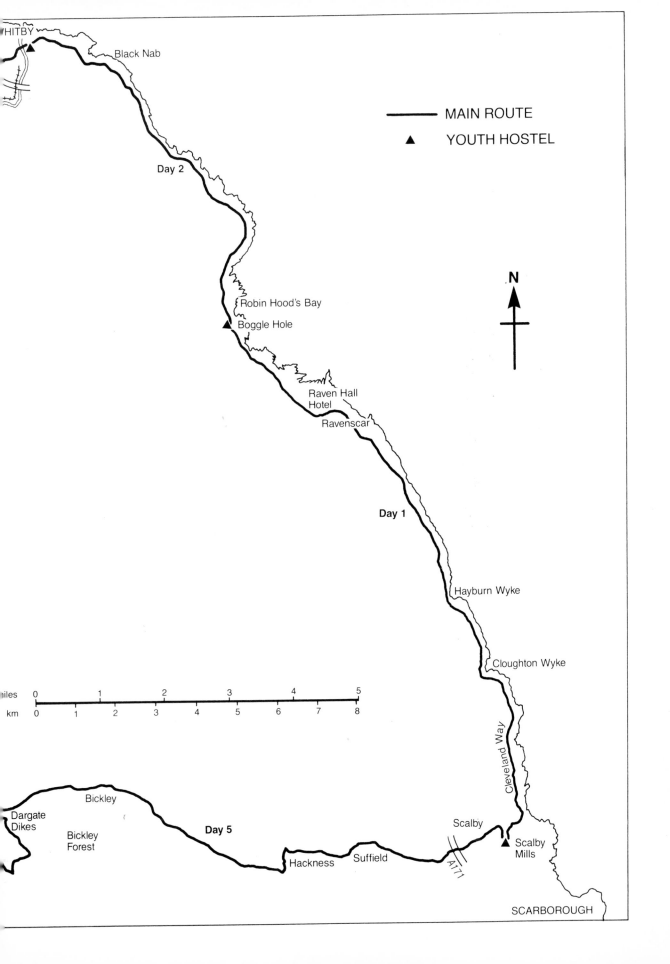

WHITBY

Black Nab

Day 2

Robin Hood's Bay

Boggle Hole

Raven Hall
Hotel

Ravenscar

Day 1

Hayburn Wyke

Cloughton Wyke

Cleveland Way

Bickley

Dargate
Dikes

Bickley
Forest

Day 5

Scalby

Scalby
Mills

Hackness

Suffield

A171

SCARBOROUGH

MAIN ROUTE

▲ YOUTH HOSTEL

N

miles 0   1   2   3   4   5
km   0   1   2   3   4   5   6   7   8

To continue the walk turn L from the Hostel down 199 steps and follow Church Street to the main road. Turn R over the swing bridge and L past the upper harbour, the railway and the bus station. Continue on past Pannett Park and up the hill to the junction. Turn R at the traffic lights (A171 Middlesborough) and L soon after onto a footpath, signposted to Ruswarp. This path runs through Esk Dale and is today's route as far as Grosmont, just over 5 miles (8km) from Ruswarp.

In Ruswarp turn L and go down to St Bartholomew's church, turn R and follow the road along the River Esk to Sleights. Cross the A169 and go forward down the private road past St Hilda's School. After passing the school take the first footpath on your L. Follow this to Thistle Grove and carry on past the front of the farm. Take the next footpath on the L, about 200 yards (180m) after Thistle Grove.

Continue forward until you come to a stile, next to a gate. Cross the stile and follow a stone path until you reach a footbridge. Cross the bridge and follow the path until you come to a lane, cross this and go through the gate opposite. Continue up a muddy path past some mature trees until you reach a stone path again. Go through the gate and follow the path along the top of a wood, walking at the field's edge. About ½ mile (800m) later you will come to Newbiggen Hall Farm, a seventeenth-century hall with high gables and studded doors.

Follow the farm track until it starts bending to the R. There is a stile on the L at this point, go over it and follow the stone path round the edge of the field across the top of a wood. Go through the gate at the end of a field and descend the steep, slippery stone path until you come to a farm track. Cross the stream on the footbridge and continue along the track past Grosmont Farm to the main road. Turn L on the road and follow it to Grosmont.

Grosmont is the start of the North York Moors Steam Railway. The line is 18 miles (29km) long and runs through beautiful country. The village has cafes, a pub and shops.

Continue the walk by going over the level crossing, through a gate on your R. Cross the river by suspension bridge and follow the path to the L, past the church and across the railway tunnel.

Start of the 199 steps, Whitby.

Turn L through a gate and go down to the railway, following the path to the hamlet of Esk Valley. At Esk Valley the track follows the line of the original railway, which was built by George Stephenson as a horse-drawn tramway and opened in 1836. Follow the track to the delightful hamlet of Beck Hole, where there is an inn and a cafe.

At Beck Hole the path joins the road. Go forward on the road, downhill, over the bridge and past the inn. Take the next footpath on the R, which is opposite the cafe. This leads you back to the dismantled railway. Cross over the old track bed and take the footpath signposted to Mallyan Spout. Follow this path for ¾ mile (1km) to the spectacular waterfall of Mallyan Spout. After seeing the waterfall retrace your steps for about 110yds (100m) to the footpath signposted to Goathland and walk to the village.

At Goathland the moors come in among the grey houses and sheep graze in the village. Wheeldale Lodge, the next Hostel, is about 2 miles (3km) from Goathland. Where three roads meet by the church follow the path up onto the moor and past the stone cross. Follow the broad path above the road to Egton Bridge, cutting across the shoulder of the hills until you meet the road to Hunt House. If the visibility is poor it is advisable to ignore the moorland path and follow the Egton Bridge Road from Goathland, turning L onto the road to Hunt House. When the road to Hunt House ends, follow the track signposted 'Roman Road via stepping stones'. The Hostel, a former shooting lodge in the heart of the moors, will soon come into view.

• DAY FOUR •

Wheeldale to Lockton (8 miles, 13km)

Today's route combines forest and open moorland and walks through the beautiful valley from the Hole of Horcum.

Take the Lyke Wake Walk track, almost due east from the Hostel, and follow it for 1 mile (1.5km). Just before you reach the summit of Simon Howe a bridle path on the R leads south down the ridge. Follow it across the moor for just over a mile (1.5km) to Wardle Green at the edge of a plantation. Continue walking south along the bridle path across fields and on the edge of forest until it meets a minor road. Turn L onto the road and follow it until it turns sharp R. At this point a track forks L. Follow the track around the edge of Killing Nab Scar to Needle Point.

A steep path down through the forest from Needle Point leads you to a crossing on the railway line. Cross with extreme care and climb through the woods on the other side. You emerge to a flat heathery expanse below a steep hill. There is a confusion of paths here, but if you want a break you can get to the Saltersgate Inn by following the path on the edge of the gully. It takes you past a farm to the pub which is about ½ mile (800m) away to the south east on the A169. From the pub follow the main road south up steep Saltergate Bank. At the top, where the road takes a sharp turn to the L, there is a track on the R, which leads down the other side of the ridge into the natural amphitheatre that is the valley known as the Hole of Horcum.

Follow the track beside the beck down the valley past Low Horcum Farm (½ mile, 800m).

Continue to follow the path as the valley narrows. About 2 miles (3km) from the farm the beck swings to the R to follow the gorge, but on your L a tributary joins it. Follow the tributary path until you climb steeply up to a minor road at Lockton. Turn L onto the road, and Lockton Hostel is in the old school house in the centre of the village.

• DAY FIVE •

Lockton to Scarborough (15 miles, 24km)

The route from Lockton to Scarborough goes through Dalby and Bickley Forests. Although the walking is not difficult, forest paths can be confusing to follow and navigating amongst rows of identical trees difficult. Unless you are an experienced navigator, it is recommended that you follow the Forest Drive through the forest.

From the Hostel turn L along the Lockton road

The Beggar's Bridge in Glaisdale.

to the A169. Cross the main road and go through a gate onto a path alongside a field. Continue through a gate into wooded Green Dale. Once out of the trees continue along a farm track for a short distance and then take the first footpath on the R across fields to Low Pasture Farm. At the farm turn R along a track to Low Staindale. Continue along the track until it joins the Forest Drive road through Dalby Forest.

Follow the road until it makes a sharp R hand bend about ¼ mile (400m) further on. At this point you can either continue along the Forest Drive to Bickley (4½ miles, 7km) or, if you are experienced at navigating in coniferous forest, you can take the following route.

Where the road bends R carry on eastwards up Grain Slack until the forest track forks. Turn up Dargate Slack, which will take you north to the ancient earthworks of Dargate Dikes and the excellent viewpoint at Crosscliff on the edge of the escarpment. Once you have managed to find your way there and enjoyed the view, continue north down the path and then turn R at the next junction of paths. Follow the footpath to Noddle Farm and from there back to the Forest Drive at Blackwood Bungalow.

Whichever route you choose, follow the Forest Drive out to Langdale End, where the Moorcock Inn will provide excellent refreshment. From the inn the easiest way back to Scarborough is to follow roads for the remaining 7 miles (11km) to the Hostel. Go via the beautiful village of Hackness, which nestles deep in the Derwent valley. If you have time to linger, it is well worth exploring. From Hackness continue on minor roads through Suffield and head for Scalby, where you cross the A171. Continue along Station Road to Burniston Road and back to Scarborough Hostel.

• PACK-FREE DAYS •

Scarborough

Scarborough is one of the oldest seaside resorts in Britain and has something for every visitor. After five days of walking you could spend another night at the Hostel and explore the many things which are on offer.

It has a rich history. Bronze Age man settled here, the Romans used it as a signalling post and the Vikings gave it its name. William le Gros

• LOCAL INTEREST •

Heather moorland
The North York Moors are the largest area of continuous heather moorland in England and Wales. When the National Park was formed in 1952 its primary purpose was to preserve this unique habitat. Three types of heather are found here: ling is the most widespread and hazes the moors with pinkish-purple in the late summer; bell heather, which is deep purple, and the pale pink heather are less common and bloom earlier in the year.

The red grouse feeds on new shoots of heather and to ensure a plentiful supply the heather is burned in controlled patches on a rotation system. The flames destroy the old plants above ground but leave the roots and the peat around them undisturbed. The plant then produces new shoots and the grouse prosper for the shoot.

In wet and boggy parts of the moor cotton grass is common and there is plenty of sphagnum moss. You may also be lucky enough to find the insect-eating sundew, or the bog asphodel. Of course, it goes without saying that you do not pick any of these plants.

Since 1952 the moors have lost over a quarter of their area to pasture and conifer forest. Bracken is a problem too and is encroaching on the heather at the rate of about 300 acres per year.

The North York Moors Railway
The enterprising spirit of Yorkshire people brought railways to this area as early as 1835 and they ran uninterrupted until Beeching swung his axe in their direction in the 1960s. With enthusiasts' great determination the 18-mile (29km) section of the line between Grosmont and Pickering was saved from obliteration and was opened as The North York Moors Railway in 1973. It is now run privately and takes visitors and local people on an unforgettable trip through the remote wooded valley of Newton Dale.

On Day Four of this walk you could catch the train at Newton Dale Station and ride as far as Pickering before returning to Levisham Station and walking to the Hostel at Lockton. Steam and diesel services operate regularly from Easter to October.

Robin Hood's Bay
At low tide Robin Hood's Bay reveals its ancient history. The rocks sweep in concentric curves through the bay. This geological pattern is formed of the oldest rocks in the National Park, which have eroded more than the limestone and ironstone between them. It is a haunt of geologists and fossil hunters.

began its castle in 1136 and the Parliamentarians seized it in 1645.

In the seventeenth century its waters were recognised as health-giving and the Victorians turned it into an important watering place, building the ornate Spa, which was restored in 1981.

Today there are beach amusements, shops, a promenade, a natural history museum, an open air theatre, an opera house and an entertainment complex. Children can visit the local playpark or waterpark. At the theatre you may be lucky enough to catch a play by the local playwright Alan Ayckbourn.

Whitby

Smugglers, pirates, heroes, explorers and Dracula are all associated with Whitby. If you want to take a break from walking, Whitby is an excellent choice, although you will probably have to climb the famous 199 steps more than once as you climb through the steep town.

The pirates are buried in St Mary's churchyard, with the skull and crossbones on their tombstones. It is thought that Bram Stoker used them as inspiration for one of the scenes in his novel *Dracula*, which he wrote while staying in Whitby in the 1890s.

Whitby is inseparable from the sea and still has a fascinating harbour, where fishing boats from many countries jostle. Captain Cook's ship, the Endeavour, was built here and the great explorer sailed from Whitby, bound for Tahiti, in 1768. Cook lived in Whitby as a young apprentice and you can see the house where he lodged, in Grape Lane. Whitby has an excellent lifeboat museum, a tribute to the astonishing bravery of her crews, who have won more medals for gallantry than any other lifeboat men in Britain.

The sea shore gave Whitby the raw material for a thriving jewellery trade. Whitby jet, a black fossilised wood, is found on the beach and in the cliffs. During the nineteenth century, when jet jewellery was all the vogue, there were over 1000 people involved in the finding and carving of jet. Today there are about three jet workers left in the town, but you can still buy exquisitely carved brooches, earrings and bracelets in the town. The history of Whitby's jet trade is traced at the Pannett Park Museum.

St Mary's Church and the ruins of Whitby Abbey dominate the town. It was a religious centre for centuries and the famous Synod of Whitby, which determined the method for dating Easter, was held here in AD 664. Caedmon the poet brought his poems to the monks of Whitby Abbey in the seventh century. You can climb the 199 steps to the cross, which is his memorial. It stands in the churchyard of St Mary's, from where there is a tremendous bird's eye view of the packed red roofs of the town.

• YORKSHIRE DALES •

THE EASTERN DALES

Open moorland, wooded dales, rock-strewn rivers and waterfalls are all encountered on this walk. It crosses Littondale, Wensleydale and Swaledale, and Goredale Scar, Malham Cove, Aysgarth Falls and Kisdon Force are all visited. Much of the walk is through Wharfedale, with dramatic limestone scars towering above the River Wharfe and delightful villages such as Linton. The going varies from easy riverside walking to tougher moorland paths.

(89½ miles, 143km)

• DAY ONE •

Skipton to Linton (11½ miles, 18.5km)

There is no Hostel at Skipton so you will need to arrive in time to walk to the next Hostel at Linton. Skipton is a pleasant market town and the walk starts from the northern end of its broad main street, overlooked by the impressive gateway of Skipton Castle.

Take the main road past the castle for about ½ mile (800m) then turn L onto a minor road to Embsay. At the Elm Tree Inn turn L through the car park and go over a stile onto a footpath, which heads for the church. Rejoin the road and just past the church take the footpath on the R through fields to the minor road at Eastby. Turn R and walk along the road for about 200yds (180m), then take a footpath on the L to Eastby Moor. A steep climb with good views leads over two stiles onto the moor itself.

Once on the moor follow the line of grouse butts to a shooting hut. Beyond the hut turn L onto a track and then shortly afterwards turn R onto a path which leads to Upper Barden Reservoir. Follow the track for about 1 mile (1.5km) to the reservoir. Cross the dam and turn L at the footpath sign to Burnsall. Continue along this path for about 1½ miles (2.5km) to a very small reservoir and a junction of paths. At the junction follow the yellow footpath marker past several boundary stones, downhill to a wall. At the wall turn L to a footpath which goes through a wood, down to a minor road.

Turn L on the road and follow it to the attractive village of Burnsall, in Wharfedale. Go into the village and turn R onto the Dales Way. Follow the Dales Way along the L bank of the River Wharfe until you come to a suspension bridge. Cross the river and continue along the Dales Way for about 2 miles (3km) to Linton Falls, just before Grassington. Recross the river via the iron bridge, then continue uphill on a minor road. Cross the B6160 and go forward on the B6265 to Linton and the Hostel. Linton is one of the most delightful villages in the Dales.

• DAY TWO •

Linton to Malham (10 miles, 16km)

From Linton Hostel turn R and cross the bridge over the stream. Turn R onto the footpath to Threshfield about ¾ of a mile (1km) away. When you reach a road turn R, then almost immediately L onto a path to Skirethorns Lane. Turn L on Skirethorns Lane for about ¼ of a mile (400m), then L again onto a track to Wood Nook Caravan Site. This attractive path continues to Bordley, just over 2 miles (3km) away. At first it follows the R bank of a beck through woodland and then crosses Malham Moor.

At Bordley keep straight on through the farmyard to a footpath sign with a blue marker. Go through the gate on the L onto the path which skirts Kealcup Hill. Follow the track for about a mile (1.5km), down to Lee Gate, where it joins a tarmac road. Bear L down the road, which descends to Gordale Bridge (1½ miles, 2.5km).

Just before the bridge is a footpath on the R, leading to Gordale Scar. It is a short detour and shouldn't be missed. Gordale is a spectacular limestone gorge, created when a cave system collapsed. At the head of the ravine, Gordale Beck tumbles 300ft (90m) over the limestone. If there is not too much water in the beck it is possible to scramble halfway up the waterfalls for a breathtaking view back down the gorge. Return to Gordale Bridge. On the other side of the road, a little below the bridge, is Janet's Foss. This is a fairytale waterfall set amongst mossy rocks and trees. Janet is the fairy queen who, legend says, lives behind the foss. Finally return to the road, continuing down into Malham and to the Hostel.

Previous page: *The Swale.*
Opposite: *Gordale Scar.*

• DAY THREE •

Malham to Kettlewell (12 miles, 19km)

Walk down to the village, turn R and take the road, then a footpath, to Malham Cove. This great curved cliff of limestone was created by gigantic upheavals in the earth's surface during the Ice Age. It is 240ft (73m) high and a waterfall once poured over its lip. Long ago the water took a less flamboyant route through the fissures in the limestone pavement at the top of the cliff. A stream now flows from the base of the cliff.

Climb steeply up L to the top of the cove and pause to look at the remarkable limestone pavement, cracked and fissured by water. Follow the path through the now dry valley for about ½ mile (800m) to where there is a footpath off to the R, signposted to Water Sinks and Malham Tarn. The stream which flows from Malham Tarn sinks underground here and reappears at Aire Head Springs, south of Malham village.

Malham Tarn is 1½ miles (2.5km) from the top

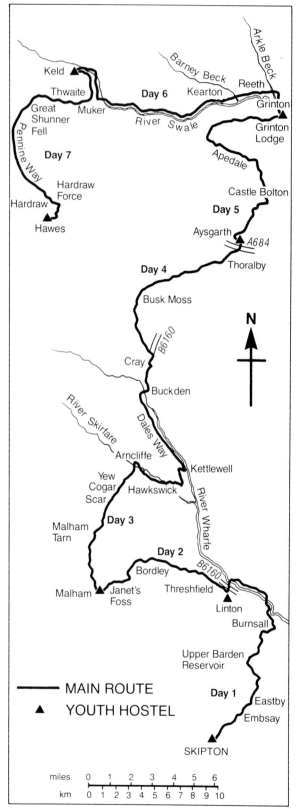

Keld

Thwaite

Day 6

Great
Shunner
Fell

Muker

Kearton

Reeth

Barney Beck

Arkle Beck

River Swale

Grinton

Grinton
Lodge

Day 7

Hardraw
Force

Apedale

Castle Bolton

Day 5

Aysgarth

▲A684

Thoralby

Day 4

Busk Moss

Cray

B6160

Buckden

Dales Way

River Skirfare

Arncliffe

Yew
Cogar
Scar

Hawkswick

Kettlewell

River Wharfe

Day 3

Malham
Tarn

Day 2

Bordley

Threshfield

Malham   Janet's
Foss

Linton

Burnsall

Upper Barden
Reservoir

N

Pennine Way

Hardraw

Hawes

▲

▲

▲

▲

——— MAIN ROUTE

▲ YOUTH HOSTEL

Day 1

Eastby

Embsay

SKIPTON

miles   0   1   2   3   4   5   6

km   0 1 2 3 4 5 6 7 8 9 10

of Malham Cove. Once you have reached the tarn follow the footpath along the R side of the tarn for ½ mile (800m) to a gate in a wall by a wood. Turn R to a footpath sign to Middle House. Cross the wall via a stile and look for a track on the L up the hillside to a gate. Continue along the track for just over ½ mile (800m) to the abandoned farm, then follow the footpath signposted to Arncliffe. You are now on an ancient footpath known as Monks' Road. The monks from Fountains Abbey had extensive grazing rights in this area.

Arncliffe is 3 miles (5km) away. Follow the path as it runs above Yew Cogar Scar, with spectacular views down the steep valley of Cowside Beck with Fountains and Darnbrook Fells sweeping above it. On reaching Arncliffe turn R past the Falcon Inn and then L down the road to the church where the names of men who fought the Scots at Flodden in 1513 are recorded. Some of their descendents still live in the dale. At the church turn R along the footpath to Hawkswick. The path goes through fields and follows the course of the River Skirfare. Keep the river on your L until you come to a footbridge. Cross it and turn R on the minor road to Hawkeswick and L at the footpath signposted to Kettlewell.

The path climbs steadily up to the R to the crest of the moorland ridge dividing Littondale and Wharfedale. At the highest point there is a fine view down Wharfedale to the imposing overhanging buttresses of Kilnsey Crag, an exacting challenge for rock climbers. From the ridge the path swings round to the L and descends to the road (B6160). Follow the road to the L, over the bridge to Kettlewell and the Hostel.

• DAY FOUR •

Kettlewell to Aysgarth (16 miles, 25.5km)

Return to the bridge over the River Wharfe and cross it. Turn R onto a footpath which runs along the bank of the river. This is the Dales Way and the route follows it beside the river to Buckden, 4½ miles (7km) away.

Buckden is one of Wharfedale's picturesque villages. It got its name from the deer which used to inhabit the area and in Norman times was in a hunting reserve. When hunting ceased the valley was given over to sheep farming and the farmers

Arncliffe from Brayshaw Scar.

brought their wool to the Buck Inn to be sold. Some of the ancient weighing equipment can still be seen at the inn.

At Buckden make for the National Park car park and take the footpath which runs north out of the car park above the B6160. It swings R towards Cray and descends to the road past the village at Cray High Bridge. Turn R along the road and follow it, climbing steadily for the next ¼ mile (400m), then leave it for a track on the L over Stake Moss. After a gentle climb the track crosses the flat top of the moor to join a lane. Do not take the footpath indicated by a signpost but turn R along the lane which is followed until just before it starts to descend. Leave it here for a short lane on the R leading up to a gate with a stile. Go over the stile to a second gate, after which you will see a foot-path sign 'Thoralby 4½ miles' (7km). The path is not clear at this point but continue in the general direction indicated by the signpost and you will soon see a wall with a gate. Once through the gate a faint path materialises and when you pass between two wooden gateposts in a broken wall the way is reasonably clear again, and descends to Thoralby with good views over Wensleydale.

At Thoralby, turn L on the road and go past the Post Office. When the road swings L uphill leave it for a lane on the R, continuing along it for about 1 mile (1.5km) to where it joins a road coming over the bridge on your R. Turn L and almost im-mediately L again onto a footpath through fields to Aysgarth and the Hostel, just across the A684.

• DAY FIVE •

Aysgarth to Grinton (12 miles, 19km)

Today's walk takes you past Aysgarth Falls, one of the most popular beauty spots in the Dales, and onto open moorland.

Take the road past the church and the Yorkshire Museum of Carriages and Horsedrawn Vehicles. The museum has a very comprehensive collection and is housed in an old mill. Cross the bridge, and just before the road climbs and turns L, go through a gap in a wall on the R and follow the river closely, near the middle falls. From here climb steeply to join the main path, which runs through trees to the most impressive section of Aysgarth Falls, where the River Ure rockets over limestone steps.

Retrace your steps to the main path and continue on to a stile and a signpost pointing away from the river to Castle Bolton. Follow the path for just over a mile (1.5km), when it emerges onto a minor road. Turn R and follow the road, turning L into the village. The castle, which dominates the village, was built in the fourteenth century and has been partly restored.

From Castle Bolton the route lies across the moors to Grinton. Take the lane close to South View, which heads over the moor to the north of the village. The path is signed but not until you are actually in the lane. Go through the gate into a large pasture and head uphill, passing a small plantation. Where the wall turns to the L the path becomes a distinct track. Continue uphill, turning R, then L to go through a gate onto moorland. Continue on the track for another ½ mile (800m) when it goes downhill to Apedale Beck but our route turns L up the valley.

This valley was once littered with mines and you will see evidence of this near the head of the dale. Do not, under any circumstances, venture underground. Once at the top the sheer spaciousness of these moors, stretching to the distance in an undulating carpet of purples and browns, lures you on. Continue forward to a fence. Just before it the track veers to the L to cross the fence, close to a large mound with a curious pit in the centre.

The track now veers back to the R before turning L over the gravelly remains of spoil heaps,

Upper Swaledale from Crackpot Hill.

where cairns indicate the way. Leave this path when you reach some shooting butts. The way is not clear at first, but turn R, keeping between the butts on your L and a small stream on your R. The stream soon becomes well-defined, splashing over a small waterfall. Follow the line of the butts, crossing the stream. At the second butt after the crossing, a narrow path swings away to the R. Follow this around the contours of the northern flank of Gibbon Hill, with splendid views of Swaledale. The path continues and widens into a green track, heading along the edge of the heather towards a prominent cairn. From the beginning of Apedale to here is about 3½ miles (5.5km).

From the cairn, smaller cairns lead the way across a limestone outcrop before the path descends slightly and continues on for just over ½ mile (800m) to a substantial shooting box, reached after crossing a wooden bridge over a stream. Follow the footpath sign but after 330yds (300m) do not follow it downhill but continue slightly uphill. The track zig-zags to the summit of High Harker Hill, which is marked by a large mound, topped with a bridleway sign.

After 55yds (50m) the path becomes clearer and leads off across the moor with a steep-sided 'hush' (see page 90) on your R. In about ½ mile (800m) the track descends steeply between cairns in the direction of Grinton. The Hostel can be seen in a group of trees about 1 mile (1.5km) away on the edge of the moor. The track now changes direction, curving away to the L, so look out for a small cairn and a faint path leading straight ahead, down the slope at this point. It is not very clear, so remember to keep in the general direction of the Hostel. Cross another track, where a tongue of close-cropped turf leads into the heather. Bear slightly L towards a patch of reeds from which a faint path emerges. This soon becomes an obvious track, which crosses a stream then goes through a gate. Follow a clear bridleway to the road. Turn L and after 150yds (140m) turn R onto a track to Grinton Lodge.

• DAY SIX •

Grinton to Keld (15 miles, 24km)

Swaledale runs a sinuous ribbon between high

• LOCAL INTEREST •

Limestone landscape

As you tramp the Dales it is hard to imagine that you are walking on what was once the sea bed. Millions of years ago the skeletons of sea creatures formed the basis for the rock that is now the limestone of the Dales. Other rocks were formed on top of the limestone but where these have been eroded the limestone is exposed in scars and pavements typical of the area. The limestone pavements are criss-crossed with crevices called grikes, formed by erosion. Grikes are usually between 9 and 12 inches wide (20–30cm) and can be as deep as 12ft (3.7m). They are a haven for shade-loving plants such as harts tongue fern.

Hushes

A hush is a man-made valley created in the search for minerals. Streams were temporarily dammed and once a considerable amount of water had collected uphill behind them they were breached. The waters cascaded down the fellside scouring away the soil to reveal minerals beneath. Much of Swaledale has a history of lead mining and it must have been a spectacular sight when very large dams were breached and the water roared downhill.

Wensleydale cheese

The perfection of Wensleydale cheese has taken 700 years. It is thought that it was first made by the monks of Jervaulx Abbey during the Middle Ages. The recipe was handed down by word of mouth until recently, when the method was written down. The cheese was originally made during the summer by Wensleydale women. Before the seventeenth century these farmhouse cheeses were made from ewe's milk but with the introduction of more cows into the area production moved to cows milk and sheep were left to produce wool and mutton.

It was not until the end of the nineteenth century that the cheese was commercially produced at the first Wensleydale cheese factory in Hawes. There is still a creamery in Hawes today and together with others at Kirby Malzeard and Coverham they produce hundreds of tons of the delicious cheese annually.

hills. Today's walk takes you right through it on a delightful path, mostly by the River Swale.

Leave the Hostel and go downhill into Grinton. Grinton church is often called 'The Cathedral of the Dales'. If you have time it is worth a visit. Originally Norman, it was added to in the thirteenth and fourteenth centuries. Cross the river and immediately turn L on a path through the fields to Reeth. Rejoin the road and cross Arkle Beck. Reeth is a pleasant village with a large village green. It was once the centre of the area's lead mining industry. The Swaledale Folk Museum on the green shows how life in the dale used to be.

To continue the walk look for an alley near the bridge, signed 'To the river'. Through the alley a waymarked path leads through fields to the next hamlet of Healaugh. Just through the village take the minor road to Kearton. This crosses Barney Beck. Once on the other side take the footpath on the L, which follows the contours of the hill and descends to the B6270. Walk along the road for a few yards and then take a footpath on the L, which follows the river bank all the way to Gunnerside, 4 miles (6.5km) distant.

At Gunnerside cross the road and continue along the river bank. The path swings away from the river, through the hamlet of Ivelet, and then returns to follow the Swale. From Ivelet, follow the river for 2 miles (3km). It swings in from the R at Muker, coming from the narrowest part of the dale. About ½ mile (800m) above Muker is a footbridge, cross it to the west bank of the Swale and continue north along the river. This is a delightful section of the walk. The fells crowd in and the river cuts through its limestone bed in a series of waterfalls. The best is about 2 miles (3km) further on, near Keld. You approach Kisdon Force through woods. The river spills over the waterfall in a deep, wooded gorge. Keld and the Hostel are less than ½ mile (800m) away.

• DAY SEVEN •

Keld to Hawes (13 miles, 21km)

The Pennine Way passes through Keld and is followed all the way to Hawes.

Return towards the bridge over the Swale but do not go down to the river, take the Pennine

Way, which leads off on the R. When path forks L down to Kisdon Force keep R and climb above a line of limestone cliffs. The path swings south high above the River Swale, with magnificent views of Swaledale. Follow the Pennine Way over several stiles and gates, to Kisdon Farm (2 miles, 3km).

At the farm turn R (west) and descend to Thwaite (1 mile, 1.5km). At Thwaite turn R on the road for a short distance and then L into a walled lane. Continue to the end of the lane and out onto the open fell. The path climbs steadily to the summit of Great Shunner Fell, just over 2 miles (3km) away. Great Shunner Fell is a magnificent viewpoint. Strategically placed between Swaledale and Wensleydale, you can look north across the headwaters of the Swale to Nine Standards Rigg, to the west is the escarpment of Wild Boar Fell, and to the south-west the Three Peaks of Whernside, Ingleborough and Pen-y-ghent.

The long descent of 5 miles (8km) to Wensleydale begins across peat hags, heading for a prominent cairn. The popularity of the Pennine Way ensures a clear, if sometimes soggy path down the broad ridge to enter a walled lane for the final part of the descent to Hardraw. In the wooded ravine to the L of the path is England's highest waterfall, Hardraw Force.

From Hardraw follow the Pennine Way signs through fields, across the River Ure on the road bridge and onto a flagged footpath to Hawes.

THE WESTERN DALES

Yorkshire's Three Peaks, Pen-y-ghent, Ingleborough and Whernside, are climbed on this classic walk. The route follows the epic Pennine Way and part of the Coast to Coast path too. There are some steep ascents – even opportunities for scrambling among rocks, and some of the tracks are rough, but the route is well marked. There are no stop-overs on this walk, one night is spent at each Hostel.

(90 miles, 144km).

• DAY ONE •

Gargrave to Malham (7 miles, 11km)

Gargrave is easily reached by bus or train from Leeds and Bradford via Skipton. The first day's route is short, to allow time to get started. It follows the Pennine Way to Malham and is well signposted all the way.

Leave Gargrave along West Street, the first part of the walk is through fields to Eshton. From Eshton the route follows the bank of the River Aire. Between Airton and Hanlith it stays on the east bank of the river through delightful parkland. At Hanlith the Pennine Way crosses the Aire to the west bank, passing an old manorial mill before entering Malham on a footpath through fields. When the path meets the minor road at Malham turn R, the Hostel is along on the L.

Malham is a particularly popular tourist spot but it is still a pretty village and seems to have survived the onslaught of visitors very well. There is an excellent information centre nearby.

• DAY TWO •

Malham to Stainforth (19 miles, 30km)

The summits of Fountains Fell and Pen-y-ghent can be climbed today but the walk begins at Malham's famous cove.

From Malham follow the resurfaced Pennine Way to Malham Cove. The path climbs to the top of the spectacular natural amphitheatre (fully described in the Eastern Dales Walk). Do be careful on the limestone pavement at the top. Limestone

Previous page: *Malham Cove.*

is notoriously slippery when wet and the fissures are just the right size to take a leg and snap it like a carrot if you lurch out of control.

The path follows a dry valley behind the cove to where a stream flowing out of Malham Tarn sinks in a ruckle of boulders. It then joins the road which skirts Malham Tarn and passes through the grounds of Malham Tarn House. The house is now a centre for the Field Studies Centre which runs courses for students mostly from schools and universities. Charles Kingsley stayed at the house in the nineteenth century and the scenery around him was the inspiration for his book, *The Water Babies.*

Pennine Way signposts continue to point the way through fields past the isolated farmhouse of Tennant Gill, about 1½ miles (2.5km) north of the tarn. From the farm it starts a gentle climb up Fountains Fell. Fountains Abbey once held grazing rights to the fell and gave it its name. On the plateau at the summit there are curious pits. They are the remains of old coal shafts.

The way goes across the wall just north of the summit and meets a minor road. Turn L on the road for ¼ mile (400m) and then R at Dale Head. About ½ mile (800m) along the path is Churnmilk Hole, a pothole. If you wish, you can avoid the climb up Pen-y-ghent by turning L here and following a walled lane to join the Stainforth to Horton road near Helwith Bridge. Turn L along the road and follow it for about 2 miles (3km) to Stainforth Youth Hostel, which is just south of the village on the B6479.

However, it would be a pity to miss Pen-y-ghent as it is one of the finest summits in Yorkshire. Seen from Churnmilk Hole it crouches as if ready to spring across the landscape. Keep R on the Pennine Way, which climbs steeply towards the summit about 1½ miles (2.5km) distant. You need to scramble through some gritstone outcrops to the top but the rewards are well worth it.

From the summit cross the wall and descend in a northerly direction on a well defined path which swings L across a soggy moor past Hunt Pot. Don't be tempted in, it drops about 90ft (27m) at first and then descends another 70ft (21m). The path reaches a gate into a lane on the L. Before going into the lane it is worth turning R for about 200yds (180m) to look at the chasm of Hull Pot. In wet weather the northern rim has a fine waterfall.

Crina Bottom on Ingleborough.

Retrace your steps to the gate and follow the lane down to Horton. You could take a break in the village before turning L to walk 4 miles (6.5km) along the B6479 to Stainforth and the nearby Hostel.

• DAY THREE •

Stainforth to Ingleton (13 miles, 21km)

The highlight of today's route is the summit of Ingleborough.

Turn L from the Hostel and walk in the direction of Horton. Just through Stainforth turn L onto a lane which crosses the railway bridge and descends to cross the River Ribble over an old packhorse bridge with a graceful arch. Below the bridge is Stainforth Force, where the river plunges into a wide pool. Follow the lane up to Little Stainforth, where there is a rather grim seventeenth-century hall. Turn R onto a minor road. Follow this for 500yds (450m) and then turn L on a footpath signposted Hargreaves Barn. The path goes through fields in the direction of the prominent peak of Smearset Scar. A mile (1.5km) further on the path meets a lane. Turn R and follow the lane past Higher Bark House and Lower Bark House to a road. Turn L and go down to Wharfe. This little hamlet is well off the tourist tracks and has several delightful old houses.

From Wharfe turn R up a walled lane which

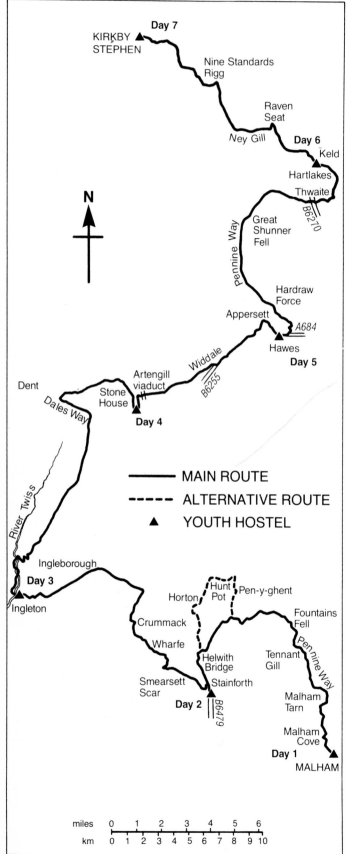

KIRKBY
STEPHEN
Day 7
Nine Standards
Rigg
Raven
Seat
Ney Gill
Day 6
Keld
Hartlakes
Thwaite
B6270
Great
Shunner
Fell
Pennine Way
Hardraw
Force
Appersett
A684
Hawes
Day 5
Artengill
viaduct
Widdale
B6255
Dent
Stone
House
Dales Way
Day 4
River Twiss
Ingleborough
Day 3
Ingleton
Horton
Hunt
Pot
Pen-y-ghent
Crummack
Fountains
Fell
Wharfe
Helwith
Bridge
Tennant
Gill
Pennine Way
Smearsett
Scar
Stainforth
Day 2
B6479
Malham
Tarn
Malham
Cove
Day 1
MALHAM

—— MAIN ROUTE
------ ALTERNATIVE ROUTE
▲ YOUTH HOSTEL

miles 0 1 2 3 4 5 6
km 0 1 2 3 4 5 6 7 8 9 10

forks after ¾ mile (1km). Take the L fork over the clapper bridge crossing Austwick Beck. Continue up the muddy lane to a farm road where you turn R to Crummack Farm. After ½ mile (800m) skirt the farm on the L and follow the track which climbs the hill on your L. After the climb the path swings R along the top of the grey limestone scars. There is quite a network of paths here but keep to the R. The path continues along sheep-cropped turf between low limestone scars and crosses a wall over a ladder stile. In about 200yds (180m) you will come to a crossroads of paths, with a signpost to Horton to the R, Ingleborough to the L. This is the well-known Three Peaks Walk (Ingleborough, Whernside and Pen-y-ghent).

Turn L on the path, which soon gains the open fell near an old shooting hut. Ingleborough is now clearly ahead and the path climbs towards it across the flank of Simon Fell. Helicopters were used to carry the stone to restore the path here. The distinctive, flat-topped summit is a huge hill fort rich in historical remains. It was probably fortified in the Iron Age and was used by the Brigantes in their defence against the Romans.

From the summit cairn turn L and follow the well-defined path for about 3 miles (5km) down to Ingleton. The views from the upper part of this path are very far-reaching. Away to the east are Fountains Fell and Pen-y-ghent, to the north are the rounded hills of the Howgills and nearer still is the long summit of Whernside.

Ingleton was once a coal mining village but is now a popular tourist venue. The Hostel is near the River Doe.

• DAY FOUR •

Ingleton to Dent (14 miles, 22.5km)

Whernside is the third of the Three Peaks and is climbed today.

At Ingleton the River Twiss tumbles through a wooded ravine in a series of waterfalls. Start the day along the Falls Walk. It is Ingleton's main attraction and is privately owned so there is an entrance fee. The wooded gorges are impressive and bridges cross and recross the river, giving excellent views of the waterfalls. The final fall is Thornton Force, which is spectacular after there has been heavy rain.

When the footpath joins a lane, turn R and after 200yds (180m) leave the lane by turning sharp L along a grassy path which zig-zags up the steep fellside. The path soon levels out and winds through little limestone scars, eventually running close to a wall on the L. Follow this wall, apart from one or two minor diversions, for the next 3½ miles (5.5km). It climbs gently up the long south-west ridge of Whernside. The gradient is gentle until just before the summit and the views improve with each step. The view back across Chapel-le-Dale to Ingleborough is particularly fine.

The village of Malham.

At the summit (2415 feet, 736m) you are standing on the highest mountain in Yorkshire. The descent follows the wall to the north. After 1 mile (1.5km) it turns R, but our route continues straight on in the direction of Three Tarns. It may seem strange to find tarns in a limestone landscape but at this level they are sitting on a cap of impervious millstone grit. Continue past the tarns in a northerly direction, descending close to another stone wall. About 1 mile (1.5km) from the tarns you will reach a track running across in a north-westerly direction. This is the Dales Way. Turn L onto it and head down into Dentdale. When you reach the road you have to make a tough decision. You can

either turn L for 2 miles (3km) to the charming little village of Dent, with its cobbled streets and the extreme attraction of cafes and pubs, or you can turn R to the Hostel, which is four miles in the opposite direction.

• DAY FIVE •

Dent to Hawes (10 miles, 16km)

Walk down the road in the direction of Dent for about ¾ mile (1km). At Stone House Farm cross the River Dee and take the green track beneath Artengill viaduct. The track skirts Dent Fell for 1 mile (1.5km), running between Great Knoutberry Hill and Wold Fell. Even in this remote spot there are the remains of old industries – coal pits and quarries – scattered on the fells and dales. The quarries here produced Dent marble, a distinctive, dark limestone much in demand for Victorian fireplaces.

From its highest point the path descends into Widdale for 1½ miles (2.5km) before entering a wood. Continue through the wood, out and down to the beck at Widdale Foot. Cross the beck and turn L onto the B6255. After 2 miles (3km) take a minor road on the L to Appersett. There is pleasant river and woodland scenery around Appersett viaduct and excellent views ahead across Upper Wensleydale to Great Shunner Fell. At Appersett turn R on the A684 and walk to Hawes. The Hostel is on the B6255, which meets the road you are on before you enter the town.

• DAY SIX •

Hawes to Keld (14 miles, 22.5km)

Today's route crosses Great Shunner Fell on the Pennine Way.

Walk into Hawes and turn L to cross the River Ure. The Pennine Way leads off to the L shortly after the bridge. It goes through fields to Hardraw. Behind The Green Dragon Inn is Hardraw Force, the highest above-ground waterfall in England and worth seeing.

The route continues along the Pennine Way along a walled, stony lane which gives access to the wild and often boggy moor and the long but easy climb to the summit of Great Shunner Fell. It

• LOCAL INTEREST •

The Pennine Way

From Edale in Derbyshire to Kirk Yetholme in Scotland the Pennine Way wends 250 miles (400km) over the backbone of Britain. It crosses some of the wildest and most majestic landscapes in the country and is the ultimate challenge to walkers in Britain. The section which passes through the Yorkshire Dales is one of the most varied and exciting.

The Pennine Way is not an ancient track. It was created by the National Parks Commission in 1965. But the credit for its existence should go to Tom Stephenson, first secretary of the Ramblers' Association, who put forward the idea as long ago as 1935 and battled for ramblers' rights to long-distance paths.

Hardraw Force

J. M. W. Turner painted Hardraw Force, capturing the incandescence of its plunging water. The waterfall is 96ft (29m) high. There are higher waterfalls underground – Gaping Gill for one – but Hardraw is the highest fall in England above ground. The force of the water has scoured the rock back and created a space behind the fall so that it is possible to walk behind the roaring force. Expect to get sprayed by the brownish water if you venture in.

During the nineteenth century the amphitheatre created by the waterfall was used as a natural auditorium for brass band contests. The bands must have had hard competition from the thunder of the falls. You can still see the remains of the bandstand and the tiers cut for the spectators. The entrance to Hardraw Force is through The Green Dragon pub and there is an admission charge.

Wildlife in the Dales

The captivating beauty of the Dales is enhanced by its wildlife, particularly its birds. On the upland moors you can expect to hear the harsh call of grouse, the sorrowful cry of peewits, and, if you are lucky, catch sight of curlews and golden plovers. On clear days lark song will accompany your walk. Buzzards and ravens inhabit the remotest spots, while kestrels hover over lower ground. Malham Tarn and the area around it is a wildlife sanctuary. The tarn is the nesting ground for many wildfowl, including mallard, tufted duck, and golden eye. The rivers are the habitat of dippers, common sandpipers, and grey and pied wagtails.

A packhorse bridge near Hardraw Force.

is a bleak summit and, although it is higher than Pen-y-ghent, lacks its drama. In good weather the views are compensation, especially those down into Swaledale.

From the summit the Pennine Way descends for just over 2 miles (3km) to a walled lane which joins the road at Thwaite. The direct route to Keld is to turn L on the B6270, but the Pennine Way takes a better route. From the centre of Thwaite follow the Pennine Way signs along a natural limestone shelf high above the River Swale. You won't be disappointed in the views, and if you have time, a short detour to Kisdon Force is worth the effort. The distance from Thwaite to Keld Hostel is just over 2 miles (3km).

• DAY SEVEN •

Keld to Kirkby Stephen (13 miles, 21km)

Keld is the crossroads of two important long-distance paths, the Pennine Way and the Coast to Coast Walk. The final day of this walk leaves the Pennine Way and continues on the Coast to Coast.

Leave Keld on the Kirkby Stephen road and after about ½ mile (800m) take the road on the R, signposted to Tan Hill. A stile on the L takes you onto a footpath along the top of Cotterby Scar and swings in a northerly direction above Whitsundale Beck, following the stream to Ravenseat Farm. Cross Whitsundale Beck on the farm road and soon after turn R onto a footpath. After ½ mile (800m) cross Ney Gill, then follow it for about 1 mile (1.5km) to a shooting hut.

Shortly after the hut the path turns down to the road but our route turns R and strikes off up the fell towards a conspicuous stone pillar on an outcrop of rock 1½ miles (2.5km) distant. The steepness of the ascent begins to ease once you reach the pillar. Continue along the path for 1½ miles (2.5km) in order to reach the summit of Nine Standards Rigg.

The collection of cairns, or standards, which give the hill its name are a unique feature. They are shown on eighteenth-century maps but their origin is uncertain. One theory is that they were built to give the marauding Scots the impression that an English army was encamped on the hill.

From the summit continue the walk by heading south before swinging west to join a bridleway which descends to Hartley, a distance of 4 miles (6.5km) from the summit. From Hartley the route follows a short lane and then a path across fields to Kirkby Stephen. This is a pleasant market town with an unusual cloistered market place.

A WEEKEND WALK IN THE YORKSHIRE DALES

This delightful weekend walk takes in some glorious limestone scenery and is guaranteed to make anyone want to see more of the Yorkshire Dales. Each day's walk starts and finishes at Stainforth Hostel.

(22½ miles, 36km)

• DAY ONE •

Stainforth, Feizor, Sulber Nick, Wharfe, Stainforth (15 miles, 24km)

Turn L from the Hostel to reach the B6479. After about ¼ mile (400m), turn L over the railway bridge and cross the superb packhorse bridge over the River Ribble. Continue along the minor road to Little Stainforh and imposing Stainforth Hall. Cross the minor road and go ahead along the lane signposted Footpath to Feizor. The lane becomes a footpath through fields and climbs a gentle gradient, crossing a couple of walls. As

Previous page: *The Stainforth packhorse bridge.*

you walk, the shapely peak of Smearsett Scar comes into view on your R.

The path levels out and gradually descends to the attractive little hamlet of Feizor. When you reach a minor road, turn L, then almost immediately R over a stile. Follow a footpath signposted to Austwick, through fields. Where the field path joins a lane, turn R to a crossroads of lanes. Go straight across to Austwick Beck, cross the footbridge and go up the lane to a junction with a road.

Turn R and after 400 yards (365m) leave the road by a lane on the L. At the top of the hill turn R over a stile onto a footpath and follow it through two fields. Cross a minor road and follow the footpath signposted to Norber. It keeps to the L of a wall, crosses some low cliffs and continues up a field to a stile. Go over the stile into a large field which is scattered with hundreds of boulders. These are the Norber Boulders, deposited in the Ice Age. The whole area has a maze-like quality and it is easy to lose your sense of direction. To

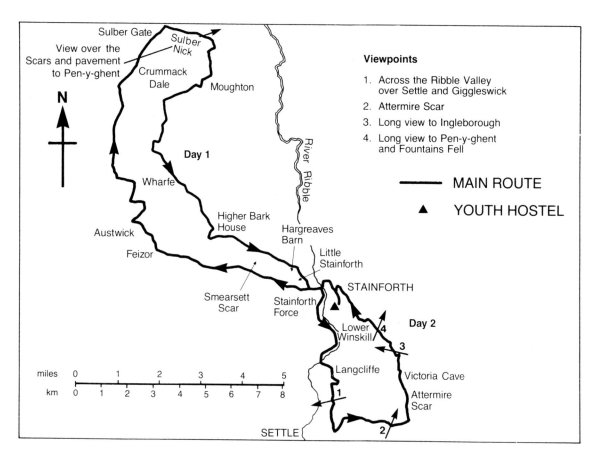

escape from the maze keep going uphill, aiming for the northernmost corner of the field. There is a step stile in the wall which is not easy to spot until you are almost on top of it.

Go over the stile and turn R. Follow the path. It eventually climbs over stony ground with good views to the R over Crummack Dale. The path becomes indistinct, but keep more or less straight ahead and avoid descending to the R. Eventually you will come to a junction with the track coming up from Crummack Farm. Turn L (uphill) along this track until you come to a path. Turn R for about 1 mile (1.5km) of level walking over beautiful short-cropped turf. The view from this path across the head of Crummack Dale towards Pen-y-ghent is very fine, the long rows of vertical scars contrast strongly with the broad acres of white limestone pavements.

When the path reaches a gate and a stile, go over the stile and follow the path for 300 yards (274m) to a signpost R to Horton. Turn R down the well-trodden Three Peaks path. The Three Peaks are Ingleborough, Whernside and Pen-y-ghent. The path runs down a groove in the plateau known as Sulber Nick. Cross a wall and leave the main path by bearing R around a small hill to rejoin the wall. Follow the wall south to cross a stile and continue along a path through the limestone to the head of Crummack Dale. Descend from the edge of the escarpment to where the path becomes a walled lane. Follow this all the way down to the lovely little hamlet of Wharfe.

The network of paths around the houses is confusing but keep bearing L and you will eventually join the road at a sharp bend. Turn L along the road for a few yards, then turn R over a stile onto a footpath through fields. Cross a small stream, two walls and a farm lane before climbing up the hill to the L of a wood. Continue over a series of stiles to reach a farm lane near Higher Bark House. There is a good view over Ribblesdale from here.

Turn R up the track and L onto a footpath signposted to Hargreaves Barn. This is a clear path through fields which form the northern flank of Smearsett Scar. After crossing a wall below the scar, the path disappears, but keep straight on across rough pasture to a stile into more fields. The path follows the field wall down to a stile into a short lane at Hargreaves Barn. The lane leads to a road. Turn R to Little Stainforth and L at Stainforth

• LOCAL INTEREST •

Glaciation
The Yorkshire Dales were once covered in a sheet of ice as much as one kilometre thick in places. As climatic changes occurred the ice responded by thickening or melting. When the Ice Age ended, around 10,000 BC, glaciers flowed out from high land, carving valleys in the soft limestone and carrying debris and soil which were deposited on valley floors. Differing rock strata created a variety of soils and the vegetation reflects this, from the calcium rich limestone to the acidic millstone grit of the uplands.

Stainforth
The two settlements of Little Stainforth and Great Stainforth which lie on either side of the Ribble, were once linked by a stony ford which gave them their name. The packhorse bridge, built by Samuel Watson, replaced the bridge in the 1670s. Downstream the river cascades over Stainforth Force (a North country word for waterfall) rushing into a huge cauldron-like pool. It is possible to swim here but it can be dangerous after heavy rain or unhealthy during drought.

The Norber Boulders
These massive boulders were torn from Ribblesdale and Crummack Dale by passing glaciers at the end of the Ice Age. When they were eventually deposited they protected the immediate countryside from the eroding effects of the weather. Blocks of Silurian slate weighing as much as 20 tons and supported by limestone, create a sculptural addition to the landscape.

Hall. Recross the river and go back up the hill to the Hostel.

• DAY TWO •

Stainforth, River Ribble, Attermire Scar, Winskill, Stainforth (7½ miles, 12km)

Retrace yesterday's steps to the packhorse bridge. Cross it and turn L on the field path to Stackhouse past Stainforth Force. The next mile (1.5km) is a delightful walk along the river. In summer the meadows are knee high in buttercups and the river burbles over its limestone bed. On the opposite bank is a paper mill, a reminder of the area's industrial past.

At the lane to Stackhouse turn L across the footbridge. Follow the lane up to the B6479, and turn R over the railway bridge. The road bypasses Langcliffe but the village is delightful and well worth a short detour. Rejoin the main road as far as the Bowerly Hotel. Take a minor road on the L opposite the hotel. There are good views across Settle and the green dome in the distance is the chapel of Giggleswick school.

Continue along the minor road. Before it descends into Settle, turn L up a lane to climb past a ruined barn into fields. A signpost to Malaham points the way up the hill by a broken wall. It is steep going at first but the gradient soon eases as the prominent three-tiered buttress of Attermire Scar appears on the skyline.

Through a gate the path forks, take the upper path to a tiny cave. Just round the corner the full splendour of Attermire is revealed. This is superb limestone scenery, and although the cliffs here do not have the same massive grandeur as Malham Cove or Goredale Scar, their variety is exquisite.

Continue along the path below the crags and cross a wall. Where the path to Malham goes R, turn L keeping close to the wall up a stony valley. As the path levels out Attermire Scar and Victoria Cave are seen straight ahead. If you have a torch, Victoria Cave is safe to explore but very muddy. The path continues over a stile and descends to a track. Turn L onto the track, through a gate, and then immediately R keeping more or less parallel to the Scars.

A faint path soon appears leading to a stile. Go over it and across wonderful, short-cropped turf to a road. Turn R over the cattle grid and immediately L on a minor road to Upper Winskill. When you reach Upper Winskill (Higher Winskill on farm gate), turn L down a lane to Lower Winskill. Go between the farmhouse and a barn, over the stile, then diagonally R across a field to another stile. In summer, the next meadow is an alpine delight with wild thyme, rock roses, buttercups and various hawkweeds. The path goes into a wood and descends a series of smooth limestone steps to emerge into a field. Cross the field and enter a short lane leading to Stainforth. Turn L and L again at the B6479 for the Hostel.

SHROPSHIRE CHALLENGE

The Shropshire hills have inspired painters, musicians and poets, but walking them is still the best way of experiencing their beauty. This walk begins and ends in Ludlow and climbs Titterstone Clee Hill, Wenlock Edge, Caer Caradoc and the Long Mynd.

(76 miles, 122km)

• DAY ONE •

Ludlow to Wheathill (10 miles, 16km)

From the Hostel cross Ludford Bridge and turn R along Temeside. Turn L up Weeping Cross Lane to Sheet Road and then turn R. Follow the road as far as a walkway by a telephone kiosk. Follow the walkway into the housing estate and where it joins a road turn R. At house number 62 turn R, then L and follow a footpath alongside number 54. Where path ends at a field turn L and follow the path uphill to join a road. Turn R up the road for about 240 yards (220m). Where the lane bears R go through a gap in the hedge to L of gate. Follow the line of the hedge to a large tree then turn L to a stile in corner of field. Cross stile and keeping the hedge on R follow the edge of the field to the A49.

Cross the road with care and go over a stile into a field. With the hedge on R cross three more stiles to reach a road near Little Ledwyche Farm. Turn L and follow the road to Ledwyche Pool. Follow the farm track along R side of the pool. Continue along the path now waymarked with Shropshire Way signs to pass Ledwyche Covert on your R. Continue along the field boundary until the gap into the next field. Turn sharp R and follow the path to where three fields meet. Bear L and head for a stile straight ahead. Cross this stile and field to a footbridge over a stream. Go uphill and turn L across the field to the stile, go into the next field and cross it to the stile at top R hand corner. Follow the farm track up to the brow of the hill where you turn L across field to gap in the hedge. Turn R and follow the edge of the field to a footbridge. Cross the stream and head for the top R hand corner of field. Go over the stile and follow the field boundary to a stile out onto a minor road. There is a good view back across Ludlow from this stile.

Turn R along the road and after 160 yards (150m), turn L up a green lane. Follow this to St Paul's church, Knowbury (worth a visit if you have time). Cross a stile into church grounds and then another into a field. Contour round the hill to a stile in the far fence. Continue by crossing a number of stiles and small fields until you reach a lane. Turn R and at the end of the lane cross a stile into a field. Cross the field to the stile at L of house and follow the track to the A4117 at GR579758.

Cross the road and follow the lane signposted to Dhustone Inn. At the first bend go straight ahead across a cattle grid and down a farm track. When the track bends go forward into a green lane. At the end go through a gate and cross the field to Shop Farm. Pass R side of farm and cross the footbridge. Cross the field and then the next field to a gate at the top L hand corner. Through the gate, turn R and follow the field boundary until you pass under overhead power cables, then turn half L. Cross to a stile into a field near Nine Springs Farm. Over the stile, follow the R hand boundary of the field to a small gate at top L. Through the gate, follow the path to a footbridge over Benson's Brook.

Cross the bridge and continue along the path onto open land. Cross the stony track and walk across rough pasture to Titterstone Incline. To reach the top of Titterstone Clee Hill, follow the old incline up to the quarry and walk round its L rim and up to the trig point at the summit. In bad weather it is wiser to turn R at the quarry and follow the track up to the aerials at the top.

Titterstone Clee Hill is the second highest hill in Shropshire (Brown Clee, which you can see to the north, is the highest). In good weather the views from the top are superb. To leave the summit, look north-east for a red roof at Callowgate and descend to it. Just to the L of the cottage enter a farm track between hedges and follow it to road at Bromdon Farm.

Turn L past the farm and then R over a stile into a field, the graveyard of numerous old vehicles. Cross the field to a gate at top R, then cross the next field to a metal gate then a wicket gate. Go through this wicket gate, across two fields and you will reach the track to Coveridge Farm. Turn L along the track then almost immediately R through a gate into a field. Keep the hedge on

Previous page: *Ludlow and Titterstone Clee.*
Right: *Corndon Hill.*

your R and follow it to a stream, cross and go through a gate. Keep the old hedgerow on your L and walk to the wicket gate into the wood. The path is now clear, follow it to a minor road. Turn R on the road and Wheathill Hostel is about 100 yards (90m) on the R.

• DAY TWO •

Wheathill to Wilderhope Manor
(13 miles, 21km)

Retrace yesterday's steps as far as the road at Bromdon Farm where you turn R uphill. Just over the brow turn L onto the track to Knapps Farm. Just short of the farm turn R across a field and bridge over a stream. Bear R uphill towards the cottage and then through the gate to L of it. Turn L down the track to the road. Turn R, then immediately L down the track next to the large house. Follow the track to Y-junction, turn R. Follow the track past Newton Cottage to the minor road.

Cross this road into a sunken lane and follow uphill to two gates. Go through L gate and continue uphill. There are good views of Titterstone Clee Hill to the R of track. Follow the track across the moor heading for two aerials. When you reach them go through a gate and follow the wall, keeping it on your R for about ¾ mile (1km), then go through the gate onto the open ground of Brown Clee Hill. Take the track straight ahead (with the broken fence on your L), then turn R to the summit. It's a good lunch spot – the views are stunning.

Retrace your steps to the broken down fence and go through the gap and over the stile in the fence on L. Follow track through gate and then down to road at GR585869. Turn R and shortly L. Continue along the road turning R at the signpost for Earnstrey. Follow the road for about 1 mile (1.5km) then take first on L. Continue forward then take the track on L past Earnstrey Hall. Go through the gate into field and follow the hedge on L, then go through the next gate. Turn L and go through another gate. Follow the hedge on your L until it ends, then go half R, heading downhill for the gap in the hedge. Cross the next two fields heading for the line of trees in hedge. Look for a cottage on your L and follow the field boundary

until you are level with it. Cross the stile and with the hedge on your R make for a metal hurdle and cross it. Cross the small wooden bridge and follow the track to another stile, cross this and the field to a gate into a farmyard. Find the track to R of the farm buildings and follow it onto the road at the hamlet of Holdgate.

Turn R along the road to the church, then turn L through the gate into field. Go downhill and through a gate to stepping stones over a stream. Cross the stream and head for the road, cross it and go through a gate into a field. Cross and go over the bridge across the River Corve. Walk uphill to the B4368 at Hopescross. Turn R and then L. Just past the black barn turn R over a stile. Cross the field and the bridge over a stream, then turn L. Follow the path over two stiles. About 33 yards (30m) past the second stile turn L over a small bridge, then R over a stile. Follow the path to a farm lane. Turn R towards Lower Stanway, cross the bridge and turn L following the path to cross another bridge. Continue to yet another footbridge and once over this go uphill. You are now approaching the beautiful escarpment of Wenlock Edge and you should be able to see Wilderhope Manor Hostel ahead of you. Follow the edge of the field and turn L when the hedge ends, following edge of the next field and turn R behind some trees. Follow the track over a stile and past the front of the farm to a stile by the Hostel.

• DAY THREE •

Wilderhope Manor to Bridges (17 miles, 27km)

Today's walk climbs to the hill fort on Caer Caradoc and goes across the Long Mynd. These hills are some of the most spectacular in Shropshire.

At the end of the Hostel drive cross the road and go down the bridleway into a wood. Continue for about ½ mile (800m) and then bear half right down the path which emerges to a field. Cross the field and go through a gate onto an old railway line. Go over it and through another gate onto a farm track. Follow the track to Coats Farm and then onto the B4371.

Turn R along the road and just past a white house on L turn L through a gate into a field and cross to a gate in the top R corner. Continue to the black metal gates in the top R corner of the next field and out onto a lane. Turn R and after about 160 yards (150m) turn L onto a bridleway. Follow this to the road near Gilberries. Turn R along the road and after ½ mile (800m) turn L down the signposted track to a cottage. Turn L past the cottage and cross the footbridge. Cross the stile into a field and turn R through the hedge. Go from field to field over the next five stiles. After the fifth stile, follow the edge of the field to the bridge. Cross the stream and follow the track. Where it meets the farm track turn L and continue to the road. Turn L and walk to Cardington. There is good beer and excellent bar snacks at the Royal Oak in the village.

Continue the walk past the Royal Oak car park and at the post box turn L and follow the road to a T-junction. Turn L and then immediately R onto the road signposted 'No Through Road' (it is a right of way). At the entrance to the Old Vicarage turn R down the track over a stile into a field. Continue north-west over three stiles heading for a line of hills. Turn L after the last stile and follow the path out onto the road at GR495960.

Cross the road and go up a wide dirt track to the stile. Cross and turn L along the ridge. This is The Wilderness and from here there are superb views of the rugged cap of Caer Caradoc Hill ahead and The Lawley to its R. Follow the ridge to

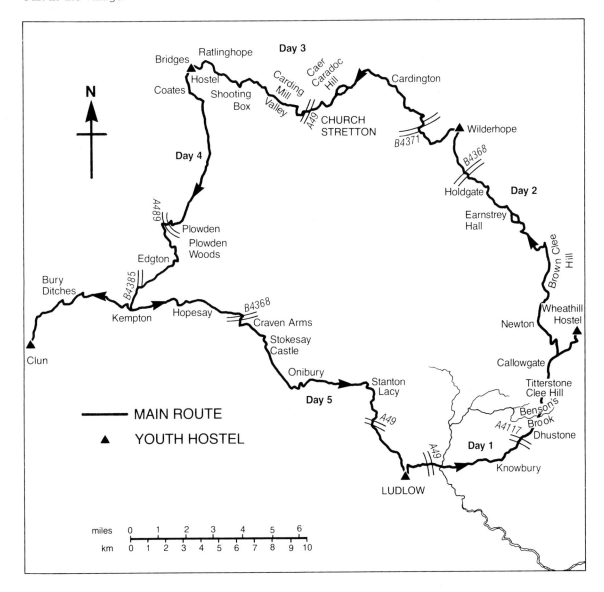

• LOCAL INTEREST •

The Long Mynd

For 10 miles (16km) the high ridge and gorse clad moors of the Long Mynd dominate the Shropshire landscape. Deep valleys have been etched by springs which rise from its rounded crest. Lying so near to the Welsh border these 4530 acres of countryside have been of strategic importance. The very name underlines the Welsh connection – from 'mynydd' meaning mountain.

Ludlow

Ludlow is a town well used to fame. Painted by Turner and described in the poetry of A. E. Housman, it stands on a steep hill by which two rivers flow. The defensive strength of the town was recognised as early as the eleventh century when the castle, now in ruins, was built by Roger de Lacy. Prince Arthur brought his bride Catherine of Aragon here six months before he died and it is said that the sons of Edward IV, the 'Princes in the Tower', made their last journey from its secure walls. The story of Ludlow is well documented at the town museum at Butter Cross.

Stokesay Castle

To call this attractive fortified manor house a castle is something of an exaggeration. It would not hold out long from a determined assault. Fortunately today's visitors come with more peaceful intentions. The castle takes its name from the twelfth century owners, the De Saye family. The structure is unique; stone towers stand topped by a timber framed house and surrounded by a moat. It is open from May until October.

a stile onto a farm track. Turn R downhill to a second stile on R. Turn R over the stile and climb to the summit of Caer Caradoc. It is a romantic peak, its summit sculpted by the hill fort. The views from the top deserve lots of time. If the top is shrouded in mist you are advised to stay on the track.

Leave the hill on its southern side and rejoin the track just before a wood. Continue through the wood and into a sunken lane. Go over the stile onto a farm lane to New House Farm. Turn L and continue to the T-junction. Cross over the stile into a field. Go forward across the field out onto the A49 at Church Stretton. Cross the road with care to the double stile and follow the path to a railway line. Cross this with extreme care, go over the stile and follow the path to the road. Turn L and follow the road to the main road near Church Stretton fire station. Turn R for the town centre.

To leave the town follow the main street to the crossroads by a bank and turn R along Shrewsbury road. Continue until you see a sign for Carding Mill Valley, turn L and follow the road up the valley. This deep-cut, rugged valley is now owned by the National Trust. It is a very popular beauty spot so expect many visitors at the height of the season. The road ends in a car park. From there take the path up the valley until a Y-junction of paths and streams. Cross the stepping stones and with the stream on your R take the R path uphill towards the Long Mynd.

Once at the summit you can enjoy the magnificent views across Shropshire. Take your time and then turn L along the wide track to the road near the Shooting Box. Turn R and follow the road for ½ mile (800m), then turn R onto the track signposted Ratlinghope. Keep on to a large house where you turn L down the track to a road.

Turn R and continue to the T-junction. Opposite the manor house, turn R onto the signposted path and continue to the bridge over Darnford Brook. Cross and turn L along a wide green track, go over the stile onto the road. Turn R and you will find Bridges Hostel 220 yards (200m) on L.

• DAY FOUR •

Bridges to Clun (16 miles, 26km)

Turn L from the Hostel and after 100 yards (90m)

Near Bridges.

turn L and go past the Three Horseshoes pub. Follow the road through the gate to Coates Farm. At Coates, turn R through the gate and follow the road to Medlicott. At the hamlet, bear R and remain on the road for another mile (1.5km) to the junction to Kentnor and Bishop's castle. About 100 yards (90m) beyond this junction go through the gate on L and walk uphill onto the Long Mynd.

As yesterday, the views are spectacular, especially to the west where the Stiperstones, Cordon Hill and the Welsh hills can be seen in the distance. Turn R along the road as far as the entrance to the gliding club and turn L past the club buildings. Walk along a rough track which runs close to the escarpment on your R. Continue down the tip of the Long Mynd until the path meets a road. Turn L and follow this road to Plowden.

At the A489, turn R and walk for ¼ mile (400m). Turn L onto the minor road to Lydbury North. Cross the bridge over the River Onny and take the first L up a private road. Continue uphill for 600 yards (550m), then turn L through the gateway into Plowden Woods. Take the broad central track uphill. After 550 yards (500m) this track turns east and rises very steeply. Almost at the top of a steep climb look for a narrow path on R. Follow this to the edge of the woodland. Go through the gate into a field and go downhill to a minor road at Edgton. Turn R and walk to the centre of the village. At the crossroads turn R, go to the top of the hill and then bear L, continue to the next crossroads.

Go forward and after ½ mile (800m) go through two farm gates. The road becomes an unfenced track and meets the B4385 opposite the entrance to Walcot Park. Turn L and follow the road into Kempton. Turn L beside Kempton Stores and after 55 yards (50m) turn R onto a concrete farm road. Go through two gates and diagonally across a field to the bridge over the River Kemp.

Through the gate marked 'Private' (it is a PROW), walk across the field to a group of lime trees. Turn L onto the track, then almost immediately R onto a track running parallel with a stream. Keep this stream on your L and follow the track through Walcot Park for just over ¾ mile (1km). About 55 yards (50m) before a gate at the top of the track, bear L down another track. Go through the farmyard and uphill to the road.

Turn R and after 100 yards (90m) turn L along the forestry track below the hill fort, Bury Ditches. After just over ½ mile (800m) this track turns sharply round the head of a steep valley. After another 330 yards (300m), where the track descends, turning to R, turn L onto a minor vehicular track and follow it out of the forest to a tarmac road. Follow the road past Guilden Down to Clun Hostel, which is the first building on the L as you enter Clun.

• DAY FIVE •

Clun to Ludlow (20 miles, 32km)

This is a long day, but the route can be cut short by catching a bus or train from Craven Arms to Ludlow. Intrepid walkers can trudge the whole way! Much of the route is easy to follow as it is waymarked with the buzzard signs of the Shropshire Way.

On leaving Clun retrace yesterday's route as far as the village store at Kempton. From Kempton follow the Shropshire Way waymarks to Hopesay.

In Hopesay, turn L and then R onto the road to Round Oak. Follow to a National Trust sign, then turn R onto Hopesay Common. Head for a group of fir trees from which there are marvellous views. Keep the trees on your L and join a faint grass track on R. Follow this to a gate on L of wood. Through the gate, follow the field boundary with wood on R to a gate by the clump of old pine trees. Through the gate, follow the field edge, with the

wood now on L, for a few yards, then turn R downhill to a stile by an old cottage. Cross the stile and field to a gate onto the farm drive. Turn R then L through the kissing gate, cross the field to a double stile. Cross this onto the road and then the stile into the next field, cross this to top L hand corner. Go through the gate. At the end of the hedge on R, go through the gate and cross both field and stile. Turn R onto the road and follow to the B4368, Craven Arms to Clun road.

This is the point to leave the walk if you prefer to take public transport to Ludlow. Turn L into Craven Arms and catch a bus or train, but first try to include a visit to Stokesay Castle.

To continue the walk, cross the B road and take the minor road under the railway bridge. Turn L over a stile into a field. Cross the field into a wood and follow the path inside the wood boundary, then the field boundary, to the railway line. Turn R and follow this for a short distance to a bridge under the line. Go under the bridge to the road at Stokesay Castle which is well worth a visit.

From the castle, follow the Shropshire Way buzzard signs to the village of Onibury. From Onibury, continue to follow the Shropshire Way from the lane near the Holly Bush pub. The Way goes through Stanton Lacy, follows the River Corve and emerges at Ludlow Racecourse, where it crosses the railway and the A49. A field path on the south side of the A49 joins the B4361 on the outskirts of Ludlow. Turn R and follow the road into the town.

• PACK-FREE DAYS •

The Hostel at Wilderhope Manor is an excellent place to stop for a second night. From here it is possible to explore more of Wenlock Edge. There are many excellent walks around Bridges and Clun too, so a second night at either of these two Hostels would be good choice to explore the area more fully.

PASTURES AND HILLS OF SHROPSHIRE

From Shrewsbury to Bridges, the first day of this walk passes through the rolling farmland of Shropshire. The second day is in complete contrast: the route crosses the Long Mynd and descends to Church Stretton through the steep-sided and beautiful Cardingmill Valley. (20 miles, 32km)

· DAY ONE ·

Shrewsbury to Bridges (15 miles, 24km)

From Shrewsbury Hostel take the A49 south-west to Bayston Hill (2½ miles, 4km). Turn R into the village and follow the road round past the library and the shopping centre. Just past the shopping centre the road turns sharp R. Immediately opposite this bend is a footpath between houses. Follow this path for a short distance, then turn off R towards a football pitch, then immediately L to cross a stile into allotments. Continue to another stile and go forwards, crossing a stream and another stile. At the far corner of the field do not follow the obvious route to the R, but cross a patch of rough ground to a stile in the L corner.

With the hedge still on the L continue along the track and pass through a gate and then cross another stile. Pass behind a bungalow and cross two more stiles before coming to a road. Turn L on the road and go a little way uphill to a farm track on the R. Turn down the track, the last house on the R has a satellite receiver and an astronomical observatory.

The track skirts a coppice and eventually crosses another track by a white cottage. Turn R and continue to a minor road. Turn L along the road and a little farther on take a waymarked track by a telegraph pole on the R. Just beyond a triangular green, take the R fork in front of Hurst Bush House. Cross the stile on the R, near a delapidated chapel and immediately cross a stile on the L into a field. Aim for the electricity pylons at the point where they cross the L hand hedge and a stile can be seen in the L hand corner of the field, beside some houses, cross the stile and turn R onto the road at Lower Common.

Follow the road for a short distance and then turn L along a waymarked track. Enter the farmyard at the end of the track and turn R by a tumbledown barn, continue along the farm track to a ford. At the ford the path goes slightly R between two fields, but continues in the same direction. Cross over a two-bar hurdle and continue along an overgrown but obvious path. Ignore tempting diversions on either side and plough resolutely on!

Cross over a farm track (which goes to Castle Place) and go over the stile opposite. Aim diagonally across the field, for the far L hand corner of the copse. Cross two stiles, a road and then another stile into a field. With a hedge on your R, continue over a footbridge and then over another stile onto a road at GR449031. Cross the road and go forward on a footpath across a stream and fields for about ½ mile (800m) to a house and a minor road.

Turn L and follow the road for ½ mile (800m) to a junction at GR446017. Go L down a little lane, passing a small wood on the R. Follow the lane round a sharp R bend and continue along the lane to a minor road at Coppice Farm. Turn L and go downhill along the lane. Keep R at the fork, turn L at GR446005 and R at the crossroads at GR446003.

Follow this lane to Picklescott which lies at the northern edge of the Long Mynd. Turn R in the village and R again to follow the road west with the Long Mynd on your L. At GR 427995 take the L lane by a small stream and go up towards a farm. After 110 yards (100m), take the L fork uphill along an unfenced lane which climbs up the Betchcott Hills. Continue to the end of the lane and then cross the open hillside in a south-westerly direction.

Where the path forks go L along a vehicle track and come to another track. This is the Portway, an ancient track which is said to have been used for at least 3000 years. However tempting it may be, cross over it and continue down the hill to Darnford Brook. At the farm track, just above the house by the stream junction, take the path south-west along the bottom of Ratlinghope Hill. Follow it for ¾ mile (1km) until it becomes a track which leads to a group of houses. Once you are on the main lane, turn R following the road round to the L past more houses. Pass the turning on the L up to the Long Mynd, and keep on the lane for 1 mile (1.6km), to Bridges Hostel which is in an old schoolhouse on your L.

Previous page: *View of fields near Shrewsbury.*

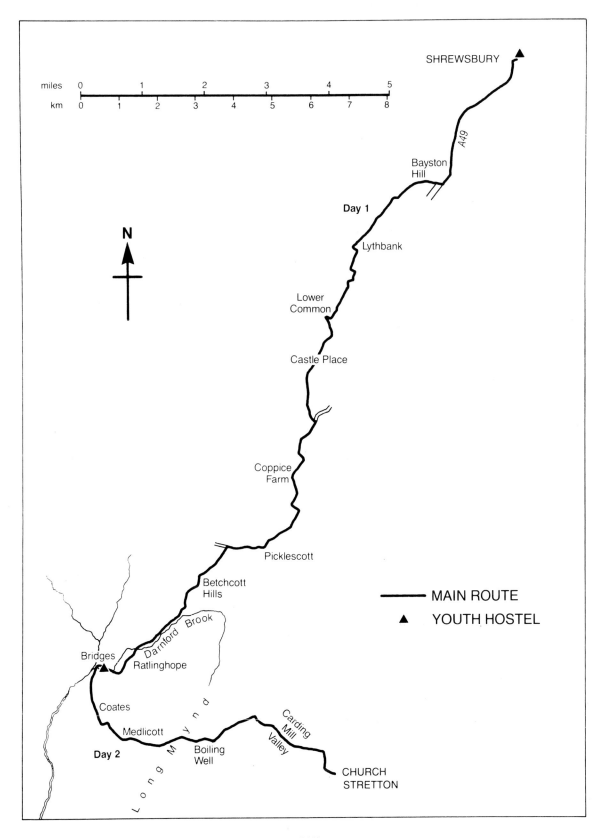

• DAY TWO •

Bridges to Church Stretton (5 miles, 8km)

Turn L out of the Hostel and go down the lane to the pub. Turn L at the pub and continue along the lane to Coates farm. Go straight over the cattle grid, keeping on the lane and continue uphill to Medlicott.

At Medlicott keep L and continue uphill onto a track to Pole Bank, about 1 mile (1.5km) away. At Pole Bank you are right on the top of the Long Mynd and, as long as the weather is good, you should be able to enjoy breathtaking views across the Shropshire Hills.

From Pole Bank continue downhill to a minor road at the stream head called Boiling Well. Turn L along the road and continue to a fork. From this point you can either go R down the busy narrow lane to Church Stretton or you can head off L across the heather, slightly north of east for about 1 mile (1.5km) to a small reservoir and a track which goes down into Carding Mill Valley. Follow the valley down to the B4370 and turn R to the centre of Church Stretton. At the next major junction turn L along the main street to the railway station.

• LOCAL INTEREST •

A Shropshire Lad?

The poet who portrayed the landscape and villages of Shropshire so vividly was actually born and brought up in Worcestershire. Alfred Edward Housman, who was a professor of classics at Cambridge, wrote 'The Shropshire Lad' in 1896 whilst living in Highgate. This slim volume of poems soon found popularity with a wide public. Housman may have idealised the countryside in his poems but he captured the serenity of the 'blue remembered hills' of the Long Mynd and Wenlock Edge in his verse.

Acton Scott

The Shropshire farming year, in the days before mechanisation, is brought to life at the working farm museum at Acton Scott. Here visitors can trudge through the farmyard and help with the chores or visit the dairy to watch the laborious process of butter making. The tools and techniques of nineteenth-century farming are displayed as well as some unusual breeds of livestock. Craft demonstrations take place at the weekends. (Closed November to March.)

Church Stretton

This attractive town takes its name from the church of St Lawrence. The northern entrance of the Norman church has a rather macabre name, the 'corpse door', so called because the dead were carried through it. Edward III granted Church Stretton a weekly market which still takes place today. At one time an attempt was made to turn the town into a spa. This resulted in a proliferation of hotels but did not have any lasting effect as the waters were not popular.

SNOWDONIA

Much of walking in Snowdonia is across rugged mountain peaks. Mountain walking is not for the inexperienced and you should not attempt this route unless you are very fit, can read a map and use a compass. If you are an experienced mountain walker Snowdonia is an exhilarating challenge and the rewards in terms of scenery and achievement are great.

Each route has a bad weather alternative as these mountains are not safe when visibility is poor. It is also advisable to use a 1:25,000 scale map for this area.

(38½ miles, 61.5km)

• DAY ONE •

Llanberis to Snowdon Ranger (6 miles, 9.5km)

This walk over Moel Eilio (2381 feet, 726m), Foel Gron and Foel Goch to the next Hostel on the shores of Llyn Cwellyn is a short distance to warm you up for the challenge later in the week. You can either stay at the Llanberis Hostel overnight or travel to Llanberis and then begin walking.

The walk starts from the junction of the High Street and Ffordd Capel Coch. Moel Eilio dominates the skyline to the west. Walk up the street to the imposing church, Capel Coch and turn R at the small bridge. Follow the minor road which turns L at a sharp bend and continue up the lane. Continue uphill and after ¾ mile (1km) the tarmac road becomes a cart track.

From here the landscape opens out giving fine views of the Snowdon massif, Anglesey and the edge of the Lleyn peninsula. The old slate quarries brought industry to the area in the nineteenth century but it was inhabited long before this. On the crest of the hill on the R of the path is an ancient hill fort.

Continue along the cart track for a farther ½ mile (800m) to reach Bwlch-y-groes. Here there are some old slate quarries and extensive forestry. Turn L (south) onto a faint track which begins the ascent of Moel Eilio. It leads to a line of modern fencing after which follow a clearer grassy track up the L hand side of the fence to the summit (2381 feet, 726m). There is a cairn at the summit and the views of Snowdon are panoramic. The western slopes of Eilio are smooth and round but

Above: *View from Cwm Idwal.*
Previous page: *On the Snowdon Horseshoe.*

the eastern slopes form a series of cwms and rocky slopes where sheep become intriguing and amusing acrobats.

From the cairn walk along the grassy, broad-backed ridge to Foel Gron (2053 feet, 629m) and Foel Goch (1984 feet, 605m). This outlying ridge of Snowdon is the haunt of wheatears and buzzards. From the summit of Foel Goch descend to Bwlch Maes Gwm (GR573559). From here turn R to

· DAY TWO ·

Snowdon Ranger to Bryn Gwynant
(7 miles, 11km)

A magnificent walk to the summit of Snowdon and down to the next Hostel.

From the Hostel retrace your steps to the Snowdon Ranger Path. Continue to the summit of Snowdon which will probably take about 2 hours. The path covers four types of hillside: the zig-zag path, the edge of the cwm, the spur, and then the final slopes. Each section takes about half an hour to walk, with plenty of good places for photography and rests. The large cwm on the R is Cwm Clogwyn which is superb glaciated scenery. As you climb, the scenery in all directions is magnificent and marvellous to walk in.

After approximately 3 miles (5km) the path levels off and meets the Llanberis path at the mountain railway. Follow the track up to the summit of Snowdon where you are standing on the highest mountain in England and Wales (3559 feet, 1085m). From here you can see the full vista of the Snowdon Horseshoe. The ridges of Crib Goch and Lliwedd dominate Cwm Glaslyn and Llyn Llydaw. It is an ancient landscape and unless you have a heart of mountain rock, one that cannot fail to move you. If it is a clear day it is possible to see Ireland and Scotland from the summit. The hills of the Lake District can also be seen.

From the summit pick up the Watkin Path by descending about 200 feet (60m) on the south ridge, Bwlch Main, to a pillar at GR609543. Keep to the path as diversions onto the scree are very difficult. Continue down and after approximately half an hour you will be in Bwlchysaethau or Pass of the Arrows. Arthurian legend says that this was the scene of King Arthur's last battle.

The Watkin Path continues on a high-level promenade which skirts the rim of Cwm y Llan to Bwlch Ciliau (GR619536). Turn R and the Path takes you past Gladstone Rock where William Gladstone addressed crowds about justice for Wales in 1892. The path continues past old mine workings to the small waterfalls in Cwm Llan. The lower reaches of the Watkin Path sweep into Nant Gwynant, one of the most beautiful valleys in Wales.

The track joins the A498 road at Bethania. The Post Office sells tea and coffee so you can stop for

continue downhill for about ½ mile (800m) to join the Snowdon Ranger Path. From now on the path is waymarked so turn R and continue zig-zagging downhill to the Snowdon Ranger Hostel. The waters of Llyn Cwellyn and the Nantlle Hills form a dramatic backcloth to the Hostel.

Bad weather route (4 miles, 6.5km)

From Llanberis Youth Hostel continue along the track to Brithdir and Tynyraelgerth, following the path over Bwlch Maes Gwm and on to Snowdon Ranger.

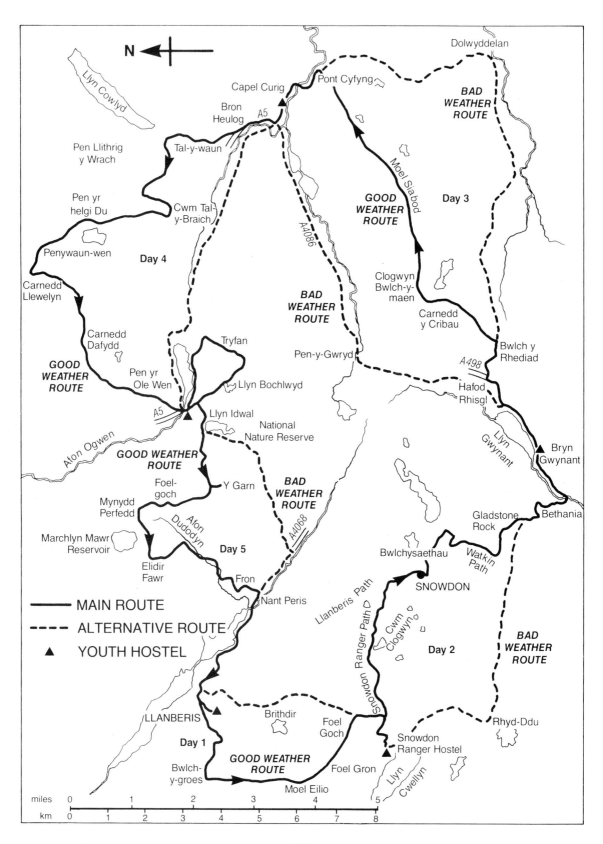

Sheepfolds.

a drink before going to the Hostel which is 1 mile (1.5km) to the L along the main road.

Bad weather route (7 miles, 11km)

From the Snowdon Ranger Hostel take the old railway track to Rhyd-Ddu and from there join the path over Bwlch Cwm Llan to the Watkin Path below Gladstone Rock. From there the route is the same as the fair weather route.

• DAY THREE •

Bryn Gwynant to Capel Curig (9 miles, 14.5km)

Another good mountain walk across Moel Siabod (2860 feet, 872m). You will probably need about three hours to reach the top of Siabod and another two hours to get to Capel Curig.

Leave Bryn Gwynant and turn R onto the A498 and walk past Llyn Gwynant. After about 1½ miles (2.5km), just before Hafod Rhisgl, take a footpath on the R through oak and ash trees. From the old sheep fold there is an excellent view back down the valley with the Hostel framed by trees. Continue to Bwlch y Rhediad at GR658526. At an old fence turn L (north) and follow the path up to

Carnedd y Cribau. There is some very easy rock scrambling along the way. From the highest point descend steeply to the col at Clogwyn Bwlch-y-maen (GR676542). There is a series of excellent stiles on the way after which bear R (east) along the shoulder of Moel Siabod.

Underfoot the grass is short and the going easy but beware of this mountain. It seems innocuous but the mountain rescue teams call it 'Heart Attack Mountain'. The long haul will really get your heart and lungs working but the effort is worth it. The grassy slopes of the summit ridge are crowned by a rocky crest and the eastern slopes are heavily glaciated. From the summit look back to Snowdon. In fine weather you will see the mountain in its full glory. The magnificent view from here also includes the Llanberis Pass, the Glyders and the Carnedds to the north and east, while to the south lie the Moelwyns, Cnicht and the pretty Lledr Valley.

Descend Siabod down the north-east ridge heading for Rhos Farm and Pont Cyfyng at the bridge next to the A5. At Pont Cyfyng take the riverside footpath on the south side of Afon Llug-

The Watkin Path by the Gladstone Rock.

wy. In contrast to the mountain paths this is a pastoral delight, particularly the section through the woods near the Hostel at Capel Curig. On emerging from the woods, cross the bridge and turn L on the A5. The Hostel is a little way along the main road, on your R.

Bad weather route

These are not easy on this route. You could continue forward from Bwlch y Rhediad through forestry to Dolwyddelan and stay at the Lledr Valley Youth Hostel, climbing Siabod the next day. Or you could walk from Bryn Gwynant to Pen-y-Gwryd on paths and tracks but this route is the A4086 for the last 3 miles (5km) to Capel Curig.

• DAY FOUR •

Capel Curig to Idwal Cottage
(10½ miles, 17km)

There is a bit of scrambling today. The highest summit reached is Carnedd Llewelyn at 3485 feet (1064m). There is also a steep descent to the Idwal Cottage Hostel which needs care. Allow about five hours.

Turn R along the A5 through Capel Curig. Keep on the A5 for another ¾ mile (1km). Just past Bron Heulog take a footpath on the R. It goes north to skirt Tal-y-waun Farm and climbs moorland towards Llyn Cowlyd, a reservoir. You may be lucky enough to see wild goats in this area. After about an hour's walking you will meet a leet – a feeder drain – which flows more or less east–west across the lower slopes of Pen Llithrig y Wrach. The leet has a path and a series of stiles.

Join the leet just south of Lyn Cowlyd and follow it, traversing Cwm Tal-y-braich. The leet runs between fences in a sheep-free zone and the vegetation is quite different from the heavily grazed moorland outside the fences. The leet zone has a rich profusion of heather, bilberry and gorse. The moor is sparse with grass and rush.

Leave the leet after approximately 1½ miles (3km), at the point where it is crossed by a path coming up from Tal-y-braich. Turn R onto this path and climb Y Braich which is the southern spur of Penyrhelgi Du. Keep to the path along the grassy ridge to a cairn. As you scramble down the east spur to the col below Penywaun-wen, the holds are plentiful and the views are exciting.

Continue forwards and climb the spur of Penywaun-wen and continue scrambling up to the shelter cairn on Carnedd Llewelyn. At 3485 feet (1062m) it is a stony wilderness but majestic in its barren grandeur. After a rest leave the summit and walk 2 miles (3km) south-west along the rocky ridge to Carnedd Dafydd. To the north high crags sweep into the cwm.

From Dafydd follow the cairns south-westwards to the summit of Pen yr Ole Wen. There is a very steep descent from this summit to the Hostel at Idwal Cottage. Take care, lean well back and test suspect-looking holds. If any scree is dislodged shout the warning 'Below!' If you keep to the L side of the slope the ground is easier to negotiate. The views are tremendous.

The path ends at the bridge over the Afon Ogwen on the A5. Cross to the Hostel. It is a good place to stay two nights.

Bad weather route (5 miles, 8km)

The old A5 from Capel Curig to Idwal is now a track and provides a safe and easy way to Lyn Ogwen. Follow the lakeside path along the northern bank until you reach the bridge on the A5.

• DAY FIVE •

Idwal Cottage to Llanberis (6 miles, 9.5km)

Three more summits to conquer today and then back to the comforts of Llanberis.

The route starts at the back of the hostel. Take the path to the R of the gully and follow this across

the moraine north of Llyn Idwal, bearing west to the spur of Y Garn. Climb the spur which is rocky but safe. It will probably take you about an hour to reach the summit at 3104 feet (947m). There is a shelter cairn where you can take a break.

From the summit retrace your steps to the top of the spur, then bear north on a track which follows the ridge to Foel-goch and then to Mynydd Perfedd (2665 feet, 813m). The ridge is mainly short turf and the walk is airy and lofty. At Perfedd bear west across Bwlch Brecan and pick up the rocky ridge to Elidir Fawr. This is enjoyable scrambling leading to a jagged summit (3030 feet, 923m), full of boulders to bound over.

Below is Marchlyn Mawr Reservoir, and Anglesey comes into view again. From the summit, follow the crest of rocks to where they meet a stone wall. Keep going downhill following the line on the wall. Cross a stile to a footbridge over the Afon Dudodyn and follow the stream along a track down to Fron Farm and then to Nant Peris village where you can get a cup of tea at the Post Office.

From Nant Peris you can either turn R along the A4068 for 2 miles (3km) to Llanberis or you can follow the rights of way through the old slate quarries. They are a fascinating aspect of industrial archaeology and there is a museum explaining their history. By the time you reach Llanberis you will be ready for a well-earned shower, supper and sleep.

• PACK-FREE DAY •

A circular walk from Idwal Cottage (3 miles, 5km)

Experienced walkers may want to climb the Glyders while they are here. However, the purpose of this route is to give people with less experience a chance to climb Tryfan, a thrilling and beautiful mountain.

From the Hostel turn R along the A5 and walk 1 mile (1.5km) to the Milestone Buttress lay-by. Take the path which leads out of the lay-by to the foot of Milestone Buttress of Tryfan. Bear L onto the east side of the mountain. After 33 yards (30m) or so, the path divides. Turn R towards the North Ridge and begin the climb to the main ridge. At first it looks awesome but the route is well marked. You will have to do some real scrambling but it is very safe with lots of footholds and handholds.

Tryfan stands in the centre of an arena of mountains with stupendous views in every direction. The Carnedds, Glyders and Y Garn clamour for attention. After feasting on the view descend via Bwlch Tryfan to a footpath which leads to Llyn Bochlwyd. From this mountain lake the path goes straight back to Idwal and the Hostel.

If you have time and energy left it is worth visiting Cwm Idwal. This is a National Nature Reserve around Llyn Idwal. It is renowned for its alpine flowers.

Idwal Cottage Hostel

MOUNTAINS AND RIVERS AROUND LLANGOLLEN

This fairly strenuous weekend walk offers a dramatic contrast between the rugged splendour of the Llantisilio Mountain ridge and the tranquil beauty of the Dee Valley. It begins and ends in Llangollen and stays one night at Cynwyd Hostel.

(30½ miles, 49km)

• DAY ONE •

Llangollen to Cynwyd (16½ miles, 26.5km)

Turn R at the end of the Hostel drive and follow the minor road round to a footpath on the L through the woods of Pen-y-Coed. At the second stile, take the lower of two tracks. Once out of the trees, bear R across a field, to a track leading down to Brook Street. Turn R along this road to reach the A5, where turn L and then R into Church Street. Go past St Collen's church, where the Ladies of Llangollen are buried, to Castle Street. Cross the River Dee on the Bishop Trefor Bridge and turn L along the A539.

Turn R past Bryn Melyn Garage and come to the Llangollen branch of the Shropshire Union Canal. Walk L along the towpath past the Eisteddfod site and continue beside the canal to its source at Horseshoe Falls. The Falls were designed by Telford to create a head of water to feed the canal. About 12 million gallons of water a day are diverted into the canal here.

Continue along a clear path to the ancient church of Llantysilio. Turn L up the narrow lane to pass Llantysilio Farm. Follow the road as far as Rhewl and turn R up a lane next to the Conquering Hero inn. On the R of this lane the impressive bulk of Maesyrychen Mountain looms over the landscape. At the end of the metalled road continue through a gate and go forward on a track. Where the track divides go R and follow an old drovers' road round the hillside. The views back down the Dee Valley are superb from this track, while Llantysilio Mountain rises ahead.

Where the path is crossed by a broad track turn L to begin the ascent to Moel y Gaer, the ancient Celtic hill fort. The track continues south-west along the undulating ridge to the summit of Moel Morfydd. At 1800 feet (548m) this is the

Previous page: View across the Dee Valley.

highest point on the walk and the views of the Vale of Clwyd, ringed by hills, are stunning.

Descend on the other side of Morfydd by continuing along the same broad track. It reaches a stony plateau from which several paths drop down to a narrow mountain road. Turn R on the road for about ¼ mile (400m) and where the roadside fence ends, turn L into a field. Follow the ridge again, keeping the fence on your R. When this fence comes to an end, pass through a gate ahead to some rough pasture. Bear L to pick up a faint path around the hillside. Cross a stile into a crop field and turn R. Follow the fence round the field until just before a small pond, here a gate leads onto grassy land. Bear L across this to an old quarry by Coed Tir-llanerch woods. It is a lovely sheltered spot to stop for lunch. A clear track leads to the edge of the woods, where it forks, bear L and go down through the trees to the road.

Turn R along the road towards Carrog. The River Dee, on your L, flows beneath a handsome seventeenth-century bridge. In Carrog take the third turning on the R. A short way up this lane is a white house on the L. Climb round the back of the house and take the path which leads south-west along the bottom of one wood and across the top of another, keep the fence on your L. Where the woods end, turn down to the L to join a grassy track leading down to the B5437.

Turn R along the road, past the swimming pool and at the top of the hill take a signposted footpath on the L, down to the salmon-filled Dee. Turn R along the river bank to Corwen Bridge. Cross the river into Corwen and turn R along the A5, following it for about ½ mile (800m). Turn R along a signposted footpath, back to the river bank. Follow the river until it turns R, then go forward on a clear path across fields to Cynwyd. Immediately before the bridge, turn L and walk through the village to the Hostel which is on the bank of the River Trystion.

• DAY TWO •

Cynwyd to Llangollen (14 miles, 22.5km)

A gentle, but steady climb through Cynwyd Forest will get you onto the moors north of the Berwyn Mountains by late morning. This is a day for relaxing and enjoying the fine scenery. Leave

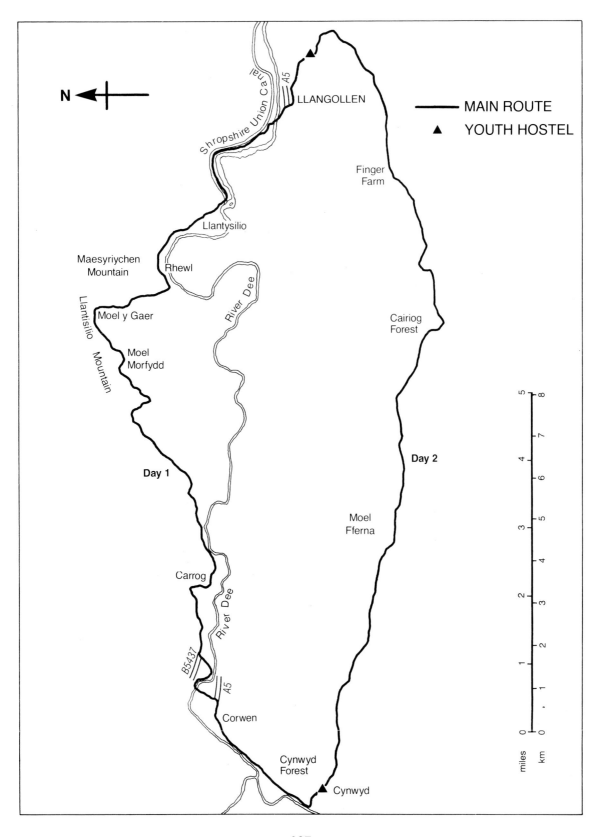

N

MAIN ROUTE

▲ YOUTH HOSTEL

Shropshire Union Canal

A5

LLANGOLLEN

Finger Farm

Llantysilio

Maesyriychen Mountain

Rhewl

River Dee

Moel y Gaer

Cairiog Forest

Llantisilio Mountain

Moel Morfydd

Day 1

Day 2

Moel Fferna

Carrog

River Dee

B5437

A5

Corwen

Cynwyd Forest

Cynwyd ▲

miles km

Cynwyd on a minor road which leads up to Cyn-wyd Forest, about ¾ mile (1km) from the Hostel. Continue along the forest road and where it divides, take the L fork. Where this track is crossed by another, broader road, continue straight on to reach the edge of the forest. Here a clear path crosses a short stretch of moorland to a stile into more forest. Cross the stile onto a forest path which soon joins a good track to emerge from the trees about 2 miles (3km) from the beginning of the forest. Pass through a gate on your R to continue on the track across rough moorland.

This stretch of the walk is beautiful in summer when the heather is in flower. The track runs straight across the moor for about 3 miles (5km) with fine views of the rugged Berwyns to your R and the rounded hill of Moel Fferna close on your L. The track reaches a stile into Ceiriog Forest. Cross the stile and go forward on a forest path for about 50 yards (45m), then turn R and drop down onto a clear forest track. Turn L on the track and follow it for ½ mile (800m) to a junction of tracks. Take the second on the R which leads out of the forest and runs along its boundary to a pleasant and little-used picnic site. Continue around the edge of the forest to a junction with a metalled road. Turn L (signposted to Vron) and follow the road along the edge of the forest for 1 mile (1.5km). Then continue along the road across the ridge of the Pengwern Hills. If the day is clear you should be able to see Snowdon back on the L from this ridge. Pass Finger Farm after 2 miles (3km), and continue along the road for 1¼ miles (2km) where a road leads off to the L to Llangollen. About 100 yards (90m) past this junction turn L through a gate onto a path leading down through forest. Leave the forest through a wooden gate and turn L to follow a track downhill to a metalled road. Llangollen Hostel is straight ahead, about ¼ mile (400m) down the road.

LONELY ELENITH

E lenith, in mid-Wales, is a green wilderness cut by rivers and streams, punctuated by reservoirs, its mountains cloaked in forest. It is one of the least well-known areas in Britain and the walker can trudge for hours with only sheep and birds for company. It is a lonely, mountainous area and walkers should be experienced map-readers and be fit before they tackle it. The Hostels are among the most isolated in Britain but if you want peace and solitude then this beautiful walk in south Elenith really cannot be bettered.

(21 miles, 34km)

• DAY ONE •

Bryn Poeth Uchaf to Ty'n-y-cornel (10 miles, 16km)

Leave the Hostel on the footpath that goes west through the forest to the Royal Oak pub at Rhandirmwyn, about ¾ mile (1km) away. Turn R on the minor road through the village and follow it north-west for 1½ miles (2.5km), then turn L to the Twyi bridge. Cross the bridge and turn R. (If you turn L there is an excellent pub with bar meals.) Continue on the road north-west for 330 yards (300m) and then take the small metalled road on the R, north across a tributary of the River Twyi. Turn R onto a track which follows the contours of the land along the Twyi. Follow the river bank for just over a mile (2km) then cross the river on the bridge at GR776471. Turn L and follow the metalled road north of the river until the farm at Troed-rhiw-ruddwen is reached.

At the farm, turn L along a clearly defined path, keeping to the east of the Afon Doethie. The path goes west for a short distance then turns north, skirting the lower slopes of Graig Ddu. The scenery here is superb and there are many places to make a lunch stop. Among the many birds to be seen in the area you may be lucky enough to see the red kite. Keep the river on your L and follow the path for about 3½ miles (6km) to a wide vehicular track at GR757534. Turn L (west) along the track and cross the ford of the Doethie Fach (small Doethie). The path climbs uphill to Ty'n-y-cornel Hostel about ½ mile (800m) away.

Previous page: *Woodland in Elenith.*
Right: *Llyn Brianne.*

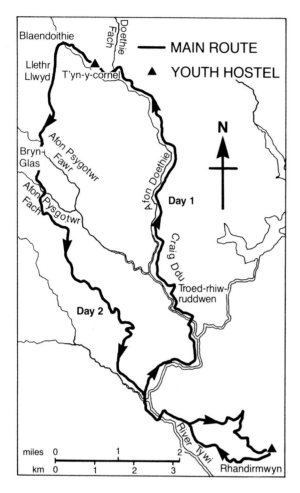

and only just visible. Continue through the forest for about 1½ miles (2.5km), heading south-east, then south and ignoring paths to L and R. Emerge from the forest and join the forestry road at GR746483. Continue along the edge of the forest to the standing stone at GR755473. Turn L for 330 yards (300m) and then R and follow the track down to the metalled road. Turn R and follow it to a minor road at the Twyi Bridge.

From the pub here, head back to the Hostel on a different route from that of the day before. Cross the river and turn R for 660 yards (600m), and take the third turning on the L – a metalled track through a gate. Follow this forestry road for about 1 mile (1.5km) to an area of disused mines. Continue on the track to GR789448 then turn due south on a track to a junction of forestry tracks at GR786443. Turn L and follow the track back to the Bryn Poeth Uchaf Hostel.

• DAY TWO •

Ty'n-y-cornel to Bryn Poeth Uchaf
(11 miles, 18km)

Set off from the Hostel by turning R on the track which goes north-west. Follow the track for just under ½ mile (800m) to GR744539 where turn L to the farm at Blaendoithie (GR742538) which is about 1 mile (2km) from the Hostel. At the farm turn L on a path which follows the course of the Pysgotwr Fawr. Follow the path for 1½ miles (2.5km) up and across Llethr Llwyd and drop down to a metalled road at GR738516. Turn L for a short distance and then R on a track to cross the Afon Pysgotwr Fawr before arriving at Bryn-Glas.

After the farm, bear L (south) to skirt round Hafod Las and drop down to the Afon Pysgotwr Fach with forestry ahead of you. Go through a gate and bear L down a drovers' trail. It is sunken

THE PEMBROKESHIRE COASTAL PATH

If you long to be a skywalker the nearest you may ever get is to walk the majestic clifftops of the Pembrokeshire Coastal Path. It travels through a landscape of noble headlands, huge skies and a sea dotted with islands and fringed with sculptured rocks and secret coves. Solitude, myriad wild flowers and the sound of the sea and the birds accompany it.

Although this walk is not the full 168 miles (270km) of the path, the 104 miles (167.5km) from the deep harbour of Milford Haven in the south to Poppit Sands in the north are a tremendous challenge. Don't undertake its entire length unless you are a fit and experienced walker. Those who tackle it will be well rewarded by the spectacular coastal scenery and a great sense of achievement on arriving at Poppit Sands.

(104 miles, 167.5km)

· DAY ONE ·

Milford Haven to Marloes Sands
(18 miles, 29km)

This first day's walk provides a stark contrast between the industrial areas of Milford Haven and the rocky beauty of the Pembrokeshire Coast. Milford Haven was chosen as the starting point because it is easily accessible by rail. However, there is no Hostel at Milford Haven and the first stretch is long, so walkers may need to find overnight accommodation so that they can begin early the next day.

From Milford Haven Station turn R onto the A4078 and almost immediately R again at a junction with a minor road. Follow it for about ½ mile (800m), then turn L and L again to go south to Gelliswick Bay. Turn R along the bay and on the far side, just before a long jetty, pick up the Pembrokeshire Coastal Path, about 1½ miles (2.5km) from the station. Follow the path along the coast, past the oil refinery, to Sandy Haven Pill, just over 2½ miles (4km) away.

At low tide it is possible to cross Sandy Haven on the causeway. At high tide, you will have to turn inland to Herbrandston and walk round to Sandy Haven by road, a detour of 4 miles (6.5km).

From Sandy Haven the Path continues through pleasant wooded countryside until Great Castle Head, where the cliffs and rocks form an impressive landscape. The Path continues over the cliff-top to Musselwick, where it crosses the beach and mud flats to Dale. If you want to avoid another long detour, cross the River Gann, via stepping stones, at low tide. From the mud flats, continue into Dale on the B4327.

Dale has a pub, shops and a Post Office. It is also a popular centre for sailing. If you are short of time it is possible to cross the neck of the peninsular from Dale to Westdale Bay, but it would be a pity as St Anne's Head, 2½ miles (4km) along the Coastal Path from Dale, is wild and rocky. The sea thunders round the head and breaks at the foot of dramatic cliffs. In 1485, Henry Tudor landed at Mill Bay to begin his claim to the throne.

From St Anne's Head to the Hostel at Marloes Sands is a distance of about 5 miles (8km) and the path is good for most of the way. Take care at Great Castle Head (another one!), just south of Westdale Bay, as the sheer cliffs of Old Red Sandstone make the path prone to erosion. There is a large Iron Age fort on the headland at Great Castle Head.

Continue along the path to Marloes Sands, a marvellous stretch of beach which is well known for its larva, or edible seaweed. Two-thirds of the way round the bay turn R, away from the coast along a path to a farm lane. Follow the track to a minor road, where turn L and shortly fork L to the Hostel which is further along the track on the L.

· DAY TWO ·

Marloes Sands to Broad Haven
(12 miles, 19km)

Turn L along the land beside the Hostel. It becomes a footpath which leads back to the coast opposite Gateholm Island. Beyond this little island is Skokholm Island, and to the R is the much larger island of Skomer. The two names are pure Norse, and date from Viking settlements here over 1000 years ago.

Continue along the Coastal Path, round the headland, known as the Deer Park, where there are fine views of Skomer. At Martin's Haven, 2½ miles (4km) from the Hostel you may be lucky and see some grey seals. During the summer you can take a boat from Martin's Haven to Skomer.

Previous page: *St David's Cathedral.*
Right: *The estuary at Milford Haven.*

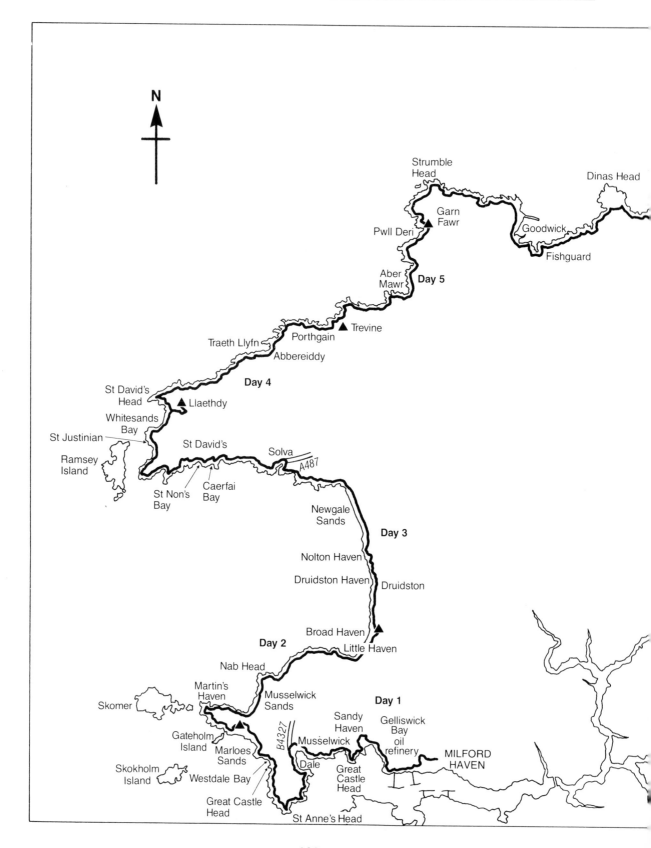

N

Strumble
Head

Dinas Head

Garn
Fawr

Pwll Deri

Goodwick

Fishguard

Aber
Mawr

Day 5

Trevine

Traeth Llyfn

Porthgain

Abbereiddy

Day 4

St David's
Head

Llaethdy

Whitesands
Bay

St Justinian

St David's

Solva

A487

Ramsey
Island

St Non's
Bay

Caerfai
Bay

Newgale
Sands

Day 3

Nolton Haven

Druidston Haven

Druidston

Broad Haven

Day 2

Little Haven

Nab Head

Martin's
Haven

Musselwick
Sands

Day 1

Skomer

Sandy
Haven

Gelliswick
Bay
oil
refinery

Gateholm
Island

Marloes
Sands

B4327

Musselwick

MILFORD
HAVEN

Skokholm
Island

Dale

Westdale Bay

Great
Castle
Head

Great Castle
Head

St Anne's Head

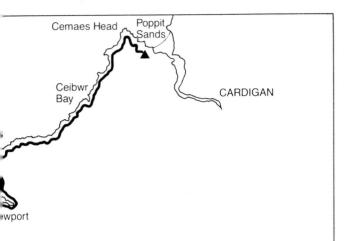

Cemaes Head
Poppit Sands

Ceibwr Bay

CARDIGAN

wport

MAIN ROUTE

▲ YOUTH HOSTEL

| miles | 0 | 1 | 2 | 3 | 4 | 5 | 6 |
| km | 0 1 2 3 4 5 6 7 8 9 10 |

The wild coastline of the headland continues with the sheer, graphite-coloured cliffs which back Musselwick Sands and onto Nab Head where early man mined flints. From Nab Head to Little Haven (6 miles, 9.5km) the Path is overgrown in places and passes through sections of woodland which stretch down to the sea. At Little Haven there are shops and pubs with good food, but you may want to plough on to Broad Haven where the Hostel is at the north end of the village.

• DAY THREE •

Broad Haven to St David's (25 miles, 40km)

The first 2 miles (3km) from Broad Haven to Druidston are easy walking. At Druidston the Coastal Path turns R away from the coast and joins a minor road past the Druidston Hotel. After ½ mile (800m) the route follows signposts across a field back to the sea.

Follow the Coastal Path along the clifftop until it reaches Nolton Haven where it descends to the village. There is a good pub here and a shop.

From Nolton Haven the Path continues past the old Trefane Colliery. Be careful here as there are the remains of an old chimney and shafts. Newgale Sands stretch for 2 miles (3km). One of the finest beaches on the Pembrokeshire Coast, it is backed by a long bank of pebbles thrown up by countless stormy seas. The path joins a minor road for about ½ mile (800m) and then the A487, before swinging L back to the coast at a bend in the road at the hamlet where there is a pub and some useful shops.

Solva, 4 miles (6.5km) farther on, is a picturesque village with wooded hills on either side. The views on the approach to Solva are fine and Ramsey Island is visible. The tempting coves and beaches below are inaccessible because of the jagged cliffs.

If you have time to swim, Caerfai Bay, 4½ miles (7km) from Solva, is an excellent bathing beach. The beautiful purplish sandstone from this bay and from Caerbwdy Bay, just before it, was used to build St David's Cathedral. Between the two bays is a fine Iron Age fort, one of many earthworks on the Pembroke coast. Penpleidiau has four embankments which cut off the promontory to complete its defence.

The next bay is St Non's. Non was St David's mother and the small chapel in the field here is dedicated to her. Tradition says that St David, the patron saint of Wales, was born here in about AD 500. The Path is now parallel with the smallest cathedral city in Britain. St David's looks little more than a village on the map but it has had a cathedral since the twelfth century.

Continue along the Path past Porthclais, which used to be the port for St David's. This is a glorious stretch of the route and there is a marvellous sense of remoteness, even at the height of the summer season. There are many wild flowers, especially in spring and early summer. The sea pounds the shore below, carving rocky inlets and bays more and more deeply. Ramsey Island dominates the seascape. 4½ miles (7km) from St Non's you will reach the nearest point to the island. It is privately owned and the haven of thousands of birds. You can visit it from St Justinian which is just over 3 miles (5km) from the next Hostel at Llaethdy near St David's Head. The Path here is clear and easy to walk so you can concentrate on the magnificent scenery and enjoy looking for seals.

The Atlantic sweeps into Whitesands Bay, making it a fine place for surfing. The jagged, volcanic mountain to the R of St David's Head is Carn Llidi and the Hostel is just below it. At the Whitesands Bay car park turn R onto the B4583 and follow it for ½ mile (800m). Fork L at a minor road and go L again up a lane, keeping L to the Hostel at Llaethdy.

• DAY FOUR •

St David's to Trevine (11 miles, 17.5km)

Don't be tempted to cut across the headland from the Hostel – St David's Head should not be missed as it has some of the finest views on the whole walk. From the Hostel take the path to the bottom of the hill, then turn L and contour round the hill. The path leads back to the coast. Follow it to St David's Head. It is a majestic, windswept headland jutting out into the Atlantic. America is in front of you. The rocks are strewn with sea campion, thrift and heather. Above the lashing surf a profusion of seabirds wheel and dive through air and sea currents.

The tip of the headland was used as an Iron Age Fort. A stone barrier, known as the Warrior's Dyke, once sealed it off but is now broken down. You can still see the remains of stone hut circles inside the fort.

The little hamlet of Abbereiddy is 7 miles (11km) of superb scenery along the coast. The Path is easy to follow along this stretch, but there are no settlements until Abbereiddy. The Blue Lagoon here was a quarry before it was flooded.

The next 4 miles (6.5km) to the Hostel at Trevine pass a superb bay at Traeth Llyfn and Porthgain is a walker's oasis – it has a pub. To reach Trevine Hostel take the minor road away from the coast at Aber Draw and follow it to the village.

• DAY FIVE •

Trevine to Pwll Deri (8 miles, 13km)

Go back along the Hostel road to the T-junction. Turn L and then take a lane on the R. It becomes a footpath which leads down to the Coastal Path at Pwll Olfa. The Path along this wild and lonely stretch of coast is narrow and can be quite dangerous. The cliffs are very sheer near Longhouse, so take great care (or walk inland from Trevine and join the Path at Abermawr to avoid the worst stretch).

If you keep to the Coastal Path you will soon see that the area abounds in reminders of the past. Castell Coch is another promontory fort, and at Longhouse there is a famous cromlech. These great neolithic stone tombs have upright stones which support a huge capstone. They are remarkable tributes to the engineering skills of early man. Carreg Sampson is a fine example of these haunting burial chambers.

At Aber Mawr the Path is still undulating but easier to walk than the last stretch. A little further along this rocky coast are places where you are most likely to see seals, especially during the breeding season in autumn. They should, of course, never be disturbed.

From Aber Mawr to Pwll Deri, the next Hostel, is a distance of 5 miles (8km). The lonely walk is along an unspoilt coastline of great beauty. Take all your provisions with you as there are no vil-

Port Clais, near St David's.

• LOCAL INTEREST •

Paradise of birds

The emblem of the Pembrokeshire National Park is the razorbill and the area is internationally famous for its birdlife. Stacked on their high-rise breeding cliffs, razorbills, guillemots, fulmars, shags and kittiwakes fill the air with their flying and calling. Rock doves share the cliff tenements. There are thousands of gulls and there are cormorants too. Skomer is a National Nature Reserve. During the breeding season about 100,000 pairs of Manx shearwaters nest on the island while 35,000 pairs make their home on Skokholm. The endearing puffins live on both islands and Skomer has about 6500 nesting pairs.

Along the estuaries and beaches, waders and wildfowl dot the water-skimmed sands and mudflats. There are oyster catchers, curlews and many species of duck; geese are regular visitors in winter. Above the clifftops kestrels hover and ravens glide. You may even see the rare red-billed chough.

Haunt of the seal

The Pembrokeshire coast is one of the largest British breeding grounds of the grey or Atlantic seal. They are often seen as just a head bobbing in the waves, but you may spot them basking on rocks. The breeding season lasts from September to October. The calves have a white, fluffy coat when they are born, but within three weeks it changes to slate grey. Four weeks from birth these seemingly helpless and cuddly-looking creatures are self-sufficient and expert at catching their own fish.

lages on this section. The Hostel at Pwll Deri is in a marvellous setting on 400ft (122m) cliffs, overlooking the bay. Its backdrop is the great hill fort of Garn Fawr and the sunsets can be spectacular. The Coastal Path meets a minor road just before the Hostel, turn L and walk along the road to it.

DAY SIX •

Pwll Deri to Poppit Sands (30 miles, 48km)

If the distance makes you gasp it is possible to use public transport between Fishguard and Newport. It will save you about 7 miles (11km).

From the Hostel continue along the path to Strumble Head (3 miles, 5km). The going is quite rough and you need to be fit and well-shod to tackle this section. The compensation is the superb scenery. Strumble Head is a wild and rocky waste. The sheer cliffs are home to many birds including gulls, ravens and the rare chough. The lighthouse on Ynys Meicel was built in 1908 but is now automatic. If you are lucky enough to be at Strumble Head on an exceptionally clear day you may be able to see the mountains of the Snowdon range to the north. They hover in the distance like a Middle Earth mirage, a contrast with the ferocious reality of the foaming sea at your feet.

Fishguard, 7½ miles (12km) along the coast, has a rail terminus for ferries to Rosslare in Eire. It also has a delightful traditional harbour full of yachts. The last invasion of Britain happened near Fishguard. In 1797 two French ships landed soldiers on the Strumble Peninsula, but the troop got so drunk on local farmhouse alcohol that they were easily rounded up and formally surrendered in the Royal Oak Inn in Fishguard.

You can take a bus from Fishguard to Newport, but if you feel confident about walking the whole way, continue beside the old harbour and pick up the Coastal Path just before Castle Point. At Dinas Head, about 4½ miles (7km) from Fishguard, you can take a short cut across the neck of the headland and save about 2 miles (3km). The clifftop is a more attractive route with many species of birds: gulls, cormorants, shags and guillemots. Between Fishguard and Newport the Preseli Hills march towards the sea, you can see their outline on your

Porthgain on Strumble Head.

R as you walk. The cliffs are lower near Newport and the going easier, although the Path can get a bit overgrown in summer.

Newport is a pleasant village with beautiful sands. There are shops and pubs too. To continue the walk, cross the estuary over the bridge and follow the signs up the hill. The 6 mile (9.5km) stretch to Ceibwr Bay is very lonely, there are no settlements near the coast, so make sure that you stock up with provisions in Newport.

Along the way you are likely to see many sea-birds. The high, craggy cliffs make excellent nesting places. There are rock arches, caves, tiny inlets and secret coves on this sea-wrought coast. About ½ mile (800m) before Ceibwr is Pull-y-Wrach, or the Witches' Cauldron, a dramatically collapsed cliff. The Path is clear but the going is hard and has some steep gradients.

During the next 6 miles (9.5km) to the Hostel at Poppit Sands you may see plenty of wildlife but not many people. Cemaes Head, just before the Hostel is a lonely wilderness of bracken, heather and gorse swept by relentless winds. The folded rock formation here and at Pen yr Afr creates remarkable patterns in the cliffs. Just after the

headland the Path follows the course of a minor road. The Hostel is on the L, a far cry and 74 miles (119km) from the oil refineries at Milford Haven.

• PACK-FREE DAY •

St David's is an excellent place to spend a second night. It is possible to visit Ramsey Island, surf at Whitesands or just laze about on the beach. St David's itself shouldn't be missed. This little cathedral city has been a centre of christianity since the sixth century when St David founded a simple monastery here.

The cathedral can't be seen from the Path or the town. It is tucked into a little valley, possibly to shelter it from the wind or the Vikings who frequently ravaged this coast. The exterior is dour but the interior is a box of delights. It has a soaring ceiling of Irish oak and fifteenth-century choir stalls with intriguing misericords.

Henry de Gower, the fourteenth-century bishop, built the magnificent Bishop's Palace next to the cathedral. Now a ruin, it is still evident that he was a man of great wealth and influence.

THE RIDGEWAY

The Ridgeway Path was designated a Long Distance Path by the Countryside Commission and follows the prehistoric route known as the Great Ridgeway and, at its eastern end, the ancient track known as The Icknield Way. This walk covers only part of the Ridgeway Path beginning at Ivinghoe at the eastern end of the path and finishing 95½ miles (152km) later at Swindon. Much of it is walked on clearly marked paths across hilltops. The going is comparatively easy, with few steep ascents but it can be muddy in places.

• DAY ONE •

Ivinghoe to Bradenham (23½ miles, 37.5km)

Spend the night at Ivinghoe Youth Hostel. Leave the Hostel, turn R past the church and follow the road. Turn L onto the B489 and continue until you reach the foot of Ivinghoe Beacon. Climb to the top of the Beacon (there is a path if you prefer not to scramble up the hard way). This is the start of the Ridgeway Path.

From the top, walk down to the Ridgeway Path sign at the minor road. Follow the signs through woods on a clear track to a stile, onto downland, and then through fields to a road opposite. Cross the road into a car park. Turn L and leave car park at a Ridgeway Path sign pointing over Pitstone Hill. Bear L with the Path through woods, then turn down to a track which runs behind Westland Farm (not shown on all OS maps). Pass behind farm and turn R onto track down to road. Cross the road and at the junction take the road for Tring Station. Follow the road past Tring station. At a T-junction, just past canal bridge, turn L for about 100 yards (90m), turn R at Ridgeway Path sign and follow the Path between fences for nearly a mile

Previous page: *Wayland's Smithy cave.*
Below: *The Ridgeway path near Chequers.*

(1.5km) to the A41. Turn R and follow the road for a few yards. Cross the road to take the footpath on L (up a grassy bank).

Follow the Ridgeway Path signs over the hill, over stiles and out to a small road. Turn R on the road for a few yards, then take the Ridgeway Path on the L. Follow the Path over double stiles and past a trig point to a small road at the north end of Wigginton. Cross the road and take a small tarmac path by a house. Turn sharp L and follow the path behind gardens for about 300 yards (250m). Come out into a field and go straight on with a hedge on your L to reach a T-junction. Turn R and pass to the R of Wicks Farm. Keep straight on to the road. Continue straight ahead on the road to Hastoe. Go across crossroads at farm and straight on until road turns sharp L. Go straight on into woods on a wide track and follow the acorn signs.

Keep to the left-hand edge of the wood and after about ½ mile (800m) you will reach a small road. Turn L for a few yards. After a road on the R, climb a stile into a field and continue near old buildings and farm machinery. Bear L to another stile, do NOT go straight on to the gate. Over the stile follow the hedge on the L to another minor road. Cross the road and go straight into woods on a wide track. Keep to the track which becomes a sunken path with banks on either side. Follow the Ridgeway Path on this sunken track for about 500 yards (450m). At this point the Ridgeway Path turns L up the bank but do not follow it as we leave it here. Instead, continue straight down the sunken path to reach a minor road at The Hale. The distance from Ivinghoe Beacon to The Hale is about 9 miles (14km).

Turn R and walk along the road towards Wendover. Just past houses on your R turn onto a path just inside the hedge. Follow this path, parallel to the road, for about a mile (1.5km) until it joins the road again. Follow the road in the same direction until a T-junction. Turn L on the road for 200 yards (180m). Take the small road on R and walk down to Wendover Church. You have rejoined the Ridgeway Path. Follow the road round with the church on your L. Opposite the church, turn R on an urban metalled track signposted Ridgeway Path. Follow the Path to reach the A413 at Wendover. Turn R through Wendover.

The next section of the walk will take you to Princes Risborough 7 miles (11km) away. At the T-junction turn L onto the B4010, over a railway bridge and past the station. Continue for about 400 yards (360m), with houses on R. Cross the road and take Ridgeway Path up through Bacombe Hill woods. The track becomes a sunken path, and then reaches open downland with a clear track leading towards the monument to the Boer War at the top of the hill. At the monument, turn L and keep to the top of the hill, cross the fence by means of the stile. From this hill you can see the Prime Minister's house, Chequers.

Follow the acorn signs and arrows through the trees, keeping high above Lodge Hill. Ignore all the other tracks and resist the urge to turn westwards. The Ridgeway Path goes almost directly south until it meets a minor road. Turn R down the road for a few yards, and then take the Ridgeway Path at the sign on your L. Follow the acorn signs on the trees until the Path turns R onto a wide track leading to a minor road. Cross the road and take the footpath into the grounds of Chequers. Follow the path that crosses the main drive to Chequers diagonally. Continue and turn R at the end of the field. Follow the Ridgeway Path signs round with Chequers on your R. Follow the acorn signs on trees and stiles and uphill to a wide track. Turn R on track for 5 yards (4.5m) and then turn L following the Ridgeway Path.

The Ridgeway Path is not clear here but it runs uphill to your L. Watch for the signs leading you up over Pulpit Hill and then down a very steep path between fences through a wood coming onto a minor road opposite a golf club. Turn L on the road and then veer R down a lane to the Plough at Lower Cadsden. There are picnic tables across the road from the pub where you can eat your packed lunch with a drink or you can try the pub's excellent selection of cheeses.

After a break (if you stop here) turn R just past the Plough and follow the Ridgeway Path signs up the hill through the woods and out over Whiteleaf Hill. The Whiteleaf Cross was cut from the chalk in the eighteenth century but it cannot be seen from the Path. The Path is clearly marked here and turns south into woodland, eventually coming to a minor road near a car park on your L. Turn R on the road for about 20 yards (18m) and then take the Ridgeway Path on L. Follow the Path over stiles into a field. Keep straight on with wood on your L until you reach a stile. Do not go over it but turn sharp R and go down to stile into woodland. Follow the Ridgeway Path by a wire fence and down turf steps. You will come into a field. Follow the Path down through two fields until you reach a T-junction at a wide track. Turn L on the track and follow it to the road at Princes Risborough. Here you leave the Path to head for Bradenham.

Turn L on road for ⅓ mile (500m) to reach a lane on R. Turn down this lane. On reaching The Old House turn R with lane and take the bridleway between two houses. Follow the bridleway to the road at the north end of Loosely Row. Turn R on

the road and take L fork at Woodway. At the next junction take the R fork called Lower Road and follow this for ¼ mile (400m) through Loosely Row until you reach a stile on your L that advertises Gommes Forge. Go over the stile and straight ahead over the next stile into a narrow strip of woodland. Follow the white arrows on trees and stiles until you emerge into fields. Follow the path down with hedge on L. It curves round the edge of fields, goes downhill over two stiles and emerges via a stile onto a minor road near a telegraph pole. Turn L on the road for about 20 yards (18m) and

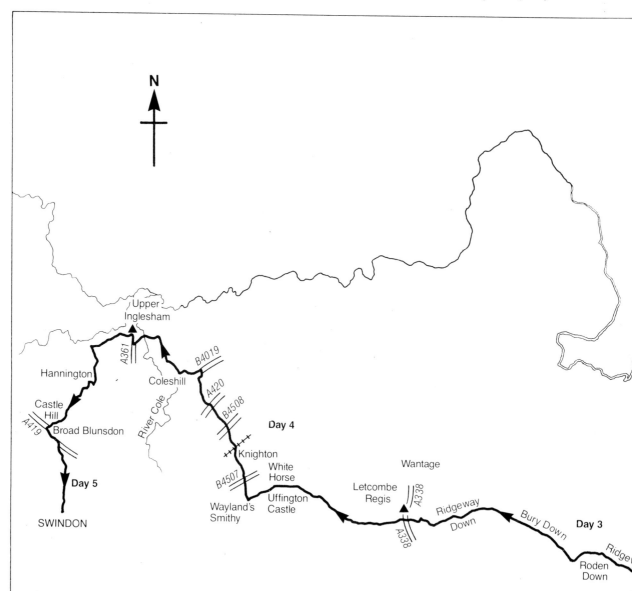

then R at footpath sign at Small Dean Farm.

Follow the path along edge of the field towards a wood. Reach the corner of the wood and turn R along edge of the wood keeping it on your L. Follow wood and fence to gate. Bear L, go on down and pass through a gap in a narrow belt of trees. Turn L up the other side of the trees for about 10 yards (9m) and then turn R along the top edge of the field with a hedge on your L. When the hedge ends, you meet a track, turn L for 50 yards (45m). Then turn R on a clear track leading to Bradenham and the Hostel.

• DAY TWO •

Bradenham to Streatley (27 miles, 43km)

Leave the Hostel and turn R on the road for ¼ mile (400m) to reach the A4010. Turn R on road for 10 yards (9m), then cross the road and take a footpath on L through a gate and across to a stile near the 'Beware Trains' sign. Cross the railway, go over the stile and up the hill through one field, over another stile and then go diagonally half R up the next large field. There is a wood along the top of the ridge, aim for a point about 20 yards (18m)

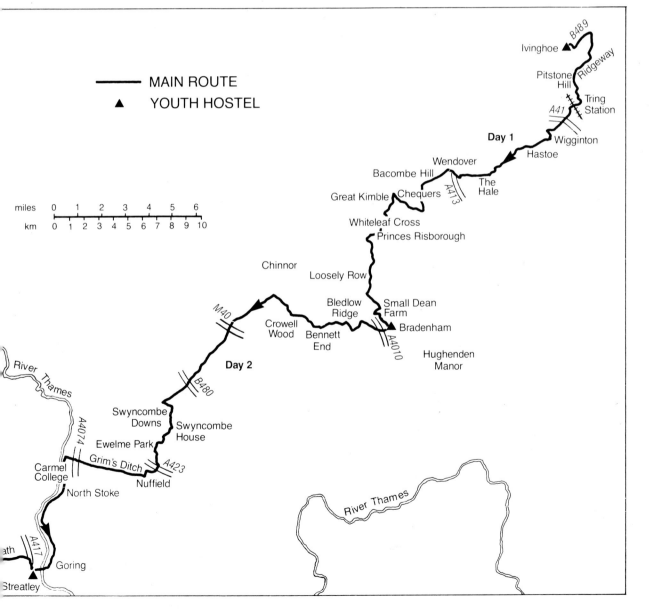

MAIN ROUTE

▲ YOUTH HOSTEL

down from the top R corner of the wood, in a narrow belt of trees running down from the top of the ridge.

Enter the woods over the stile and you will see a 'Keep dogs on lead' sign on a tree. Go past this tree, and on past a similar sign on another tree. Follow the arrows up the hill. Continue on this path to the very top of the ridge to meet a wide track. Cross this track and continue in the same direction over the top of the ridge and along the other side. Go over the stile and continue in the same direction, now going slightly downhill with a wire fence on your R. Emerge into a large field. Take the faint path diagonally down the field to reach a minor road just to the R of Bottom Farm. Turn L on the road past the farm, and where it meets a T-junction turn slightly L and leave the road straightaway taking the footpath on the R.

Go uphill to a stile at Scrub Cottage. Go ahead up the lane to meet a minor road just south of Bledlow Ridge village. Turn R and walk on the road to Bledlow Ridge – about ½ mile (800m). Turn L onto the bridleway that you will find almost opposite the junction at Haw Lane. Follow the tarmac bridleway for about 50 yards (45m), and then turn R on footpath at a large old-fashioned metal ladder stile. Follow this footpath down between fences and over the stile at the bottom. Go straight on through a belt of bushes and then turn L with the edge of the field, keeping the hedge on your R, and then turn R. Where the fence turns L downhill, turn with it down to the road. Turn R on the road and walk straight to Bennett End (ignore a L turn and a R turn near a pond).

Go straight through the crossroads at Bennett End. After ¼ mile (400m) turn R with lane to pass Pophley's Farm on L. Keep on the lane. Just past a house on the L take a footpath on the L into Crowell Wood. Follow the track through the wood with horse jumps on the L and a pond and then a farm on the R. Go straight on, crossing a track and follow the path through R hand edge of wood, with fence and field on R. When the fields end, fork slightly R to follow arrows on trees. Turn R on a track leading out of the wood near Crowell Hill Farm. Turn L at the minor road and follow for ¼ mile (400m). Where the road turns sharp R, take the second footpath (signposted) and continue for

The Manger, seen from the White Horse.

• LOCAL INTEREST •

The White Horse
The great White Horse of Uffington is carved into the chalk of the Downs that drop away just to the side of the Ridgeway Path in Oxfordshire. It cannot be seen from the Path and is not easy to see when close to. However, do not walk on the horse as thousands of visiting feet are eroding it. It is best seen from the air, but views from the B4507 give some idea of its magnificence. It is nearly 400ft (120m) long, about 130ft (40m) high and probably over 2000 years old. It is thought to date from the Iron Age, as horses of a similar shape have been found on coins of that period.

Uffington Castle
Close to the White Horse is the Iron Age hill fort of Uffington Castle. On a clear day five counties can be seen from its ramparts. Uffington Castle is just one of the many prehistoric sites along the Ridgeway Path.

Wayland's Smithy
About 1 mile (1.5km) west of Uffington Castle, along the Ridgeway Path, is a fine long barrow about 3000 years old. It stands in a ring of trees beside the Path and is a marvellous place to absorb the atmosphere and history of the Ridgeway – as long as you are not there on a fine summer weekend when there are likely to be many visitors. The name derives from the Norse god Wayland, the smith. Legend says that if a horse is left overnight at Wayland's Smithy with a coin, the animal will be shod by morning.

Wildlife on the way
Much of the ancient downland has gone under the plough, making certain plants and animals of the chalk habitat rare. Fortunately some have survived. On the upland stretches of the Ridgeway some of the most common plants are scabious, bird's foot trefoil, salad burnet, stemless thistle and ribwort plantain. Although most species of butterfly have been depleted by pesticides, among others you may see the marbled white, and the chalk hill blue. Hares and foxes can be seen but it's doubtful whether you will see badgers, although they are there in reasonable numbers.

Churches
There are some fine and ancient churches along the route. Although there won't be time to visit them all try to see St Mary, North Stoke which has medieval wall paintings; St Andrew, Chinnor and the churches of Great Kimble and Little Kimble.

about ½ mile (800m) in the same direction, downhill through woods ignoring other tracks to rejoin the Ridgeway Path (it follows the Icknield Way here) just south of the large cement works at Chinnor.

Turn L and follow the wide track of the Ridgeway Path. There is a nature reserve on Beacon Hill that preserves a chalk habitat. Go under the M40 motorway. Keep straight on, following the Ridgeway Path signs for about 3 miles (5km) and cross the B480. Continue to follow the Path crossing two minor roads and taking the Path L up to Swyncombe Downs, past Swyncombe House. There is a steep hill to negotiate between here and Ewelme Park and the going can be very muddy after rain. The Path eventually brings you to the A423. (A few yards along it is The Crown public house.) Cross the road and follow the footpath up the drive of Fairway Cottage to the golf course. The Path goes across the golf course and is clearly marked with white posts.

About a ¼ mile (400m) after the thirteenth-century church at Nuffield the Ridgeway Path turns R into Grim's Ditch. There are two paths, one in the ditch and the other on the bank. The ditch path is the right of way. Follow Grim's Ditch to the A4074. Cross the road and climb the stile a few yards to the R of the drive leading to Carmel College. Go through the wood, across the school drive and when you reach a stile, turn L and go to the grounds of Carmel College. Pass a telephone box on your R and the lake on your L. At the edge of the grounds go through a double gate and head towards North Stoke. At North Stoke church the path turns towards the river and follows the Thames to Goring. Cross the river and head up the village street at Streatley. Turn L at The Bull, the Hostel is 50 yards (45m) along on the same side of the road as the pub.

• DAY THREE •

Streatley to Wantage (15 miles, 24km)

From the Hostel turn L on A417 for ½ mile (800m). Turn L at Rectory Road and follow it for one mile (1.5km). At Lower Warren Farm the Ridgeway Path is the R lane which leads up to the Berkshire Downs. You can follow the wide, ancient track across the downs revelling in the views for about 13 miles (21km) until you reach the A338. Turn R

and walk down the main road for about ¼ mile (400m) until the minor road to Letcombe Regis. Turn L, the Ridgeway Hostel is just along on the L.

• DAY FOUR •

Wantage to Inglesham (19 miles, 30km)

Retrace your steps to the Ridgeway Path and follow it westwards. There are some excellent views on this section of the Path and you will pass many historical and legendary sites including Blowingstone Hill, the White Horse, Uffington Castle and Dragon Hill as well as many ancient burial sites. About one mile (1.5km) after the White Horse, before Wayland's Smithy turn R down a minor road towards the B4507. Cross the B4507 and follow the signposts for Knighton. Walk through the village.

After leaving it walk for about a mile (1.5km) when the road turns R alongside the railway. Follow the road under the bridge and continue on for about ¾ mile (1km). Cross the B4508 and make for Watchfield. After ¼ mile (400m) bear R opposite Old Wharf House, down a wide track. Continue straight on. The track becomes overgrown and can be muddy. Reach the A420 and cross it. Continue along the track to Tithe Farm and beyond until you reach the B4019, about 1½ miles (2.5km) further on. Turn L on the road and walk into Coleshill.

At Coleshill turn R on Lechlade road and continue along the road for about 1½ miles (2.5km). Just before you get to Broadleaze Farm there are some cottages on the L, immediately before them is an overgrown stile. Go over this and follow the track behind the cottages, then L, through a gate and along edge of a field. Go through an overgrown gate and follow hedge to R. Cross the River Cole and follow the track through double gates at a line of trees. Go diagonally across this field to more double gates into a field. Cross this diagonally to a gate on the far side. Go through, turn R and walk beside an open ditch towards College Farm. Reach the A361, and turn R (College Farm is on opposite side of road.) Walk along the road to Upper Inglesham. At the crossroads turn L and the Hostel is just along on the L.

Field landscape on the Berkshire Downs.

• DAY FIVE •

Inglesham to Swindon (11 miles, 17.5km)

This last day of walking will take you to Swindon and to public transport home. Turn L out of the Hostel and follow the street down to a LH bend. On the bend take a footpath on the R. Follow the path for about 1½ miles (2.5km) to a track that has a fence on the R. At the junction by a building turn L and go forward to crossroads. Turn L and follow farm track for just under a mile (1.5km). Just before the end of the track take the footpath to the R.

Follow the path ignoring other tracks, to Nell Farm. Follow the path round to the L of farm and within ½ mile (800m) join a track that goes round Hannington Hall. On reaching the minor road turn R and walk through Hannington. At the end of the village is a road junction, immediately before this on the R is a footpath. Follow it south for about 150 yards (130m) then fork slightly R uphill. Stay on the path for about a mile (1.5km) until you drop down to woodland. On reaching the woodland turn R and then L round end of wood, across a stream. Continue to a farm building, opposite which branch R along the footpath (NOT down farm track).

Continue towards Castle Hill where there is a hill fort. Cross the hill fort and meet a wide track at some buildings. Continue straight down this track towards the church at Broad Blunsdon. At the church continue on the minor road until you reach the A419. Turn L to walk about 4 miles (6.5km) to Swindon.

PACK-FREE DAYS •

After a long first day you could take the next day as a rest day, and spend a second night at Bradenham. If you are feeling energetic you could do a circular walk from Bradenham on an attractive part of the Ridgeway Path not included on this route. The walk is to Crowell Hill via Lodge Hill and Hempton Wainhill and is about 18 miles (29km) long. If you don't feel like walking you could visit either the National Trust property of Hughenden Manor where Disraeli lived, or West Wycombe Park where Sir Francis Dashwood, founder of the notorious Hell Fire Club lived.

The second rest day could be spent at the Ridgeway Hostel. From there you can explore the many sites of archaeological interest in the area or the villages of the Vale of the White Horse such as Uffington, Letcombe Regis or Childrey with its delightful duck pond. Kingston Lisle manor is nearby and Wantage, the birthplace of King Alfred, is an interesting town. Didcot Railway and Steam Museum is about 12 miles (19km) from the Hostel and Oxford about 17 miles (27km).

FORESTS AND MARSHES
OF SUFFOLK

Blaxhall Hostel is on the edge of Tunstall Forest, an airy forest with dappled paths and interesting wildlife. Walks in this area are not strenuous and the two days walked from Blaxhall Hostel offer a wide variety of scenery, from the forest to the marshes of the River Alde. You can also visit Snape Maltings and the Ship Inn at Blaxhall which is famous for traditional singing, and step dancing which is gypsy in origin with touches of flamenco.

(25 miles, 40km)

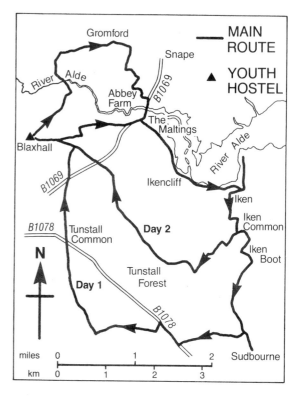

• DAY ONE •

A day's walk from Blaxhall (15 miles, 24km)

Today's walk visits Snape Maltings, Iken, the village of Sudbourne and Tunstall Forest.

From the Hostel take the rough lane east across fields to Blaxhall Heath. As you come to the heath go straight ahead and then follow the edge of the plantation on your L to a disused sandpit. Skirt the northern side of the sandpit to a track which runs due north along the top of a bank. It will bring you to a minor road. Turn R onto this and follow to the next junction. Turn L onto the B1069.

When you reach the Maltings on your R, take the green track on the R, which runs alongside the marshes. Boots are necessary on this stretch, especially at high tide. Follow the path for 1 mile (1.5km) to Iken Cliff, a popular picnic spot. At Iken Cliff, which is not a true cliff, but a low bluff, the path runs close beside the River Alde. Follow the track for just under 1 mile (1.5km) to a minor road at Iken. Turn L and follow the road to a R hand bend. Turn L on a lane beside the river to Iken church. This isolated church, standing beside the river, is one of Suffolk's earliest Christian sites. Germanic missionaries landed here and founded a priory in the seventh century.

After visiting the church retrace your steps to the minor road and turn R. Take the next L to Iken Common and Iken Boot. There are some delightful thatched cottages tucked away round here. At Iken Boot take the farm track on the R and follow it for 1 mile (1.5km). During the spring and early summer the woods on the R of the track are carpeted with flowers. The track ends at a minor

Previous page: The Maltings.

road just outside Sudbourne. Turn L along the road and walk into Sudbourne.

At the far end of the village the Chequers pub can refresh the parts that a packed lunch cannot reach. After lunch, retrace your steps to the centre of the village and take the first turning on the L. Where this lane bends sharply R take a cart track on the L which leads into Tunstall Forest.

Parts of the forest were devastated by the Great Storm of 1987, fallen timber has been cleared and young trees planted. Oaks and wild cherry punctuate the conifers in this attractive stretch of woodland. Follow the track due west for 1 mile (1.5km), ignoring the track that leads off to the L. The track meets the B1078. Turn R onto the road and follow it for ½ mile (800m) to a cart track on the L. Follow this track through the forest and where it forks turn R. This path eventually meets a wider track, where turn L. When this track leaves the forest, turn R onto yet another cart track and follow it north-west.

Continue through this delightful forest for another 1½ miles (2.5km) until you emerge at Tunstall Common. Beware of low-flying aircraft at this point, they are landing at Bentwaters, less than a mile away and can be quite alarming.

Where the track meets the B1078 go straight ahead and continue north for another mile (1.5km) to cross the B1069. Cross the road and take the first track on the L. Follow the track, along the edge of the plantation, back to Blaxhall Common. Turn L and follow the track and the rough lane back to the Hostel.

• DAY TWO •

Blaxhall and Tunstall Forest (10 miles, 16km)

As you leave the Hostel turn R onto a minor road. At the first crossroads continue straight over (signposted Stratford St Andrew and Saxmundham), pass Grove Farm and then turn L (signposted Saxmundham 4) and cross the River Alde. Continue under the railway bridge and immediately turn R on the road which is signposted to Saxmundham.

After 200 yards (180m) turn R onto the track to Botany Farm. Recross the railway line by the level crossing and take the path to the L of a clump of trees. Before you reach the farm buildings turn L and follow a path for 50 yards (45m) to a stile beneath a line of electricity pylons. Cross the stile to a white-railed footbridge over a little river. Cross this and continue through trees and then turn L on a track which soon becomes a metalled road into Gromford.

Follow the road for a short distance and look for South Lodge Cottage on your R. Turn R beside it and go onto a rough track. After 100 yards (90m) join a footpath on the L. Continue through trees and onto another track. When you reach a minor road turn R for 75 yards (67m) and then turn R onto another lane marked 'No Through Road'. At the end of this road continue on a footpath. After 25 yards (22m) turn L at the side of a field. Continue over a stile and at the top corner of the field turn R. Do not join the lane, but follow the field edge until you can see Abbey Farm over on your L. Continue to follow the path until you pass the farm on your R and join the farm track to the B1069 road just north of the River Alde. Turn R to cross the river and reach the Maltings.

At the Maltings there is a pub, a cafe, souvenirs and crafts in the main season. After a break turn L out of the Maltings along the main road for 150 yards (140m) then turn L onto the Orford Road. Almost immediately take the path to Ikencliff and

follow it to the picnic site. Go through the picnic site and follow the path along the river until it meets a minor road. Turn R and after 150 yards (140m) take the road on the L to Iken Common.

In just under 1 mile (1.5km) there is a very sharp L hand bend. Leave the road on the bend to take a track on the R. Follow the track for 250 yards (225m) to a clump of trees, where turn R along the edge of the wood. Go through a shelter belt and turn R, then immediately L to walk alongside another shelter belt. Go over a stile and then through the woods for a short distance to a minor road.

Turn R on the road and after 200 yards (180m) you will come to a red and white fire post (number 13). Turn L at the fire post onto a forestry track into Tunstall Forest. At the next red and white fire post, also number 13, turn R and keep straight on this track for at least a mile (1.5km). At the first gravel track turn L towards a cottage, then turn R by the cottage. Follow the forest track until you cross a minor road. Cross it and go forward on a green track and after about ½ mile (800m) cross the B1069. Continue across Blaxhall Heath on a gravel track to the Hostel at Blaxhall.

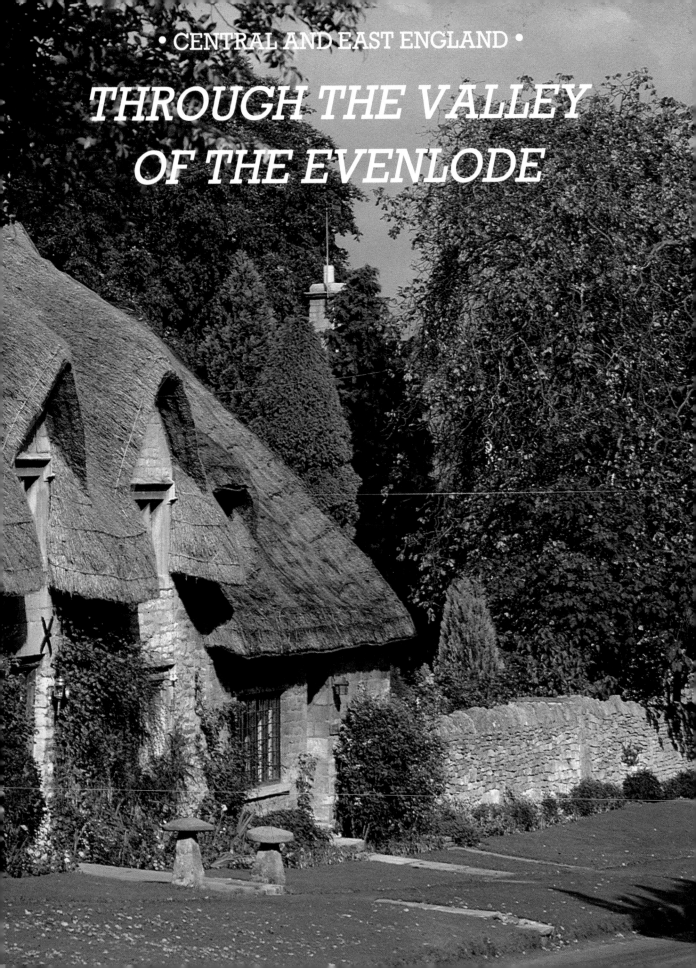

THROUGH THE VALLEY
OF THE EVENLODE

A gentle walk through the delightful valley of the River Evenlode. The route passes through peaceful Cotswold villages, past solid farms, ancient churches and magnificent manor houses. It begins in Charlbury, Oxfordshire, and stays one night in Stow-on-the-Wold, Gloucestershire.

(20 miles, 32km)

• DAY ONE •

Charlbury to Stow-on-the-Wold
(13 miles, 21km)

Turn R from the Hostel and walk through Charlbury to cross the River Evenlode on the B4437. Go past the station and take the lane on the R to Walcot Farm. Follow the farm lane which becomes a path and continue to a gate onto a minor road. Turn R for a short distance and then L onto a road to the tiny village of Shorthampton, which lies below Wychwood Forest just over 1 mile (1.5km) from Walcot. Keep on the road which leads directly to a field path.

Follow the path, which becomes a hard track, to the village of Chilson less than 1 mile (1.5km) away. Turn L through this delightful hamlet of old stone houses. About 50 yards (45m) along the road turn R onto a path across fields. From here you can see Gilbert Scott's extraordinarily unsympathetic church tower at Leafield, to the L.

Keep on the field path which eventually leads into a farmyard. Continue onto the minor road at Ascott-under-Wychwood. Turn R into the village. It is now a peaceful place but once had two castles. Turn L before the railway to Ascott Earl. Go through Ascott Earl and take a path to the R over the river and under the railway line. The path follows the railway line to the A361.

Turn L along the minor road to the edge of Shipton-under-Wychwood. Cross the river and turn first R past houses. Follow Meadow Lane until it becomes a track and then bear L over fields and stiles to a minor road (Milton to Lyneham). Cross the road and go through a gate and across a field into Bruern Wood (just over 1 mile, 1.5km, from the A361).

There is a clear route through the wood to Bruern Abbey. This was once a Cistercian found-

Previous page: A typical Cotswold cottage.

• LOCAL INTEREST •

Under Wychwood?
Wychwood was once a royal hunting forest on much the same scale as the New Forest. Henry I kept a menagerie there and royal hunting parties enjoyed the sport it offered until Tudor times. The surviving woodland overlooks the Evenlode valley and gives its name to a series of villages. Shipton-under-Wychwood, which stands on the west bank of the river, has at its centre a large green on which there is a memorial recalling a tragic loss of life. In 1874, 17 villagers joined a party of almost 500 people who were sailing to New Zealand to start a fresh life. They perished when the ship sank off Tristan Da Cunha. Ascott-under-Wychwood once contained two castles: Ascott Doyley Castle, now Manor Farm and the other at Ascott Earl to the west.

Charlbury
Overlooking the Evenlode valley, this attractive town of stone built houses and shops is well worth exploring. The medieval church of St Mary contains some fine stained glass and a stairway thought to be 700 years old. A translator of the Authorised Version of the Bible was once a vicar here. The manor house has Anglo-Saxon origins and was owned in the period before the Dissolution by the monks of the Benedictine monastery at Eynsham.

ation but was rebuilt as a mansion in the eighteenth century. Continue through parkland and through a gate to cross a minor road. Go forward over a field with woodland on your L and, eventually, the River Evenlode close on your R. Continue down a narrow path onto a lane through Foxholes Farm. There is a nature reserve at Foxholes. At the farm turn R to a bridge over a brook. Follow the L bank of the brook and the path for about 1 mile (1.5km) to a minor road. Go through a gate, turn R and follow the road which becomes the B4450. Follow it into the very pleasing village of Bledington.

In Bledington take the minor road to the L past the church. If you have time visit this lovely church. Among its treasures is an ancient hour glass beside the Jacobean pulpit. It was used to time sermons.

The road leads onto a path which follows the Westcot Brook. Cross the bridge and continue with the brook on your R. Just before reaching the

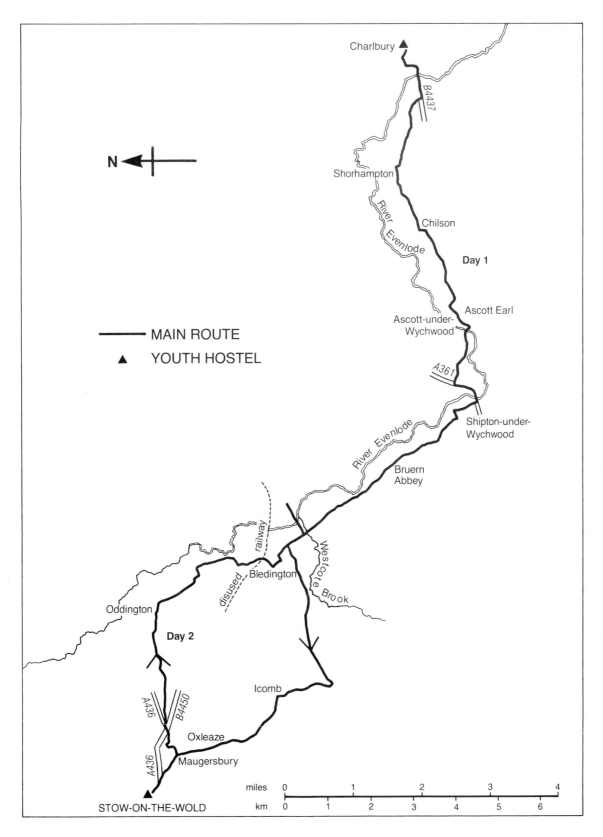

buildings of Cawcombe House, leave the path and turn R onto a path (GR216217) which runs north to join a track leading into Icomb.

Once in Icomb pass the church and take the Rand road, then turn L. Where the road forks, go R and continue on the road which eventually becomes a track leading across the flank of Icomb Hill and over Maugersbury Hill, with superb views across the Evenlode valley. The track eventually leads to Oxleaze and then over a dismantled railway into Maugersbury. Continue on the minor road to the A436 and into Stow-on-the-Wold. The Hostel is in the square in the centre of this mellow Cotswold town.

• DAY TWO •

Stow-on-the-Wold to Kingham Station
(7 miles, 11km)

Retrace yesterday's steps to the village of Maugersbury. Where the road bends sharp R, turn L and follow a small lane for ½ mile (800m) to the junction of the B4450 and the A436. Turn R onto the B road and continue along it for ½ mile (800m), past a house to a footpath signposted on the L. Go through the gate and across a field on Martin's Hill. After 200 yards (180m) turn R at a junction of footpaths and continue for 200 yards (180m), past a small tumulus, to another crossing of paths where turn R again. Follow the path to the road on the edge of Oddington. Turn L and go into

the village where the Horse and Groom is waiting to refresh you.

From the pub continue along the village street until the road bends L. Go straight ahead down a lane marked 'Dead End'. At the second footpath sign follow the path which leads close by the side of a house. A small stream flows beside the path on the R. Follow the path in the direction of the church across an open field. At the top R hand corner of the field go onto a lane that leads past the church.

The church of St Nicholas is a memorable gem. It has stood in its tranquil position at the edge of the wood for about eight centuries. If it is open, go inside and look at the fourteenth-century Doom painting on the wall.

Continue along the track with the wood on your L for about ¾ mile (1km). A bend in the track takes you into the wood. Where the track bends to the R and leaves the wood, go forward on another track to continue through the wood. Follow this path with the field fence on your R, to the end of this section of woodland with a field in front of you. Turn L on a track through the wood which emerges, turning south, shortly afterwards.

Follow this path along the field edge, passing woodland on your L and then on your R. The path joins a track which once more crosses the disused railway line and a stream before it reaches the B4450 just outside Bledington. Turn L to the village and follow the B road to Kingham station.

THE SOUTH DOWNS WAY

• EASTBOURNE TO ARUNDEL •

The best walks are not confined to the north of the British Isles. The South Downs Way traverses the Downs between the Weald and the sea and anyone who walks the sheep-cropped turf, with lark song cascading above, cannot fail to find it an inspiring journey. There is a unique sense of the past on the Downs and you are never far from evidence that early farmers tended their flocks, built forts and buried their dead here. The Romans, Saxons, Danes and Normans settled in the surrounding valleys and in more recent centuries yeoman farmers, merchants, landowners and royalty added magnificent buildings to complete the landscape.

This walk does not cover the whole length of the Way but gives routes between convenient Hostels. Once up on the Downs you will pass few cafes and pubs, unless you descend to villages, so it is advisable to carry supplies with you. As there is so much of interest to see at Brighton and in the Arundel area you could stay a second night at each of these Hostels.

(54½ miles, 87.5km)

• DAY ONE •

Eastbourne to Alfriston (11 miles, 17.5km)

Eastbourne does not have a Hostel so you will need to arrive early enough to walk to the next Hostel at Alfriston. There are alternative starts to the South Downs Way but this route begins at Dukes Drive at the western end of Eastbourne Promenade and follows the coast. A clear, well-marked path leads up the cliff to the top of Beachy Head. Continue along the cliff-top path past Belle Tout lighthouse towards Birling Gap, where there is a small diversion away from the cliff edge. Once back on the path continue on over the impressive cliffs of the Seven Sisters to Cuckmere Haven, 5½ miles (9km) from Beachy Head. Walk across the shingly beach to the River Cuckmere and turn R along the bank. Follow the river up-stream to the A259 at Exceat Bridge.

Turn R onto the A259 and follow the footpath along the road for ¼ mile (400m) to Exceat Cottages. At the cottages cross the road and go through the gate on the L of them. Continue straight up the hill to a dip or stile in the wall. Go over it and down the steps through a wood into West Dean. Continue over the first road junction. At the second junction, where the road goes R to the church, go straight up a drive for a short distance and then turn L along a path by a wall, which will eventually follow a green track through woods.

After dropping over the crest of the hill continue down the path through trees and along the edge of fields until you reach Litlington. At Litlington the Way meets a minor road. Turn R on the road and just before the Post Office take a little path on the L, which takes you to the river bank. Cross the river over the footbridge and continue on the asphalt path until you come to Frog Firle Hostel just outside Alfriston.

Alfriston is a gem of a village. It has many buildings of historical interest, including the National Trust's first property, the Clergy House. This fourteenth-century priests' house is open to the public and worth making time to visit. The church, built in 1360, is often called the Cathedral of the Downs. The Star Inn dates from 1500 and, like Alfriston, has many smuggling associations.

• DAY TWO •

Alfriston to Telscombe (11 miles, 17.5km)

From Frog Firle turn R onto the minor road to Alfriston and walk to the village. From Alfriston High Street the South Downs Way goes up the road alongside the Star Inn. Follow the road until you reach a track leading straight up a hill. Go forward on this well-defined track, pass a long barrow on the L and continue over Bostal Hill, Firle Beacon and Beddingham Hill (5 miles, 8km from the long barrow).

After a radio mast the Way swings L towards the sea and passes through several gates onto a less distinct path which descends round Itford Hill and meets a more distinct path. Follow this to Itford Farm and the A26.

Turn R onto the A26 and in 50yds (45m) turn L down a lane to a level crossing. Cross the railway with care and continue on to cross the River Ouse and arrive in Southease. The church here has a round tower and some thirteenth-century wall

Previous page: *A 'Jill' windmill, Clayton.*
Right: *Beachy Head.*

The village of Alfriston.

paintings. Go through the village and at the junction with the Newhaven road turn R then almost immediately L onto a lane. Follow this lane for 2 miles (3km) to Telscombe Hostel. Telscombe is a charming hamlet and has a fine flint church with a Norman nave and chancel.

• DAY THREE •

Telscombe to Patcham (10 miles, 16km)

Turn L up the hill from the hostel and take the first track on the R. Follow this until you reach a track on the R before a house. Turn onto the track and continue along it for ¾ mile (1km), then turn R onto a footpath across a field. Follow the path for 1½ miles (2.5km) until you reach a road. Turn L here onto a bridleway between houses. Carry on along the bridleway for about 1½ miles (2.5km), it will take you over Mill Hill, Front Hill and Iford Hill.

Eventually it joins a concrete road and where this turns sharp L towards a barn on the brow of a hill, turn R, and follow a fence for 20yds (18m).

Turn L through a kissing gate and follow the contours of the hill alongside a fence on your L. Continue just to the L of the ridge with the village of Kingston below on your R. Go L by a dew pond and cross Castle Hill and on towards Newmarket Hill. The South Downs Way turns R down the hill in a huge R hand sweep for about 1 mile (1½km) until it reaches the A27 at the Newmarket Inn, 8 miles (13km) from Telscombe.

Cross the main road and turn R. In 20yds (18m) go through a gate on your L by a small wood. At a flint wall, take the path through a wood and then continue straight across a field to a gate. Climb the track up the ridge past dew ponds and follow the path for 1½ miles (2.5km). Shortly after a line of pylons turn R between a double row of fences. Where these end go through a full-size gate and follow the fence to the crest of the escarpment. At a crossroads of paths turn L along Plumpton Plain on the edge of the escarpment. Keep on the path for 2½ miles (4km). There are magnificent views to Ditchling Beacon, 2½ miles (4km) further on.

At 813ft (248m), Ditchling Beacon is the highest point in East Sussex and the views from it across the blue haze of the Weald are splendid. There is a Neolithic earthwork on the top which was also used by the Romans. Just over 1 mile (1½km) from the Beacon, past two dew ponds, a path leads off to the L. Follow this south, away from the escarpment to Patcham Hostel, 3 miles (5km) distant, on the northern edge of Brighton. The Hostel is on the A27, opposite the Black Lion pub.

• DAY FOUR •

Patcham to Trueleigh Hill (6½ miles, 10.5km)

Cross Park Green in front of the Hostel and at the road turn L under the railway bridge, then immediately R up a metalled road. Where it bends L take the rough track up the hill on the R. Over to the R you can see the twin windmills of Jack and Jill on the hill across the valley. About 1 mile (1.5km) further on, just over the brow of the hill,

Above: *Old Priest's House, Alfriston.*
Below: *Chanctonbury Ring.*

leave the main path and keep L along a fence through gates and by a hedge (ignore the next gate on the L). You are now back on the South Downs Way.

Continue forward and after passing through the second gate across the path turn L downhill through trees. Pass between a cottage and Saddlescombe Farm and continue to a minor road. From here this route deviates slightly from the Way so that we can walk the Devil's Dyke. Cross the road, go over a stile and cross a field. Continue down a shingle path until an old pumping station comes into view. Go through the fence and follow a power line around the hill. Go over another stile and turn L up the valley. Just out of the coppice keep L up a grass track.

The path skirts round the Devil's Dyke which is a deep, natural amphitheatre. Sussex legend says that it was begun by the Devil, who wanted to destroy the Christian churches on the Weald. He began to dig a trench through the Downs to the sea so that it would pour in and drown the churches. The story says that he never completed the dike because he was scared off by an old lady who lit a candle, but I suspect that he found the job too much like hard work.

Near the top you rejoin the South Downs Way. If you detour to the R you can get refreshments at the Dyke Hotel but it is often very crowded in the summer, although there are good views over the Weald and westwards to Chanctonbury Ring. Tottington Barn, the next Hostel, is at Trueleigh Hill, 2½ miles (4km) along the ridge. The chalk track at Fuking Hill leads across Edburton Hill and Trueleigh Hill. The Hostel is on your R just before a clump of conifers.

• DAY FIVE •

Trueleigh Hill to Arundel (16 miles, 26km)

The South Downs way continues past the Hostel on the road and down to the A23 via a track across Beeding Hill. Turn L on the main road for 200yds (180m), then cross it and follow the track across the bridlebridge over the River Adur. Turn R along the river bank and then L onto a track which leads to St Botolph's church. This flint church is worth some of your time.

When the track meets a minor road turn R and

follow it for ¾ mile (1km). When the road turns R take the track on the L and follow it, keeping to the main chalk track, turning R at Annington Farm. Annington Hill is on your R, follow the track for 1 mile (1.5km) to the minor road from Sompting to Steyning.

Turn R along the road and after ½ mile (800m) where the road bears R, take the track on your L, which continues straight on. This track follows the edge of the escarpment, with splendid views across Steyning and the Weald to Chanctonbury Ring, 2½ miles (4km) distant. To the south you will see the majestic fortifications of Cissbury Ring. This impressive hill fort was built in about 250 BC.

Chanctonbury Ring is marked by a grove of beech trees planted in 1760 by Charles Goring when he was a boy. He tended the seedlings lovingly, carrying water up the hill to them. He lived to an excellent age and saw his trees reach maturity. The trees are now a famous landmark and can be seen by sailors at sea. The Ring itself is an Iron Age earthwork and has splendid panoramic views.

The Way continues past Chanctonbury down to the A24. Cross the road and go forward up the lane opposite. It leads you back onto the ridge where you can enjoy the open downland past Sullington Hill, Chantry Hill and Springhead Hill,

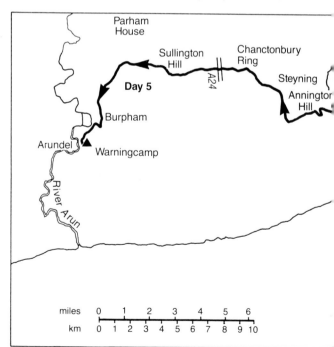

with views over Storrington and Parham Park. Beyond, the Weald stretches out in a patchwork of farms, rivers and villages and walking up here gives a marvellous sense of detachment and tranquility.

At the summit of Springhead Hill the track passes through a small wood, just after which a clear track goes forward and then swings L down to the village of Burpham. Leave the South Downs Way here and follow the Burpham track, which will take you to the Hostel at Warningcamp, Arundel, 2¾ miles (4.5km) from the Way.

Burpham stands in a romantic setting by the River Arun, with Perry Hill to the east and water meadows and Arundel Castle to the west. Burpham takes its name from the burgh or massive mound to the south of the village. It was probably built as a defence against the Danes. There is a beautiful church in the village. Originally Saxon, it has soaring thirteenth-century stone vaulting.

At Burpham go past the pub (if you can) and take the next L, which leads to a footpath to the river bank. Follow this for about ¾ mile (1km). Where the river bends R towards a railway bridge keep straight on, with a ditch on your R. Cross a stile and go through a gate, which leads to a wooded lane. Just before the houses on the L

turn up the path in front of houses and continue forward past greenhouses to Sefton Place, the Arundel Hostel.

• PACK-FREE DAYS •

Brighton

It's hard to imagine that until the late eighteenth century the vibrant town of Brighton was little more than a fishing village. The eighteenth-century's craze for sea bathing and sea air changed Brighton into a fashionable resort and gave it its Regency houses and George IV's (then Prince of Wales) royal seal of approval. His fantastic Brighton residence, the Royal Pavilion, is open to the public – try not to miss it.

There is much else to see in this elegant resort. The Lanes are the narrow remnants of the old town but their tiny shops are now crammed with antiques and gifts. There are modern shopping precincts with excellent shops, Europe's largest marina and the Theatre Royal, which sees many pre-West End runs. And then there is the sea. The beach, the promenade and the famous pier are the epitome of an English seaside resort – a lot of fun. If the weather is good and you don't mind crowds you could do a lot worse than spend the day at the seaside, indulging yourself for a while.

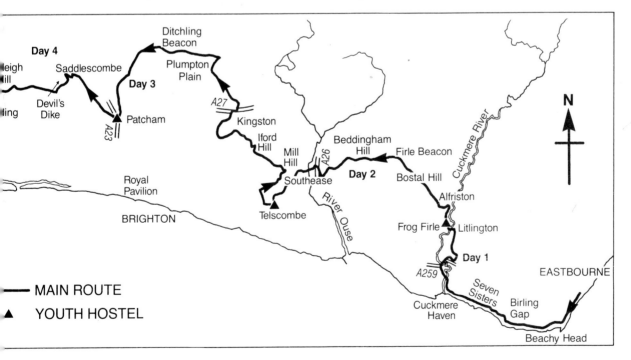

MAIN ROUTE

▲ **YOUTH HOSTEL**

• LOCAL INTEREST •

Dew Ponds

High on the Downs you will pass dew ponds. Their name is rather a misnomer as they are not filled with dew but by rain and mist. They were called shippons by the local shepherds who built them. Yes, they were man-made to bring water to the vast herds of sheep that grazed the dry tops of the Downs. Ponds scraped out of a bed of chalk ought to dry out but dew ponds often keep their water even in a drought. The secret is in their lining of flints and clay, which seems to retain water extremely well.

Parham House

Parham House is set in a delightful park just below Rackham Hill. This impressive Elizabethan house was built by Thomas Palmer, who sailed to Cadiz with Drake. The house has been restored and contains fine Elizabethan, Jacobean and Georgian portraits and furniture. But it is not a remote show-piece, it has a comfortable, lived-in atmosphere. It is open to the public during the season, but check before you visit.

The South Downs

Parts of the Way run along ancient trackways which have been used for thousands of years. The present Way is a designated long-distance footpath of 80 miles (129km), which was opened in 1972. It is waymarked with signposts or indicator posts which show the Countryside Commission's long-distance route symbol, an acorn.

Arundel and Chichester

The small, picturesque town of Arundel is dominated by the massive keep, battlements and turrets of Arundel Castle. It was built soon after the Conquest by Roger Montgomery, Earl of Shrewsbury and added to in the twelfth century. Cromwell's men almost destroyed it during the Civil War, but it was rebuilt in the eighteenth century and extensively restored in the late nineteenth century. If you climb to the top of the keep the view of the town, Downs and marshes is stunning. The grounds are open to walkers all the year round but the castle only on certain days, so check before you visit.

From Arundel it is possible to visit the cathedral city of Chichester. It is an ancient town, with a beautiful Norman cathedral. Clustered about it are many medieval buildings and some fine Georgian houses. Much of the city's Roman wall is still intact.

Just west of the city is one of the most important Roman sites in Britain. Fishbourne was a magnificent second-century palace, with superb mosaics, many of which can be seen. There is an excellent museum on the site.

Chichester harbour has several inlets, with engaging red-roofed villages. Bosham, from where Harold set sail to Normandy in 1064, is a delight. It is a fascinating area of marsh, sea and boats and worth exploring.

If you are still full of energy you could use the day to walk the next stretch of the South Downs Way, from Amberly to Cocking, although it is a distance of 17½ miles (28km) and there is no Youth Hostel at Cocking. Buses from Cocking go to Midhurst, Singleton and Chichester.

ABOVE THE KENTISH WEALD

On the first day this pleasant weekend route follows the Greensand ridge above the Weald from Crockham Hill through woodland and the deer park at Knole to Kemsing Hostel. The second day is a circular walk from Kemsing through the attractive village of Ightham.

(25 miles, 40km)

• DAY ONE •

Crockham Hill to Kemsing (15 miles, 24km)

From Crockham Hill Hostel turn L along the B2026 and take the first turning on the R after the Post Office stores. Where the lane turns L towards the church, cross a stile at the footpath sign. Cross the centre of the field to a gate on the opposite fence. Turn R. Follow the fence to a stream and cross a stile and plank bridge. Follow the hedge on L of field towards some houses.

Go over the stile into what appears to be a private garden, but is a PROW, and climb steps to a lane. Turn L. Through the gate at the end of the lane take some steps on R. At top of these steps continue along L edge of the field. At the corner of the field branch onto a path through the woods towards a cottage. Keep the cottage fence on R and turn down a broad path coming in from L.

Almost immediately take a narrow path on R to cut across Crockham Hill Common.

Continue until several paths meet at the top of a steep slope. Descend the slope to the road opposite Chartwell car park. Cross and take the stile to L of car park. Follow the path uphill into woods keeping the fence on the L until the fence corner is reached. Turn R and follow the path to a road. Cross and continue through woods, following a broad path to a narrow lane. Immediately take the path on R, which shortly goes into a lane opposite a house. You are now in French Street. Turn R along the lane, bear L at the fork and descend the hill. Continue along through this pastoral valley.

About ½ mile (800m) from French Street take L fork and go over a stile into Toy's Hill Wood. A broad path leads through beech woods and rhododendrons to a clearing with memorial stone and conifers. Go forward and follow the path towards a house. Turn R immediately before the entrance to house. You come to a road, cross it and bear R to pick up the path after 20 yards (18m). (If you need refreshment the Fox and Hounds is a few yards along the road.)

Go downhill through beeches (keep straight where other paths converge), to a stile at the edge of the wood. There is a vast view of the Weald here. After crossing the stile turn L to the corner of the field. Cross another stile into a paddock and aim for the gap in the trees diagonally across the paddock. Cross a stile next to a gate and follow R edge of the field to a footbridge over a stream. Cross and follow the hedgerow on L of the field. Continue to follow the footpath straight ahead until a vehicle track is reached. Follow the track up a hill to a gate and stile. Turn R over the stile by the gate and immediately R over a further stile in a hedge. Follow the path with the field on R and woods on L.

Enter the woods over a stile, cross the stream and climb steeply, taking L fork towards Ide Hill church. There are marvellous views over the Weald here. With the church on R, cross the green, turn R and follow the road down and out of the village. Turn L onto the main road (B2042), cross this and just before The Churchill inn turn R

Previous page: *Oast house cowls.*
Left: *Bluebells in a Kentish wood.*

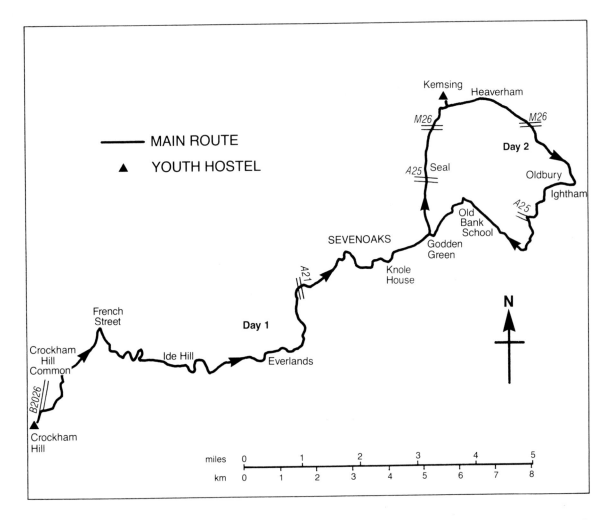

MAIN ROUTE

▲ YOUTH HOSTEL

Kemsing
Heaverham
M26
M26
Day 2
A25 Seal
Oldbury
Ightham
A25
Old Bank School
SEVENOAKS
Godden Green
A21
Knole House
N
French Street
Day 1
Crockham Hill Common
Ide Hill
Everlands
B2026
Crockham Hill

miles	0		1		2		3		4		5
km	0	1	2	3	4	5	6	7	8

and then L on a lane climbing above a cottage. Where it bears L, turn sharp L up a rough track into woods.

At the top of the rise take the path to R, following a fence on your R. Continue along this path, keeping to the edge of the hill with the road running parallel on your L. Cross a narrow lane when you come to it and take the path leading through posts into pines. The pines give way to beech wood. The path continues, still running parallel with the road on the L, with wide open views on your R, to a minor road. Go forward on the road and where it bears L, go through the lodge gate on R towards Everlands. Follow the drive between the cottages. Where it turns L, take the path ahead into the woods. Continue to the road, cross, turn L and almost immediately turn R onto a woodland path.

Where the track forks, take R branch and follow to the road. Cross and go over a stile onto a path

through a conifer plantation. Follow the path straight ahead for nearly 1 mile (1.5km). Continue to a stile onto a minor road. Turn R beneath the Sevenoaks bypass and shortly after go over the stile on L. Continue along the track for a few yards and turn sharp R just before a gate. Follow the footpath to the road on the outskirts of Sevenoaks. Cross and take the path opposite. Follow this for about 1 mile (1.5km) to a main road, turn R and follow into town.

Turn R along the main shopping street to a church on R. Just beyond it turn R down a lane signposted to Knole. Follow this into Knole Park. Keep to the drive and follow it to the front entrance of Knole House. Turn L and follow the path round to an avenue of trees. Walk through the avenue to the end, bear R and continue along the path to the boundary fence and a swing gate.

Cross onto the track and follow it past two cot-

• LOCAL INTEREST •

Halls of Fame

Chartwell

The personality of Winston Churchill is deeply imprinted on this house. During the 40 years that Chartwell was his home, Churchill made many alterations to the house and the interior has been left unchanged since his death. You can see his study, his library and the cottage studio where an unfinished painting still stands on the easel. Outside, the wall around the vegetable garden reveals Churchill's bricklaying skills and the garden contains 32 species of yellow roses, planted at the time of the Churchills' Golden Wedding.

Knole

During the 500 years of its history, Knole has been the home of Archbishops and a royal palace. One of the largest private houses in Britain, it is set in 26 acres (9.5 hectares) of parkland. The 4 acres (1.5 hectares) of buildings were extensively remodelled by Thomas Sackville, the poet and politician to whom Elizabeth I granted Knole in 1566. Sackville, a very wealthy man, brought some 300 Italian craftsmen to work on the house, creating long galleries and ornate ceilings on a grand scale. The house stayed in the possession of the family for ten generations until it passed to the keeping of the National Trust in 1946.

Ightham Mote

Surrounded by the moat which gave this medieval manor house its name, Ightham is built partly of stone and part timber. The Tudor chapel, built in 1520, has a beautiful decorative ceiling and linen fold panels. Sir William Selby, whose wife Dorothy is said to have revealed the secret of the gunpowder plot, owned the manor from 1611 and built the fine staircase to replace the original stone steps.

A woodland clearing near Sevenoaks.

tages to a T-junction. Turn R, then L onto the road. Keep on through Godden Green to Seal.

At Seal cross the main road (A25) with care, turn L. Take R turning into Church Street bearing R at the fork. Enter the churchyard on L. Take L path and go through a metal gate. Take the path across centre of the field, over a stile, and across a second field to a white gate. Cross the railway line with care, by way of stiles. Take the path leading across the field to a stile and cross the M26. Go through the next field to houses. Once out of the field take the road through a housing estate. At the corner of Park Lane turn L into Kemsing. Turn R at St Edith's Well then L up Church Lane. The Hostel is to the R of the church gate.

• DAY TWO •

A circular walk from Kemsing (10 miles, 16km)

Retrace yesterday's steps through Seal to Godden Green. At the village look for a small wooden garage set back on L hand side of the village green and follow the public footpath running through L of green into the woods. Take the R path at a fork, and continue to a gate. Go through this gate, skirt the field on the R side, then follow the path, by the drive, to a pedestrian gate onto a road. Turn L for ½ mile (800m) to Old Bank School. Turn R onto a signposted footpath beside a school drive. A narrow rocky path now climbs 300 yards (270m) to a metalled drive. Turn R, then immediately L on a wide track between chestnut fencing.

The ridge path you follow runs the whole length of some rough woodland, fern and bramble known as Seal Chart. There are beautiful intermittent views to the south. After 600 yards (550m), cross the road and continue by R fork of the paths opposite. Keep strictly to the main track for ½ mile (800m) to the church of St Lawrence. 50 yards (45m) past the church, take a path that forks L through woodland. It becomes a sunken cart track and goes uphill to the edge of a large sand-pit on R.

Almost past this turn L onto a sunken path and follow it down through woods to a road. Cross and turn R for 150 yards (140m). Take the wide stone-paved track on L parallel with road. Take the first wide track up a short steep slope on the R. This track continues to run parallel to the road. Once a wooden marker is reached in the middle of a crossroads of tracks, turn sharp R down a sunken path to the main road (A25). Turn L down the A25, passing The Cobb Tree on the L.

Turn L and bear L past a chapel. Continue through the fringe of Heron Shaw Wood. Once out of the wood turn L onto a vehicle track and follow this up a slope, round a curve to the L, then R. At the point where it bears sharp L to some farm buildings walk straight ahead for a few yards then turn R and follow the line of old oak trees on your R. Then turn R again still following the line of trees (heading towards the motorway). Look out for a path on the L cutting diagonally across a field. Follow this to the railway line, turn L passing through a light screen of trees for about 350 yards (320m) to a crossing.

Cross with care and walk diagonally L across a large field. At the ditch cross the plank bridge, turn R to the corner of the field. Walk L with the motorway on your R, to a bridge across the M26. Once over the bridge, follow the concrete road for a short distance, then again walk diagonally L across a large field to a hedge. Cross the plank bridge over the ditch, continue diagonally across the next field to another ditch and bear L. The path emerges onto a road next to the Chequers pub. Turn R into Heaverham.

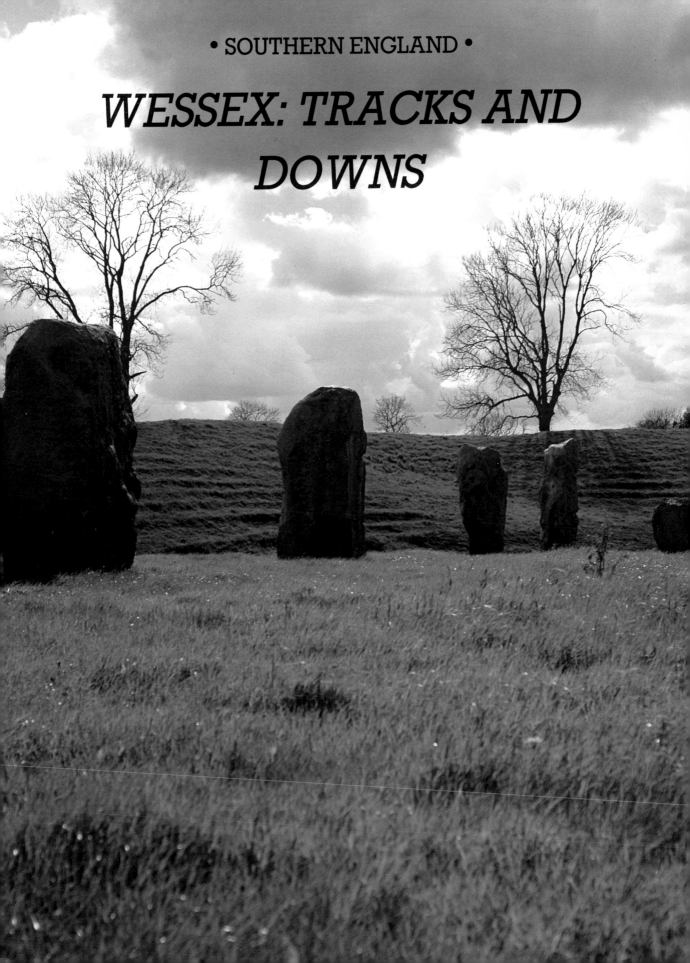

WESSEX: TRACKS AND DOWNS

The great sweep of the Downs to the south of Salisbury is excellent for a weekend walk. It is an area rich in ancient history, with Iron and Bronze Age relics, including many tumuli and some impressive earthworks. Salisbury is full of delights with tea shops, book shops and the magnificent cathedral.

(32 miles, 51.5km)

• DAY ONE •

Salisbury to Cranborne (16 miles, 25.5km)

From Salisbury Hostel head for the southern end of Churchill Way to the roundabout leading into East Harnham. From the roundabout follow St Nicholas Road. Cross the River Nadder and continue into Harnham Road, crossing New Harnham Road to Old Blandford. Climb the hill out the Nadder valley and head for the Downs. Continue along Old Blandford Road for ½ mile (800m) to a by-way sign which points west along the Old Shaston Road. Turn down it and leave tarmac, lamp-posts and cars behind.

The cart track along which you walk was the old road to Shaftesbury. As you walk you will see a fine view of Salisbury cathedral. In summer the track is a fragrant corridor of violets, traveller's joy, white campion, wild rose and honeysuckle. Further along the track you see the edge of Salisbury racecourse. After 2 miles (3km) on the track turn L at a junction with a tarmac track. (Allow yourself about an hour to reach this point from Salisbury.)

After 100 yards (90m) on the tarmac track, turn R onto a field track leading towards Stratford Tony. This is part of an old Roman road. Follow the grassy track past a conifer plantation on your L and cross a farm track to join a field path to Stratford Tony. Walk through the village, which has a thatched bus shelter, and cross the River Ebble by a footbridge at Kingfisher Cottage. Head for the church and turn R onto a bridleway, following it to Manor Farm. At a junction of tracks (GR088264), turn L and follow a concrete track south, past a group of modern barns on your L. In just under ½ mile (800m) turn R onto a field path which leads to a small wood.

Previous page: *Avebury Stone Circle.*

Go through the wood and cross a field to a rough farm track. Follow the track south across Fulston Down to join the Ridgeway at GR082234, just over 1 mile (1.5km) away. There are fine views across the Downs and rippling wheat. Continue to the edge of Knighton Wood which you should reach in 2½ hours from Salisbury.

Pass Knighton Wood Farm and enter the wood following a blue bridleway sign. The path follows the course of the Roman road again. The wood is delightful with bluebells, cowslips, brown owls, cuckoos and deer. Cross a minor road and continue along the south side of Vernditch Chase to the car park at Martin Down. You are now about 3½ hours from Salisbury and more than half way!

The landscape here opens out to give panoramic views. Martin Down is an extensive area of heathland. It stretches south, fringed by Blagdon and Pentridge Hills. There are many long barrows and tumuli in the area as well as sections of Grim's Ditch and Bokerly Ditch, a large Romano British earthwork. Much of the area is also a National Nature Reserve.

Cross the A354 and head south for about 1 mile (1.5km) towards Bokerly Ditch. At a junction of paths take the signposted track to Pentridge. It will take you over Pentridge Hill and then all the way to Cranborne. The view from the hill is superb and scans a green and wooded landscape. From the top of the hill its downhill all the way to Cranborne Hostel in the village centre.

• DAY TWO •

Cranborne to Salisbury (16 miles, 26km)

A different route back to Salisbury via Knoll Down and Clearbury Ring. From the Hostel turn R into Water Street and follow the path along the river Crane. Near the second bridge is an electricity sub-station, turn L and go through into Penny's Mead. Turn R and follow the farm track turning first L at a junction of tracks (GR060134). Walk up the side of the field following a line of small oaks to the B3078. Cross the road into Burwood, following the signs to Boveridge.

Leave the wood and reach Boveridge church. In the north-east corner of the churchyard, almost hidden by yew trees and undergrowth is a small stile created from a tree stump. Go over it and

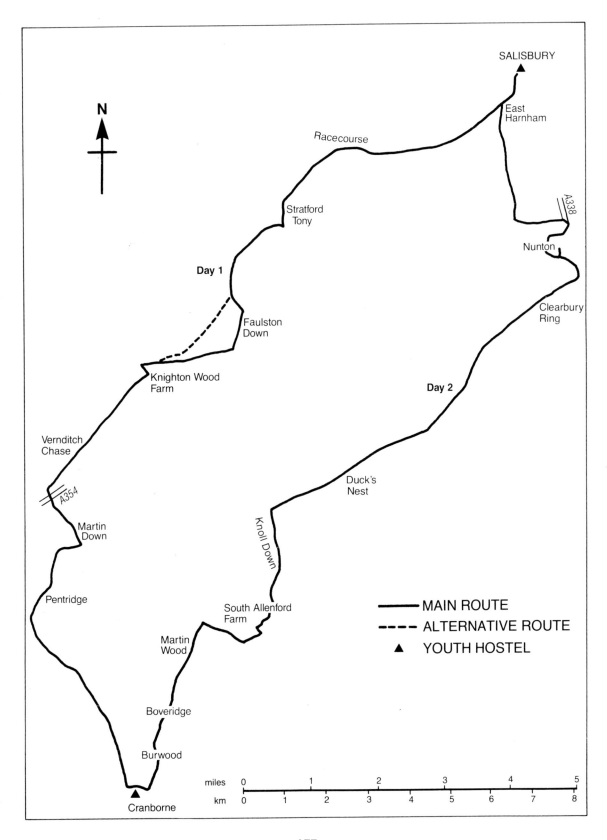

N

SALISBURY

East
Harnham

Racecourse

Stratford
Tony

A338

Nunton

Day 1

Faulston
Down

Clearbury
Ring

Knighton Wood
Farm

Day 2

Vernditch
Chase

Duck's
Nest

A354

Martin
Down

Knoll Down

Pentridge

South Allenford
Farm

MAIN ROUTE

Martin
Wood

ALTERNATIVE ROUTE

▲ YOUTH HOSTEL

Boveridge

Burwood

miles 0   1   2   3   4   5

Cranborne

km 0   1   2   3   4   5   6   7   8

follow the path north to Noddle Hill over a series of stiles. Continue through to the farm and pick up a track northwards into Martin Wood. Follow it to the north end of the wood and a small triangular plantation next to a farm track at GR074173.

At the track turn R and walk along a shallow valley to the first track on the L by some new farm buildings. Turn L and walk up a concrete track which climbs out of the valley to the tree-crested ridge. At the wood (GR087169), turn L and after about 200 yards (180m) turn R at an old, small barn. Descend the ridge following the track to South Allenford Farm. Look out for where the doves roost!

Cross the minor road and turn L. Within 100 yards (90m) turn R up the footpath to Knoll Down. The track soon becomes a path leading you over the infant River Allen. The path is a delightful contrast to the concrete tracks which now criss-cross the countryside.

Climb to the top of Knoll Down and drink in the space and scent of wild thyme. To the west lie the hills of Blagdon and Pentridge; to the north, beyond Martin Down the rolling chalklands leading to Salisbury Plain; to the south the edges of Ringwood and the New Forest and to the east, open downland crossed by ancient tracks.

Go east and cross part of Grim's Ditch and pass a series of tumuli and Beggar's Bush. At the northern end of the ridge of Knoll Down (GR090199) turn R at the junction with a farm track. Descend to a minor road. (Allow an hour, including rests from South Allenford Farm.)

Cross the minor road and take the R hand track, not the drive to Tenantry Farm. The R fork takes you along a grassy track past a long barrow and an area called Duck's Nest. Walk over the ridge, crossing a shallow, dry valley and climb up the other side to a crossroads of paths by an L-shaped copse. This is the southern end of Whitsbury Down, and you will see much evidence of horse training. Continue east following the bridleway and signs to a junction of five tracks (GR126215). You are now half way and at a good spot for lunch.

Continue by walking to the tiny, triangular copse and take the L hand track for 1½ miles (2.5km) to where a path leads off the Clearbury Ring. Turn R onto the path and make for the mas-

Salisbury Cathedral.

sive earthwork. It was probably constructed in the Iron Age and is still a marvellous vantage point. Salisbury can be seen to the north.

Descend the hill on the east slope, using a bridleway. When you reach an old building site near the junction of two paths (GR158248), bear L and then R to join a path down the north side of a field. At the bottom of the field, a short distance from the A338, a gate leads into a field to join a track near a line of pylons at GR164255. Turn L and follow the track into Nunton village.

Leave Nunton on the east side along the minor road which joins the A338. Then turn L and cross the bridge over the River Ebble. Almost immediately after the bridge turn L into the drive of Longford Farm. Continue through the farm and keep on the bridleway past the farm cottages. Go through two fields to join the Odstock to Salisbury road. Turn R and walk the last mile back to Salisbury along the road past Odstock Hospital. There is a frequent bus service from the hospital if your feet give up on you.

The sea, Chesil Beach, the swans of Abbotsbury, the Dorset Downs and massive earthworks are all encountered on this delightfully varied walk. It is easy to reach if you have private transport, but if you rely on Public Transport, plan it carefully. Trains go to Dorchester and there are buses to Bridport, but check the times before you set out. The walk begins in Bridport and ends in Dorchester.

(25½ miles, 41km)

• DAY ONE •

Bridport to Litton Cheney (14½ miles, 23km)

Step out of the back of Bridport Hostel and cross the playing fields. A series of tarmac paths lead to a soccer pitch and pass the grounds of Bridport Football Club. Cross the minor road to Eype by the bridge outside Palmers Brewery. The brewery harnesses the energy of the river by means of a water wheel. Follow the River Brit along the west bank.

Just south of a cottage (GR464919) is a bypass. Continue on the other side of the road across fields to West Bay. Enter West Bay through a caravan site. You are now 2 miles (3km) from Bridport.

The small harbour bustles with fishing boats and there are several cheap and cheerful cafes. To the west lie Golden Cap (a towering cliff) and the full sweep of Lyme Bay. To the east lies Chesil Beach, while the downs of Dorset unfold inland.

Head for the beach. The walk continues in the direction of Chesil Beach, an 18 mile (29km) reef of shingle. At West Bay, as elsewhere walking on the shingle is like negotiating billions of ball-bearings – very difficult. The easiest route is to

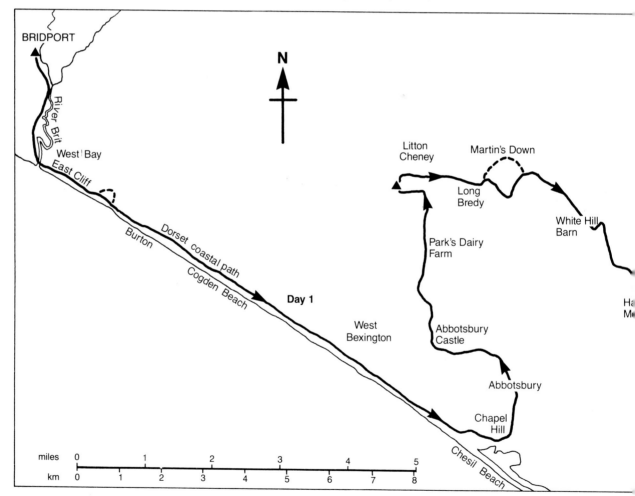

follow the clifftop path which is part of the Dorset Coastal Path. Before you climb to the top of East Cliff take a close look at these cliffs of mellow golden sandstone. They are severely eroded but dizzying as you look up.

Go up East Cliff by the path, passing a golf course on your L. Sea thrift and bird's-foot trefoil bloom at your feet. In less than an hour you should reach Burton Freshwater. There is a large caravan site on the beach. In dry conditions you should be able to walk along the beach to pick up the path to Burton Cliff, but in wet conditions you may need to follow the path inland to the footbridge at GR483896 and walk along Burton Cliff to Burton Beach.

Pass a third caravan site above Burton Beach before the route descends to the more recognisable part of Chesil Beach at Cogden Beach. On your L is Burton Mere. On maps it appears as two

• LOCAL INTEREST •

Chesil Beach
For 10 of its 18 miles (29km), this huge spit of pebbles is wedged between a lagoon (the Fleet) and the open sea. Strong tides have swept pebbles onto its bank from as far as Cornwall. These change both in size and colour from east to west; the grey pebbles at Portland gradually diminish and become brownish-yellow at the western end. Many ships have been wrecked along the bank and in 1824 two villages were devastated by a freak tide which broke the bank.

Abbotsbury
The plentiful supply of eel grass provided by the Fleet is particularly appreciated by the 800 mute swans at Abbotsbury Swannery. Originally created by the Benedictine monks whose abbey existed here until the sixteenth century, the swannery is open from May, when the eggs are incubated, until mid September. If you have time, enjoy a wicked cream tea at one of Abbotsbury's tempting teashops.

Dorchester
The rich Roman heritage of this town is exhibited fully at the Dorset County Museum. Some Hardy manuscripts and the remains of an early warrior may also be viewed in this fascinating collection. Dorchester's more infamous past includes the Bloody Assizes of Judge Jeffries in 1685, which led to the conviction of almost 300 people – of whom 80 were executed.

MAIN ROUTE
ALTERNATIVE ROUTE
YOUTH HOSTEL

DORCHESTER

Maiden
Castle

Day 2

Bronkham Hill

Previous page: *St Catherine's Chapel from Wears Hill.*

freshwater lakes but on the ground they are rafts of reeds, phragmites and iris. For the next 3 miles (5km), the route follows the inland side of Chesil Beach. There is a fine trail on the shingle which makes it easier to walk on this side. There is a cafe at West Bexington.

Continue along the Beach until you reach the coastguard lookout (GR560846) then make for the car park. From the car park follow the Coastal Path acorn signs along the track. The route is heading for Abbotsbury. Turn R onto a footpath at GR565845 and cross the lower slopes of Chapel Hill to the village. You'll be tempted to spend a long time exploring Abbotsbury but there are still 5 miles (8km) to go.

Leave the village along the track next to the chapel and go up White Hill to a series of tumuli. There are marvellous views back across the village, Chesil Beach and Portland. Turn L and follow the path along the ridge of the hill to Wears Hill and Abbotsbury Castle, an Iron Age fort at GR557865. From the castle, turn north along a tarmac farm track for ½ mile (800m) to a grassy junction (GR556873). Turn L and follow the rough track past Park's Farm to the road junction with a minor road. At the road turn L and the Hostel is less than ½ mile (800m) away at Litton Cheney.

• DAY TWO •

Litton Cheney to Dorchester (11 miles, 18km)

Turn R outside the Hostel and pass the pub to reach the road junction (GR548903). Turn R, passing a primary school. At the next junction there is a row of cottages on the other side of the road. In the middle of the row is a gap and a simple stile. Go over it and follow the path due east. The path is not very distinct but the stiles can be clearly seen across the fields. A small footbridge takes the path over a stream. Enter Long Bredy beside another row of cottages.

Head for the parish church and take the path to Martin's Down above the village. (One hour from the Hostel.) On the top you will come to Cross Dyke, an area of barrows, tumuli and earthworks (GR578904). From here, walk south-westwards

for just over 1 mile (1.5km) to White Hill Barn at a five-ways junction (GR595892). Look back down the Bredy valley, a broad, beautiful valley hidden from the outside world by the downs.

Take the path that leads in a southerly direction from the junction and turn L onto a farm track (GR596892). Then turn R onto a path at GR 598893. Follow the path through the edge of a wood and along a field edge to the corner of a plantation (GR601884). Turn L up a cart track to a minor road. Cross the road and continue along the cart track to the conifer wood of Black Down. Go through the woods to reach another minor road (GR616877). At the road you can visit Hardy's Monument by making a short detour to the R. It is a monument to Thomas Masterman Hardy, Nelson's flag captain at Trafalgar (Lord Nelson's 'Kiss me Hardy'), not the Dorset Hardy of literary fame.

From the Hardy Monument retrace your steps to the track that leads onto Bronkham Hill (GR625870). As you walk across the hill on a clear track, three lines of pylons come into view and you cross a concrete farm track. Tucked away in the fold of the downs is a large agricultural production unit – hesitate to call it a farm!

Pass the third line of pylons and follow the line of tumli. In ¼ mile (400m) there is a sharp bend in the track and in another ¼ mile (400m) take the L path down to Ashton Farm Cottages (GR658878). The route goes down into the valley of South Winterbourne across pastures and past tumuli. The massive bulk of Maiden Castle comes into view, dominating the opposite hillside. When you reach Ashton Farm Cottages go forward at the crossroads and take the Winterbourne Monkton road to a sharp bend. From here take the path up Maiden Castle.

This majestic Iron Age hill fort with its steeply undulating ditches is glorious. It is the largest earthwork in Western Europe. As you stand on the top with the wind whistling about you, it isn't difficult to imagine Roman legionaries advancing to storm it as they swept through Wessex.

From the top go down to the road which runs to the north of the hill and walk to Dorchester and a well-earned cup of tea.

DEVON HILLS AND DARTMOOR

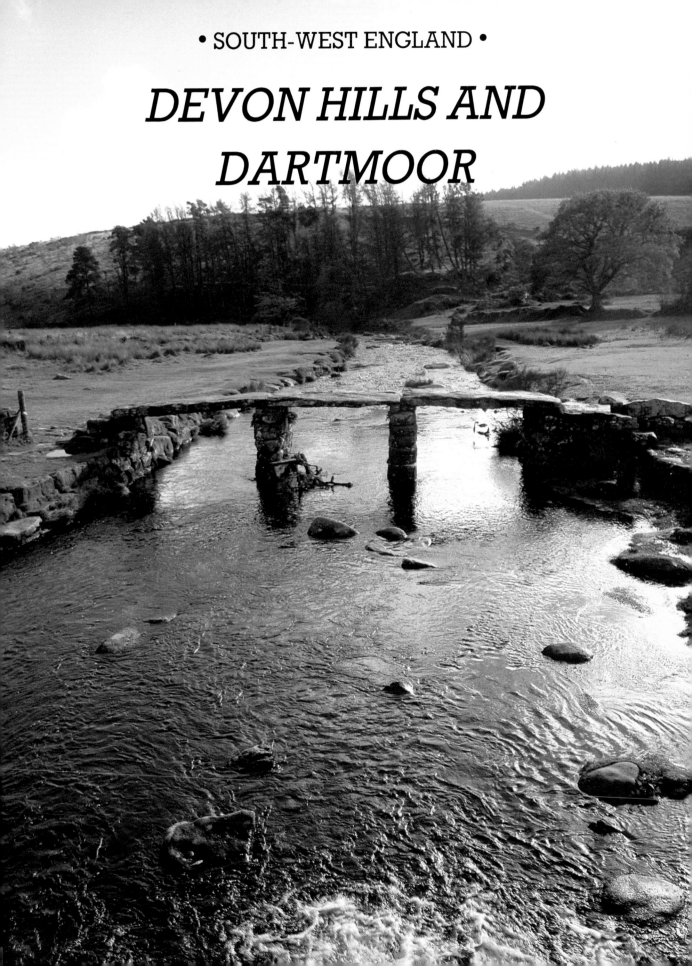

Devon has a rich variety of scenery and this walk takes you through some of its great contrasts. It crosses the lush pastures and red loams of the South Hams, climbs the open moorland of Dartmoor and follows the cliffs of the South West Coastal Path. Devon is renowned for its rolling hills so the walk is likely to be tiring at times, but there are no difficult sections and it should be within the scope of well-shod, reasonably fit walkers.

(64½ miles, 103.5km)

• DAY ONE •

Exeter to Steps Bridge (11 miles, 17.5km)

Much of today's walk is on lanes but is quite tiring because of the hills.

Turn L at the Hostel gate and at the main road turn R to cross the River Exe, then the Exeter canal, then the railway. At the roundabout turn L (A379 Dawlish) and almost immediately take the drive on the R marked Highfield Bungalow. Within 25 yards (23m) fork sharp L, go through a gate on R and follow the R hand hedge up the field. Go through the gate at the top of the field, turn L and follow the hedge past a clump of trees to the adjacent hedge. Follow this to a stile in the top corner of the field. Cross the stile and keeping the hedge on your L cross a stile in the next corner. Walk past a hut and follow the hedge to the road.

Turn R on the road and then almost immediately L. At the T-junction turn R and follow the road to the footbridge over the main road. Go over the bridge, turn L and follow the road round for ¼ mile (400m). At the next junction go R, within ¼ mile (400m) cross the dual carriageway and take the lane opposite. At the top of the lane go through the R hand gate and follow the hedge on your L. When you emerge into a lane turn R and continue until you reach Shillingford St George. Turn R and walk through the village.

At the T-junction going out of the village turn L, then almost immediately R by the stone cross. After a mile (1.5km) turn L at Manstree Cross towards Dunchideock. In ¼ mile (400m) turn R towards Doddiscombsleigh and continue along the road for about 1 mile (1.5km) to Willhayes

Previous page: Postbridge clapper bridge.

Cross. Go straight over and after ½ mile (800m) you will reach a road junction. Turn L to Doddiscombsleigh and the fifteenth century Nobody Inn for a break. You could also visit St Michael's church, which has some of the finest medieval stained glass in Devon.

Leave the village by continuing past the school (on the R). Take the next road on the R and fork L at Hereford Cottage. After the cottage turn almost immediately L into a small lane. Pass by the gate on the L and head diagonally across the field towards a telegraph pole at the top. Cross the stile and follow the path diagonally up this field too. Go through a gate and continue along the R hand hedge until you pass through a gate into a lane. Turn L down the lane for ¼ mile (400m), then turn L under a railway bridge. Go straight across the B3193 onto the minor road to Tedburn.

After ¼ mile (400m) turn L and follow the lane through the farmyard to a gate. Go through the gate onto an enclosed footpath above the River Teign. Where the path bears R uphill keep straight on through a gate and between cottages (not the path above them) to reach the B3193. Turn L over the road and in 50 yards (46m) fork R. At the T-junction go R. At the sharp L bend go over the stile on your R. Follow the L hand hedge until it turns to the L. Go straight on for a short way to pass through a gate into a wood. Follow the path straight through the wood, staying on the same side of the river, for about 1 mile (1.5km) until it comes out onto the road at Steps Bridge. Turn L and Steps Bridge Hostel drive is a few yards along on the L.

• DAY TWO •

Steps Bridge to Bellever (18 miles, 29km)

A long day, mostly across undulating countryside with magnificent views.

Turn L out of the Hostel to walk uphill through Bridford Wood. At the top pass through a five-bar gate, then turn quarter L to walk uphill over grass to a metal gate. There are good views of Dunsford L from here. Go forward through the gate and pass through two more metal gates to reach a farm track. Turn L and walk towards Lower Heltor Farm (Hel Tor is on your L across the fields). Just before the farm buildings turn L and then R to pass

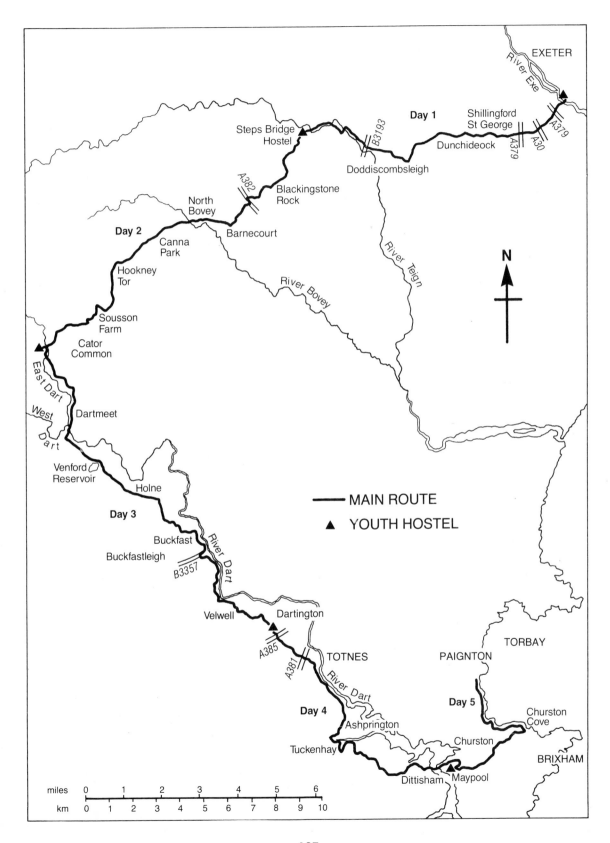

in front of them. Walk down the farm drive to the road. Cross over to a path, follow it uphill to a five-bar gate, pass through a field. Walk uphill with the hedge on your R. At the highest point look for a path on your R (it may be overgrown in summer), go along it, over two stiles to a road.

Turn R at the road and walk downhill to Westcott Farm. Follow the road uphill and where it turns R go straight ahead into a farm track. Follow the track for approximately ½ mile (800m) to a road. Turn R and walk uphill to a road junction. Take the second on the L after 200 yards (180m), go over a stile on your L and on to Blackingstone Rock. You can climb the rock up stone steps for fine views of the surrounding countryside.

From the rock retrace your steps to the road junction. Turn L and follow the road to Didworthy Cottages. Turn L and follow the road round to the R. After about ½ mile (800m) it reaches a crossroads where there are magnificent views. Continue forward on a grass track until you come to a road. Turn L and walk downhill to a road junction. Turn R into a road marked 'Unsuitable for motors'. Follow the road down a steep, zig-zag hill to a cottage. After 200 yards (180m) the road begins to flatten out and there is a fingerpost to a path on the L. You may have to search for it in summer as it is sometimes overgrown. Follow the path downhill through two five-bar gates to a bridge. Cross it and pass through another gate onto the A382. Beware of this road, it is narrow and the traffic is fast-moving.

Turn L along the road to Wray Barton Manor where you turn R into a lane opposite. Follow the lane for about ½ mile (800m) over a bridge to a T-junction. Turn L and almost immediately R at Barne Cross. The hedgerows around here are beautiful in spring. Walk along the road to Barnecourt Farm, pass between the buildings, then turn R. Follow this lane for about 1 mile (1.5km), it deteriorates into a track, then to a grass path which is sometimes very muddy. Eventually it joins a gravel track which runs parallel with the River Bovey. Pass through a gate onto a road and walk up to North Bovey. At the top of the hill is the welcome sight of The Ring O' Bells, where you can take a break.

To continue the route, turn L towards the church and walk through the churchyard with the village green on your R. Follow the path to the road, cross over and go ahead across the bridge spanning the Bovey. Follow the road uphill for about 1 mile (1.5km). There are fine views to the R here. The Manor House hotel in the middle distance was once owned by W. H. Smith. The road drops to crossroads at Canna Park. Cross over to the farm road and continue, ignoring any turnings. At West Coombe Farm continue through a gate and onto a twin concrete track, where the concrete track turns R continue forward on a grass track past a small reservoir, through a gateway (no gate) and up to a five-bar gate from which there are good views.

Pass through the gate and turn L, walk to a wall coming in from your R and follow it downhill to a road. Cross over to a sunken track and turn L. Follow the track past a dog pound on the L and soon after turn L to pass behind Meadland Warren Farm to a small gate. Pass through and turn quarter L downhill, over a farm track to a five-bar gate. Go through and turn L following a grass path to a gate in the wall. Go through that and follow the path to a wire fence. Go through to cottages and pass in front of them to a farm track.

Follow the farm track past Challacombe Farm uphill to a gateway on the L. No gate, so pass through and follow a grass path to a gate. Go through to the bridge, cross it and turn R onto a track which follows a wall to a five-bar gate. Go through and turn quarter R uphill over grass to another five-bar gate. Through it, follow the fence on your L round the edge of the field. Do not be tempted to shortcut across the field. Just before the end of the fence turn R to walk downhill to a ford. Cross the ford and continue uphill past Sousson Farm buildings on your L. Go through a five-bar gate onto a farm road. Follow it round with the forest on your R. When you come to a gate, go through onto the road, remembering to close the gate behind you.

Turn R and follow the road, where it swings R continue forward onto a farm track. The track levels out for a while with Cator Common on your L, then drops to the stepping stones across Wallabrook where there are many species of marsh plants. Once across the stream make for Pizwell Farm, pass between the buildings and turn L through a five-bar gate onto a track. Follow this R

The River Bovey.

then L to yet another five-bar gate. Go through and keeping the wall to your L, follow the track to a field where turn quarter R and walk to a pile of rocks. Turn L onto a track and walk to·a five-bar gate. Pass through this onto a farm track where turn R towards Drury farm. Just before the farm bridge, turn L and follow Drury Brook to where it joins the East Dart. Turn R at the road to cross the East Dart by a fine bridge. Turn R soon after to Bellever Hostel.

• DAY THREE •

Bellever to Dartington (17 miles, 27km)

Retrace your steps to cross the river. Over the bridge turn R and walk along the river bank. This is a very pleasant walk beside the lively river. After nearly a mile (1.5km) the path goes through a forestry plantation. Emerging, the route continues on a track which leads south-east away from the forest. Follow the waymarks to Babeny Farm. Leave the farm by the road over the bridge and after 100 yards (90m) turn R to follow waymarks along a path by a stream flowing to join the East Dart river. At the junction with the river, stop following the waymarks and do not cross the stepping stones. Instead turn L to follow the East Dart. Continue along the bank for about 1 mile (1.5km) to the car park at Dartmeet.

Dartmeet, where the West Dart and the East Dart rivers meet, is one of Devon's most famous beauty spots. If you reach it in the high season it can be awash with tourists.

Turn R onto the B3357 and cross the river bridge. Turn immediately L into the garage forecourt to follow waymarks to the stepping stones across the West Dart. The river is sometimes impassable, if this is the case, follow the waymarks R to Huckaby Farm. Leave the waymarks at the farm and go out onto a minor road, turn L and follow the Holne road 3 miles (5km) to Venford Reservoir.

If the stones are passable cross them and follow the bridlepath up the hill, keeping L at Combestone. Once out on the open moor continue south-east on a path for about 1 mile (1.5km), away from the wood on your L. The tor on your R is Combe-

Hound Tor.

stone Tor. Cross a stream by the footbridge. Turn L when you come to the road and follow it for ½ mile (800m) to Venford Reservoir. The moor hereabouts is littered with prehistoric settlements and workings.

From the reservoir continue along the road for 1½ miles (2.5km). Fork R at the signpost for Scorrington and after ¼ mile (400m), opposite the signpost to Michelcombe, turn L through a kissing gate (not the one into the recreation ground). Follow the path to Holne church and the Church House inn. Just past the inn take the Buckfast road. Fork L at Ridgeway Cross for Shutterford. Shortly after the farm turn R onto a delightfully green enclosed lane above a stream. Follow it for just over a mile (1.5km) to the road. Turn R to cross the river and after 300 yards (250m) turn L for Buckfast.

Once you reach Buckfast you still have 5 miles (8km) to walk and although you may want to explore this delightful village and the abbey it is probably better to press on to Dartington. If you stay a second night at Dartington you could return to see Buckfast properly.

To continue the walk turn south at the mini roundabout, signposted 'All routes'. After ½ mile (800m) turn R onto the B3380. After the station junction continue for 300 yards (250m), then turn L under the motorway viaduct.

Follow this road beside the River Dart for 3 miles (5km). After Velwell Farm and Higher Velwell Farm continue for 200 yards (180m), where the road bears L go through the gate on your R, just past a track. Keep the hedge on your L and go up the field, crossing stiles to pass through a wood. Follow the hedge on your L to the road. Turn L and after ¼ mile (400m), where there are two gates and a holly tree on the R, go through the first gate and follow the hedge to the bottom of the field. Go through the gap and follow the hedge on the R, through a gate and down a track to the road. Turn R, bear L over a bridge, bear L again and Dartington Hostel is 200 yards (180m) on your L.

• DAY FOUR •

Dartington to Maypool (10½ miles, 17km)

A pleasant, easy day's walking on footpaths and quiet Devon lanes. The day ends with a ferry

• LOCAL INTEREST •

The last great southern wilderness

Dartmoor National Park covers an area of 365 square miles (587km^2). It comprises moorland, bog, wooded valleys and high, windswept hills, some of which reach over 2000ft (608m). Many of the hills are topped with massive piles of granite eroded into stark shapes by centuries of weather, giving dark drama to the landscape. These are the famous tors of Dartmoor.

Humans have built settlements on the moor since prehistoric times and the evidence of stone huts, circles and forts is strewn throughout the area. Today the wilderness is fringed with comfortable market towns, while the core has isolated villages and the prison. But it is still wild, and vast tracts are used by the Army for firing ranges. The areas used have warning signs and red flags are put out on days when the firing ranges are in use.

Although the famous Dartmoor ponies live wild on the moor, they are rounded up once a year in the autumn and branded by local farmers. Some of them are sold, others return to the moor to survive the appalling winters. The ponies are known to have been on the moor for about 1000 years.

The moor was mined for copper, manganese, lead and tin during the Middle Ages. Tin continued to be mined until the twentieth century. Granite has always been quarried. Nelson's column in Trafalgar Square, London, is of Dartmoor granite.

The Dart Valley Railway

Dr Beeching closed the railway line between Totnes and Buckfastleigh in 1962. It took seven years of constant pressure by the Dart Valley Light Railway Company to allow them to operate a regular, private service on the line. Now summer visitors can enjoy the splendour of steam as the train wends its way through 7 miles (11km) of peaceful woodland beside the River Dart. The coaches are painted chocolate and cream, the livery of the Great Western Railway.

Clapper bridges

For centuries Dartmoor's rivers were crossed either by ford or by clapper bridge. Some of these ancient and distinctive bridges still stand, although more modern bridges have been built to take traffic. The walk passes three: Postbridge, Bellever and Dartmeet. The bridges are built of huge granite slabs piled on the river bed and topped with great flat sheets of rock. The clapper bridge at Postbridge is monumental and probably dates from the fourteenth century.

crossing from Dittisham to Maypool. You can travel from Totnes to Maypool by boat on a Dartmouth River Cruise. Phone Ridalls on Totnes 866125 and explain that you want to be dropped at Greenway Quay for Maypool Youth Hostel.

If you are walking, turn L on leaving the Hostel and follow the road for 300 yards (280m). Cross the A385 and go forward for about 1 mile (1.5km), heading for Totnes. Cross the A381 and take the road almost opposite. Pass under the railway bridge and immediately turn L. At the next junction bear R uphill, passing Totnes Castle on your R. At the T-junction turn L down Fore Street, along the pillared arcades of the Butterwalk.

At the mini roundabout near the river bridge turn R into The Plains. When the road bears R keep straight on and at the end of the buildings on the L continue through the timber yard on the quayside to the Steam Packet Inn. Walk round to the R of the inn and turn R up the road opposite the inn, then very shortly L along Sharpham Drive, signposted 'Footpath to Ashprington'.

The footpath runs above and roughly parallel to the river for about ¾ of a mile (1km). You will then cross a stile into an open field. Cross to another stile in the far L hand corner. After three more stiles the path veers closer to the river. Keep on the path past a wood and through a sheep enclosure and you will enter a track leading to Sharpham House. Long before the house can be seen keep a sharp lookout for a small stile on your R. Go over it and cross a steep field to another stile in the corner of a wood. Follow the path through the wood and on to where it joins the road. Turn R on the road for the village of Ashprington. Continue through the village, past The Durrant Arms and follow the road to cross the creek at Bow Bridge. Continue past two more pubs to reach Tuckenhay.

Immediately after passing the thatched cottages at the end of the village, turn L over a small stone bridge towards a group of houses. Take the track straight ahead of you, past the end house. Ignore steps to a stile on your L and come to a T-junction. Turn L and just after the next bend in the track turn sharp L off the main track. This path brings you high above a branch of Bow Creek, with Tuckenhay on the opposite bank. Continue along a well defined track which turns away from the creek to join the road at Court Prior. Turn L and follow the road for about 1½ miles (2.5km) to Dittisham.

If you have time explore the old village then make your way to the quayside (bear L at the Red Lion) and summon the boat to take you across the Dart by ringing the bell. The last boat in April and October is at 6pm but for most of the summer season it runs obligingly late.

Once over the water (this is where you should be dropped if you caught the cruiser from Totnes) follow the road up past Greenway for 1 mile (1.5km) and at the road junction turn R and follow the signpost for Maypool. The road runs straight into the drive leading to the Hostel.

• DAY FIVE •

Maypool to Paignton Station (8 miles, 13km)
and then public transport to Exeter.

A short walk to the coast where you can swim, and then a walk along the lovely South Devon Coastal Path.

Turn R out of the Hostel and shortly, by Higher Greenway farm come to a R turn opposite a pair of cottages. Turn R. The route has been waymarked, so follow the blue arrows or blue and yellow arrows for about 2 miles (3km), crossing two major roads and going through Churston. Go under the railway bridge just through the village and come to a T-junction.

Leave the waymarks here and turn R on the road for about 50 yards (46m), then turn L into a lane. You will walk counter to a set of red arrows coming in from the coast. The track ends at the entrance to a wood. Bear R across a field and follow the R hand hedge. At the fork take the gravelled path on the L through woods and down steps to Churston Cove and the sea.

The walk continues along the South Devon Coastal Path. It is clear to follow and you can join it at Churston Cove. Follow it to Paignton for marvellous views across Tor Bay. Paignton Station, where you can catch a train back to Exeter, is about 4 miles (6.5km) north of Churston Cove.

• PACK-FREE DAYS •

Dartington

Dartington is an excellent place to spend a second night as there are many places of interest within easy reach. You could take a day off from walking by catching the Dart Valley Railway from Staverton Bridge back to Buckfastleigh and visit Buckfast Abbey, a mile (1.5km) to the north. In 1907 Benedictine monks began to build the great abbey church as the centrepiece of their community. It was completed in 1937. It has some fine stained glass made by the monks. Today you can buy their famous tonic wine or their excellent honey. One monk is a world authority on beekeeping.

Dartington Hall is also well-worth visiting. It is a restored fourteenth-century manor house and superb garden above the River Dart. There are fine views along the valley to Totnes. The hall is a centre for Arts and excellent concerts are held regularly. Away from the main building is a craft centre where you can buy high quality crafts ranging from ceramics to toys and clothes made by some of Britain's top craftspeople.

Maypool

Brixham is a bus ride away from Maypool but once there you could walk some of the Coastal Path from Brixham, or explore the appealing harbour and town.

If you walked from Dartington to Maypool you could take a river cruise on the Dart as a relaxing break before the final day of the walk.

YOUTH HOSTEL INFORMATION

WINDERMERE TO AMBLESIDE
Ordnance Survey Outdoor Leisure Series sheet 7

Windermere Youth Hostel
High Cross
Bridge Lane, Troutbeck
Windermere
Cumbria LA23 1LA
Tel: Windermere (09662) 3543
Bus: Frequent buses from the surrounding area
Train: Windermere Station 2 miles (3km)

Hawkshead Youth Hostel
Esthwaite Lodge
Hawkshead
Ambleside
Cumbria LA22 0QD
Tel: Hawkshead (09666) 293
Bus: Ribble 505/15 from Ambleside (connections from BR Windermere) alight Hawkshead 1 mile (1.5km)
Train: Windermere 7 miles (11km), vehicle ferry

Coniston (Holly How) Youth Hostel
Holly How
Far End
Coniston
Cumbria LA21 8DD
Tel: Coniston (05394) 41323
Bus: Ribble 505 from Ambleside; Ribble 512 Ulverston–Coniston
Train: Frequent services from surrounding areas

High Close Youth Hostel
High Close
Loughrigg
Ambleside
Cumbria LA22 9HJ
Tel: Langdale (09667) 313
Bus: Ribble 516 from Ambleside (connections from BR Windermere), alight ¾ mile (1km) SE of Elterwater, then ¾ mile (1km)
Train: Windermere 10 miles (16km)

Ambleside Youth Hostel
Waterhead
Ambleside
Cumbria LA22 0EU
Tel: Ambleside (05394) 32304
Bus: Ribble service from surrounding areas
Train: Windermere 3 miles (5km)

WINDERMERE AND THE SHORES OF ULLSWATER
Ordnance Survey Outdoor Leisure Series sheets 5, 7

Grasmere (Butharlyp How) Youth Hostel
Grasmere
Ambleside
Cumbria LA22 9QG
Tel: Grasmere (09665) 316
Bus: Ribble 518, 555/7 Lancaster/Ulverston–Keswick, alight Grasmere ¼ mile (400m)
Train: Windermere 8½ miles (13.5km)

Patterdale Youth Hostel
Goldrill House
Patterdale
Penrith
Cumbria CA11 0NW
Tel: Glenridding (08532) 394
Bus: From Keswick and Windermere
Train: Penrith 15 miles (24km)

Grasmere (Thorney How) Youth Hostel
Thorney How
Grasmere
Ambleside
Cumbria LA22 9QW
Tel: Grasmere (09665) 591
Bus: As for Grasmere Butharlyp How
Train: Windermere 9 miles (14.5km)

NORTHERN LAKELAND
Ordnance Survey Outdoor Leisure Series sheet 4

Keswick Youth Hostel
Station Road
Keswick
Cumbria CA12 5LH
Tel: Keswick (07687) 72484
Bus: CMS 34/5 from Whitehaven (pass BR Workington) Ribble 555/8 from Lancaster (pass close BR Windermere)
Train: Penrith 18 miles (29km); Windermere 20 miles (32km)

Buttermere Youth Hostel
King George VI Memorial Hostel
Buttermere
Cockermouth
Cumbria CA13 9XA
Tel: Buttermere (059685) 245
Bus: From Keswick (May–Oct only)
Train: Workington 18 miles (29km)

Longthwaite Youth Hostel
Longthwaite
Keswick
Cumbria CA12 5XE
Tel: Borrowdale (059684) 257
Bus: CMS 79 from Keswick
Train: Workington 25 miles (40km); Penrith 26 miles (42km)

Derwentwater Youth Hostel
Barrow House
Borrowdale
Keswick
Cumbria CA12 5UR
Tel: Borrowdale (059684) 246
Bus: CMS 79 Keswick–Seatoller
Train: Penrith 20 miles (32km); Windermere 24 miles (38.5km)

HADRIAN'S WALL
Ordnance Survey Landranger sheets 86, 87

Alston Youth Hostel
The Firs
Alston
Cumbria CA9 3RW

Tel: Alston (0434) 381509
Bus: Wright Bros 681 from Haltwhistle
Train: Haltwhistle 15 miles (24km);
Penrith 19 miles (30.5km)

Ninebanks Youth Hostel
Orchard House
Mohope
Ninebanks
Hexham
Northumberland NE47 8DO
Tel: Haltwhistle (0434) 345288
Bus: Wright Bros BR Hexham–Alston,
alight Ouston 1 mile (1.5km)
Train: Haydon Bridge 11 miles (18km)

Once Brewed Youth Hostel
Once Brewed
Military Road
Bardon Mill
Hexham
Northumberland NE47 7AN
Tel: Bardon Mill (04984) 360
Bus: From Hexham, Haltwhistle (passes
BR Hexham and Haltwhistle) peak
summer only; Northumbria 685
Carlisle–Newcastle-upon-Tyne, alight
Henshaw 2 miles (3km)
Train: Bardon Mill 2½ miles (4km)

Greenhead Youth Hostel
Greenhead
Carlisle
Cumbria CA6 7HG
Tel: Gilsland (06972) 401
Bus: Northumbria 685 Carlisle–
Newcastle-upon-Tyne (passes BR
Haltwhistle)
Train: Haltwhistle 3 miles (5km)

Acomb Youth Hostel
Acomb
Hexham
Northumberland NE46 4PL
Tel: Hexham (0434) 602864
Bus: Tyne Valley 880–2 from Hexham
(passes BR Hexham); Northumbria 685,
X85 Carlisle–Newcastle-upon-Tyne,
alight Hexham 2½ miles (4km)
Train: Hexham 2 miles (3km)

THE NORTHERN WHITE PEAK
Ordnance Survey Outdoor Leisure
Series sheets 1, 24

Hathersage Youth Hostel
Castleton Road
Hathersage
Sheffield S30 1AH
Tel: Hope Valley (0433) 50493
Bus: South Yorks 272 from Sheffield
Train: Hathersage ½ mile (800m)

Edale Youth Hostel
Rowland Cote
Nether Booth
Edale
Sheffield S30 2ZH
Tel: Hope Valley (0433) 70302
Bus: No service
Train: Edale 2 miles (3km)

Castleton Youth Hostel
Castleton Hall
Castleton
Sheffield S30 2WG
Tel: Hope Valley (0433) 20235
Bus: South York/Trent 272 from Sheffield
(passes BR Hope)
Train: Hope 3 miles (5km)

Ravenstor Youth Hostel
Ravenstor
Miller's Dale
Buxton
Derbyshire SK17 8SS
Tel: Tideswell (0298) 871826
Bus: From Sheffield, Buxton (passes
close BR Sheffield and Buxton)
Train: Buxton 8 miles (13km)

Eyam Youth Hostel
The Edge
Eyam
Sheffield S30 1QP
Tel: Hope Valley (0433) 30335
Bus: Sheffield–Bretton; Sheffield–
Chesterfield–Buxton; Mansfield–
Chesterfield–Manchester–Liverpool;
alight Eyam
Train: Grindleford 3½ miles (5.5km);
Hathersage 4 miles (6.5km)

THE SOUTHERN WHITE PEAK
Ordnance Survey Outdoor Leisure
Series sheet 24

Ilam Hall Youth Hostel
Ilam Hall
Ashbourne
Derbyshire DE6 2AZ
Tel: Thorpe Cloud (033529) 212
Bus: From Derby, Manchester (passing
close BR Derby and Macclesfield),
alight Ilam Cross Roads 2½ miles (4km)
Train: Matlock 14 miles (22.5km);
Uttoxeter 15 miles (24km)

Youlgreave Youth Hostel
Fountain Square
Youlgreave
Bakewell
Derbyshire DE4 1UR

Tel: Youlgreave (0629) 636518
Bus: Silver Service 170, Chesterfield–
Matlock (passes close BR Chesterfield
and Matlock)
Train: Matlock 10 miles (16km)

Hartington Hall Youth Hostel
Hartington Hall
Hartington
Buxton
Derbyshire SK17 0AT
Tel: Hartington (029884) 223
Bus: Bowers 442 from BR Buxton
Train: Buxton 12 miles (19km); Matlock
13 miles (21km)

Bakewell Youth Hostel
Fly Hill
Bakewell
Derbyshire DE4 1DN
Tel: Bakewell (062981) 2313
Bus: Frequent from surrounding areas
Train: Matlock 8 miles (13km)

Matlock Youth Hostel
40, Bank Road
Matlock
Derbyshire DE4 3NF
Tel: Matlock (0629) 582983
Bus: Frequent from surrounding areas
Train: Matlock ¼ mile (400m)

THE DERBYSHIRE DALES
Ordnance Survey Outdoor Leisure
Series sheet 24

Matlock Youth Hostel
(see above)

Youlgreave Youth Hostel
(see above)

THE COAST AND NORTH YORK
MOORS
Ordnance Survey Outdoor Leisure
Series sheets 26, 27

Scarborough Youth Hostel
The White House
Burniston Road
Scarborough
North Yorkshire YO13 0DA
Tel: Scarborough (0723) 361176
Bus: Frequent from surrounding area
Train: Scarborough 2 miles (3km)

Boggle Hole Youth Hostel
Boggle Hole
Fyling Thorpe
Whitby
North Yorkshire YO22 4UQ

Tel: Whitby (0947) 880352
Bus: United 93A/B Scarborough–
Whitby (passes BR Whitby and
Scarborough, alight Robin Hoods Bay
1 mile (1.5km)
Train: Whitby (not Sun Oct–Apr) 7 miles
(11km); Scarborough 15 miles (24km)

Whitby Youth Hostel
East Cliff
Whitby
North Yorkshire YO22 4JT
Tel: Whitby (0947) 602878
Bus: Frequent from surrounding area
Train: Whitby (not Sun Oct–Apr) ½ mile
(800m)

Wheeldale Lodge Youth Hostel
Wheeldale Lodge
Goathland
North Yorkshire YO22 5AP
Tel: Whitby (0947) 86350
Bus: West Yorkshire 92 Malton–Whitby
(passes close BR Malton and Whitby),
alight near Goathland 2 miles (3km)
Train: Grosmont (not Sun Oct–Apr) 6
miles (9.5km); Grosmont (North
Yorkshire Moors Railway and
connecting with BR Grosmont) 3 miles
(5km)

Lockton Youth Hostel
The Old School
Lockton
Pickering
North Yorkshire YO18 7PY
Tel: (Warden) Pickering (0751)
60376
Bus: West Yorkshire 92 Whitby–Malton
(passes close BR Whitby and Malton)
Train: Malton 14 miles (22.5km);
Levisham (North Yorkshire Moors
Railway and connecting with BR at
Grosmont) 2 miles (3km)

THE EASTERN DALES
Ordnance Survey Landranger
sheets 91, 92, 98

Linton (Nr Grassington) Youth
Hostel
The Old Rectory
Skipton
North Yorkshire BD23 5HH
Tel: Grassington (0756) 752400
Bus: West Yorkshire 71/2 from Skipton
(passes close BR Skipton)
Train: Skipton 8 miles (13km)

Stainforth Youth Hostel
'Taitlands'
Stainforth
Settle
North Yorkshire BD24 9PA

Tel: Settle (07292) 3577
Bus: Whaites Settle–Horton
Train: Settle (not Sun Oct–Apr) 2½
miles (4km); Giggleswick 3 miles (5km)

Kettlewell Youth Hostel
Whernside House
Kettlewell
Skipton
North Yorkshire BD23 5QU
Tel: Kettlewell (075676) 232
Bus: As for Linton but alight Grassington
Train: Skipton 16 miles (25.5km)

Aysgarth Falls Youth Hostel
Aysgarth
Leyburn
North Yorkshire DL8 3SR
Tel: Aysgarth (09693) 260
Bus: Darlington–Hawes North East or
Lakes United Cumbrian Express
(summer only). West Yorkshire Dales
bus stop at Hostel.
Train: Darlington

Grinton Lodge Youth Hostel
Grinton
Richmond
North Yorkshire HG4 4PW
Tel: Richmond (0748) 84206
Bus: United 30 Richmond–Keld
(connections from BR Darlington), alight
Grinton ¾ miles (1km)
Train: Kirkby Stephen (exc Oct–Apr) 24
miles (38.5km); Darlington 25 miles
(40km)

Keld Youth Hostel
Keld Lodge
Richmond
North Yorkshire DL11 6LL
Tel: Richmond (0748) 86259
Bus: United 30 from Richmond,
connections from BR Darlington
(infrequent)
Train: Kirkby Stephen (not Sun Oct–
Apr) 11 miles (17.5km)

Hawes Youth Hostel
Lancaster Terrace
Hawes
North Yorkshire DL8 3LQ
Tel: Hawes (09697) 368
Bus: United 26 from Richmond,
connections from Darlington
(infrequent); Yorkshire Dales National
Park free bus from BR Garsdale in
summer
Train: Garsdale (not Sun Oct–Apr) 6
miles (9.5km). (The Settle to Carlisle
Railway might close in May 1989)

THE WESTERN DALES
Ordnance Survey Landranger
sheets 91, 92, 98

Malham Youth Hostel
John Dower Memorial Hostel
Malham
Skipton
North Yorkshire BD23 3DE
Tel: Airton (07293) 321
Bus: From Skipton (passes close BR
Skipton)
Train: Skipton 13 miles (21km)

Stainforth Youth Hostel
(see above)

Ingleton Youth Hostel
Greta Tower
Ingleton
Carnforth
Lancs LA6 3EG
Tel: Ingleton (05242) 41444
Bus: To Kendal, Lancaster, Settle (not
Sun); to Settle and Skipton daily; to
Lancaster and Settle daily
Train: Bentham 4 miles (6.5km);
Clapham 5 miles (8km)

Dentdale Youth Hostel
Cowgill
Dent
Sedburgh
Cumbria LA10 5RN
Tel: Dent (05875) 251
Bus: United 26 from Richmond
(connections BR Darlington), alight
Hawes, 8 miles (13km)
Train: Dent 2 miles (3km); Giggleswick
17½ miles (28km)

Hawes Youth Hostel
(see above)

Keld Youth Hostel
(see above)

Kirkby Stephen Youth Hostel
Fletcher Hill
Market Street
Kirkby Stephen
Cumbria CA17 4QQ
Tel: Kirkby Stephen (07683) 71793
Bus: No service
Train: Kirkby Stephen (not Sun Oct–
Apr) 1½ miles (2.5km)

SHROPSHIRE
Ordnance Survey Landranger
sheets 137, 138

Ludlow Youth Hostel
Ludford Lodge
Ludford
Ludlow
Shropshire SY8 1PJ

Tel: Ludlow (0584) 2472
Bus: Each hour from Birmingham, Shrewsbury and Hereford Midland Red West X92, 292 Birmingham–Hereford to within ½ mile (800m)
Train: Ludlow ¾ mile (1km)

Wheathill Youth Hostel
Malthouse Farm
Bridgenorth
Shropshire WV16 6QT
Tel. Burwarton (074633) 236
Bus: Infrequent from Ludlow, alight Three Horseshoes, 1 mile (1.5km); Midland Red West X92, 292 Hereford–Birmingham, alight Hopton Bank 5 miles (8km)
Train: Ludlow 9 miles (14.5km)

Wilderhope Manor Youth Hostel
The John Cadbury Memorial Hostel
Easthope
Much Wenlock
Shropshire TF13 6EG
Tel: Longville (06943) 363
Bus: No service
Train: Church Stretton 8 miles (13km)

Bridges Youth Hostel
Bridges
Ratlinghope
Shrewsbury SY5 0SP
Tel: Linley (058861) 656
Bus: Williamsons – Pulverbatch 4 miles (6.5km); Midland Red – Church Stretton 5 miles (8km)
Train: Church Stretton 5 miles (8km)

Clun Mill Youth Hostel
The Mill
Clun
Craven Arms
Shropshire SY7 8NY
Tel: Clun (05884) 582
Bus: Midland Red West 262–5 from Ludlow alight Clun ¼ mile (400m)
Train: Broome (not Sun Oct–Apr) 7 miles (11km); Craven Arms 10 miles (16km)

SNOWDONIA
Ordnance Survey Outdoor Leisure Series sheet 17

Llanberis Youth Hostel
Llwyn Celyn
Llanberis
Caernarfon
Gwynedd LL55 4SR

Tel: Llanberis (0286) 870280
Bus: Bws Gwynedd 88/89 from Caernarfon or 77 from Bangor (passes close BR Bangor), alight ½ mile (800m) NW of Llanberis; coach and mini bus hire from Llanberis village
Train: Bangor 11 miles (17.5km)

Snowdon Ranger Youth Hostel
Snowdon Ranger
Rhyd Ddu
Caernarfon
Gwynedd LL54 7YS
Tel: Waunfawr (028685) 391
Bus: Bws Gwynedd 11 fom Caernarfon (connections from BR Bangor)
Train: Bangor 16 miles (26km)

Bryn Gwynant Youth Hostel
Bryn Gwynant
Nant Gwynant
Caernarfon
Gwynedd LL55 4NP
Tel: Beddgelert (076686) 251
Bus: Bws Gwynedd 97 Porthmadog-Bethgelert, alight Bethgelert, thence 4 miles (6.5km); service extended to Llanrwst (passing the Hostel and BR Betws-y-Coed) summer only
Train: Betws-y-Coed (not Sun, except by Gwynedd CC peak shuttle) 13 miles (21km); Bangor 25 miles (40km)

Capel Curig Youth Hostel
Plas Curig
Capel Curig
Betws-y-Coed
Gwynedd LL24 0EL
Tel: Capel Curig (06904) 225
Bus: Bws Gwynedd 95/97 from Porthmadog, Llandudno, Bangor and Llanrwst (passes BR Betws-y-Coed, Bangor and Llandudno Junction and BR and Ffestiniog Rly Porthmadog) summer only
Train: Betwys-y-Coed (not Sun, except by Gwynedd CC peak shuttle)

Idwal Cottage Youth Hostel
Idwal Cottage
Nant Pfancon
Bethesda
Bangor
Gwynedd LL57 3LZ
Tel: Bethesda (0248) 600225
Bus: Bws Gwynedd 95, Llandudno–Llanrwst (summer only) passes BR Betws-y-Coed and Conwy; otherwise Bws Gwynedd 6/7 from Bangor (passes BR Bangor), alight Bethesda 4 miles (6.5km)
Train: Bangor 12 miles (19.5km); Betws-y-Coed 11 miles (not Sun, except by Gwynedd CC peak shuttle)

MOUNTAINS AND RIVERS AROUND LLANGOLLEN
Ordnance Survey Landranger sheets 116, 117, 125, 126

Llangollen YHA Field Study and Activity Centre
Tyndwr Hall
Tyndwr Road
Llangollen
Clwyd LL20 8AR
Tel: Llangollen (0978) 860330
Bus: From Wrexham (passes close BR Ruabon), alight Llangollen 1½ miles (2.5km); main bus services provided by Crosville (Wales)
Train: Chirk 5 miles (8km); Ruabon 5 miles (8km)

Cynwyd Youth Hostel
The Old Mill
Cynwyd
Corwen
Clwyd LL21 0LW
No telephone at Hostel
Bus: Bws Gwynedd 94 Wrexham–Barmouth (passes close BR Ruabon and Barmouth)
Train: Ruabon 18 miles (29km)

LONELY ELENITH
Ordnance Survey Landranger sheet 147

Bryn Poeth Uchaf Youth Hostel
Hafod-y-Pant
Cynghordy
Llandovery
Dyfed SA20 0NB
Tel: Cynghordy (05505) 235
Bus: No service
Train: Cynghordy (not Sun) 2¼ miles (3.5km)

Ty'n-y-cornel Youth Hostel
Glantuen
Ystumtuen
Aberystwyth
Dyfed SY23 3AE
Tel: Ponterwyd (097085) 693
Bus: Crosville Cymru/Roberts S1 from Aberystwyth (passes BR Aberystwyth), alight 1 mile (1.5km) west of Ponterwyd 1½ miles (2.5km)
Train: Rhiwfron (seasonal service only) 2 miles (3km); Aberystwyth (not Sun Oct–Apr)

THE PEMBROKESHIRE COASTAL PATH
Ordnance Survey Landranger sheets 145, 157

Marloes Sands Youth Hostel
Runwaysklin
Marloes
Haverfordwest
Dyfed SA62 3BH
Tel: Dale (06465) 667 or 662
Bus: From Haverfordwest or Milford
Haven to Marloes (infrequent, not daily)
1 mile (1.5km)
Train: Milford Haven 11 miles (17.5km);
Haverfordwest 14 miles (22.5km)

Broad Haven Youth Hostel
Broad Haven
Haverfordwest
Dyfed SA62 3JH
Tel: Broad Haven (0437) 781 688
Bus: Edwardes 311 from Haverfordwest
(passes close BR Haverfordwest)
Train: Haverfordwest 7 miles (11km)

St David's Youth Hostel
Llaethdy
St David's
Haverfordwest
Dyfed SA62 6PR
Tel: St David's (0437) 720345
Bus: Richards 340 from BR
Haverfordwest or 411 from Fishguard,
alight St David's on both, 2 miles (3km)
Train: Fishguard Harbour 15 miles
(24km); Haverfordwest 18 miles (29km)

Trevine Youth Hostel
11 Pfordd-yr-Afon
Trevine
Haverfordwest
Dyfed SA62 5AU
Tel: Croesgoch (03483) 414
Bus: Richards 411 from Fishguard
(passes close BR Fishguard Harbour,
connections from BR Haverfordwest on
412)
Train: Fishguard Harbour 12 miles
(19.5km); Haverfordwest 18 miles
(29km)

Pwll Deri Youth Hostel
Castell Mawr
Tref Asser
Goodwick
Dyfed SA64 0LR
Tel: St Nicholas (03485) 233
Bus: Richards 410/11 Fishguard–
Goodwick (connections from BR
Haverfordwest) alight Goodwick, 4
miles (6.5km)
Train: Fishguard Harbour 4½ miles
(7km)

Poppit Sands Youth Hostel
'Sea View'
Poppit
Cardigan
Dyfed SA43 3LP

Tel: Cardigan (0239) 612936
Bus: Richards 403/9 from Cardigan to
within ½ mile (800m) (Jul, Aug only) but
to Dogmaels, 2 miles (3km) at other
times
Train: Fishguard Harbour 20 miles
(32km); Carmarthen 26 miles (42km)

THE RIDGEWAY
Ordnance Survey Landranger
sheets 163, 165, 173, 174, 175

Ivinghoe Youth Hostel
The Old Brewery House
Ivinghoe
Leighton Buzzard
Beds LU7 9EP
Tel: (0296) 668251
Bus: 61 Aylesbury–Luton (passes close
BR Aylesbury and Luton); 505 Express
coach, Oxford–Cambridge
Train: Tring 3 miles (5km)

Bradenham Youth Hostel
The Village Hall
High Wycombe
Bucks
Tel: Naphill (024024) 2929
Bus: Beeline X14/15 High Wycombe–
Princes Risborough (passes close BR
High Wycombe and Princes
Risborough), alight Bradenham
Train: Saunderton (except Sun) 1¼
miles (2km) High Wycombe 4½ miles
(7km)

Streatley on Thames Youth Hostel
Hill House
Reading Road
Streatley
Reading
Berks RG8 9JJ
Tel: Goring on Thames (0491)
872278
Bus: Oxford/Beeline 5, Reading–Oxford
Train: Goring and Streatley 1 mile (1.5km)

The Ridgeway Youth Hostel
The Court Hill Ridgeway Centre
Court Hill
Wantage
Oxfordshire OX13 9NE
Tel: Wantage (02357) 60253
Bus: South Midland 302 from Oxford
(passes close BR Didcot Parkway),
alight Wantage 2 miles (3km)
Train: Didcot Parkway 10 miles (16km);
Hungerford 12 miles (19km)

Inglesham Youth Hostel
'Littlehome'
Upper Inglesham
Highworth
Swindon
Wilts SN6 7QY

Tel: Faringdon (0367) 52546
Bus: Thamesdown 77, Swindon–
Cirencester; Swanbrook 64, Swindon–
Burford; both pass close BR Swindon
Train: Swindon 9 miles (14.5km)

FORESTS AND MARSHES OF
SUFFOLK
Ordnance Survey Landranger
sheet 156

Blaxhall Youth Hostel
Heath Walk
Blaxhall
Woodbridge
Suffolk IP12 2EA
Tel: Snape (0728) 88206
Bus: Eastern Counties 80–82 Ipswich–
Aldeburgh (passes close BR
Saxmundham), alight ½ miles SW of
Stratford St Andrew 2 miles (3km)
Train: Wickham Market 3 miles (5km);
Saxmundham 5 miles (8km)

THROUGH THE VALLEY OF THE
EVENLODE
Ordnance Survey Landranger
sheets 163, 164

Charlbury Youth Hostel
The Laurels
The Slade
Charlbury
Oxford OX7 3SJ
Tel: Charlbury (0608) 810202
Bus: Local service only
Train: Charlbury 1 mile (1.5km)

Stow-on-the-Wold Youth Hostel
Stow-on-the-Wold
Cheltenham
Glos GL54 1AF
Tel: (0451) 30497
Bus: Pulhams Cheltenham Spa–
Moreton-in-Marsh
Train: Kingham 4 miles (6.5km);
Moreton-in-Marsh 4 miles (6.5km)

THE SOUTH DOWN WAY
Ordnance Survey Landranger
sheets 197, 198, 199

Alfriston Youth Hostel
Frog Firle
Alfriston
Polegate
East Sussex BN26 5TT
Tel: Alfriston (0323) 870423
Bus: Southdown 126 Eastbourne–
Seaford (passes close BR Seaford and
Polegate)
Train: Seaford 3 miles (5km); Berwick 3
miles (5km)

Telscombe Youth Hostel
Bank Cottage
Telscombe
Lewes
East Sussex BN7 3HZ
Tel: Brighton (90273) 37077
Bus: Brighton & Hove 14/A from
Brighton (passes close BR Brighton),
alight Heathy Brow ¾ mile (1km)
Train: Southease 2½ miles (4km);
Lewes 6½ miles (10.5km); Brighton 7
miles (11km)

Brighton Youth Hostel
Patcham Place
Brighton BN1 8YD
Tel: Brighton (0273) 556196
Bus: Brighton & Hove 773 Brighton–
Gatwick airport (passes close BR
Preston Park)
Train: Preston Park 2 miles (3km);
Brighton 3½ miles (5.5km)

Truleigh Hill Youth Hostel
Tottington Barn
Truleigh Hill
Shoreham-by-Sea
West Sussex BN4 5FB
Tel: Steyning (0903) 813419
Bus: Brighton & Hove 20/A from BR
Shoreham-by-Sea, alight ½ mile (800m)
south of Upper Beeding, 1¾ miles
(2.5km) by bridlepath
Train: Shoreham-by-Sea 4 miles (6.5km)

Sefton Place Youth Hostel
Warningcamp
Arundel
West Sussex BN18 9QY
Tel: Arundel (0903) 882204
Bus: Southdown 212 from Worthing,
alight BR Arundel 1 mile (1.5km)
Train: Arundel 1 mile (1.5km)

ABOVE THE KENTISH WEALD
Ordnance Survey Landranger
sheets 187, 188

Crockham Hill Youth Hostel
Crockham Hill House
Crockham Hill
Edenbridge
Kent TN8 6RB
Tel: Edenbridge (0732) 866322
Bus: No service
Train: Edenbridge 2 miles (3km);
Edenbridge Town (not Sun) 3 miles
(5km); Oxted 3 miles (5km); Hurst
Green 3 miles (5km)

Kemsing Youth Hostel
Cleves
Pilgrim's Way
Kemsing
Sevenoaks
Kent TN15 6LT
Tel: Sevenoaks (0732) 61341
Bus: Kentish Bus 25/6 from Sevenoaks
(passes close BR Sevenoaks), alight
Kemsing Post Office 250 yards (230m)
Train: Kemsing (not Sun) 1½ miles
(2.5km); Otford 1¾ miles (2.5km)

WESSEX: TRACKS AND DOWNS
Ordnance Survey Landranger
sheets 184, 195

Salisbury Youth Hostel
Milford Hill House
Salisbury
Wiltshire SP1 2QW
Tel: Salisbury (0722) 27572
Bus: Frequent from surrounding areas
Train: Salisbury 1 mile (1.5km)

Cranborne Youth Hostel
2, Crane Street
Cranborne
Wimborne
Dorset BH21 5QD
Tel: Cranborne (07254) 285
Bus: From Fordingbridge (connects
from close BR Salisbury)
Train: Salisbury 15 miles (24km)

WESSEX BY THE SEA
Ordnance Survey Landranger
sheets 193, 194

Bridport Youth Hostel
West Rivers House
West Allington
Bridport
Dorset DT6 5BW
Tel: Bridport (0308) 22655
Bus: Southern National 31/X31
Weymouth–Taunton (passes close BR
Dorchester South and West)
Train: Axminster 11 miles (17.5km);
Dorchester South and West 15 miles
(24km)

Litton Cheney Youth Hostel
Litton Cheney
Dorchester
Dorset DTZ 9AT
Tel: Long Brady (03083) 340
Bus: Southern National 31/X31
Weymouth–Taunton, alight Whiteway
1½ miles (2.5km)
Train: Dorchester South or West 10
miles (16km)

DEVON HILLS AND DARTMOOR
Ordnance Survey Landranger
sheets 191, 192, 202

Exeter Youth Hostel
47, Countess Wear Road
Exeter
Devon EX2 6LR
Tel: Topsham (039287) 3329
Bus: Exeter City Services K, L, T (pass
close BR Exeter Central), alight
Countess Wear Post Office ¼ mile
(400m)
Train: Topsham 2 miles (3km); Exeter
Central 3 miles (5km); Exeter St Davids
4 miles (6.5km)

Steps Bridge Youth Hostel
Steps Bridge
Dunsford
Exeter EX6 7EQ
Tel: Christow (0647) 52435
Bus: Devon General 359 from Exeter
(passes close BR Exeter Central)
Train: Exeter Central 9 miles (14.5km);
Exeter St Davids 9 miles (14.5km)

Bellever Youth Hostel
Bellever
Postbridge
Yelverton
Devon PL20 6TU
Tel: Tavistock (0822) 88227
Bus: Devon Central 359 from Exeter
(passes close BR Exeter Central), alight
Chagford 9 miles (14.5km)
Train: Newton Abbott 19 miles (30.5km)

Dartington Youth Hostel
Lownard
Dartington
Totnes
Devon TQ9 6JJ
Tel: Totnes (0803) 862303
Bus: Western National X80 Torquay–
Plymouth (passes BR Paignton and
Totnes), alight Shinner's Bridge ½ mile
(800m)
Train: Totnes 2 miles (3km); Staverton
(Dart Valley Railway) 1½ miles (2.5km)

Maypool Youth Hostel
Maypool
Galmpton
Brixham
Devon TQ5 0ET
Tel: Churlston (0803) 842444
Bus: Devon General 22 BR Paignton–
Brixham, alight Churston Pottery 2
miles (3km)
Train: Paignton 5 miles (8km); Churston
(Dart Valley Railway) 2 miles (3km)

PREPARATION FOR A LONG WALKING TRIP

A long walking trip needs to be planned carefully in advance if it is to be a success. Lack of planning usually results in lack of enjoyment.

• FITNESS •

The trip will involve walking for a number of days without a break, or at best with only an occasional rest day, with a fairly heavy rucksack. This is much more demanding than most people imagine, and it is important therefore to make some effort to become reasonably fit before the start. This is best done by taking long day walks or – better still – weekend walking trips carrying the kind of loads that will be taken on the main trip. This will improve fitness and, at the same time, be a good test of the equipment. In particular, it is important to make sure that boots are well-broken in before the start.

• BOOKING THE HOSTEL •

Some Hostels – particularly those in popular areas in the summer – become fully booked well in advance. Make sure, therefore, that bookings are made in good time. In arranging the Hostels it is important to be realistic and to be reasonably confident that a schedule can be maintained. The *YHA Accommodation Guide* is a mine of information about the facilities available at each Hostel. Remember that they are normally closed for some periods of the year and usually for one night each week at other times – this will have to be taken into account when arranging your programme. The meals supplied by Hostels are very good and at reasonable prices; the evening meal is usually served at a fixed time, however, and it is important to be sure that the Hostel can be reached by then (a cafeteria type service is offered at some Hostels which gives greater flexi-bility in meal times). If you prefer to prepare your own meals then make sure the hostel has a store or that you can obtain food locally.

• EQUIPMENT •

Equipment should be in a sound condition so that it will not fail during the trip. It may be difficult to obtain replacements or to have it repaired once you are on your way.

The following personal equipment and clothing will be necessary for a long distance trip in summer using Youth Hostels:
Boots (there is a wide variety of specialist walking boots available; obtain advice from a reputable supplier of outdoor equipment)
Thick woollen stockings
Walking breeches or thick trousers (not jeans)
Shorts (for hot days; but *in addition* to trousers or breeches, not *instead of*)
Waterproofs (anorak/cagoule and overtrousers)
Long-sleeved sweater(s)
Woollen hat (even in summer for high level routes) and/or light sun hat (for very sunny days)
Map, guidebook, compass and map case
Water or drink container
Whistle (for mountainous areas)
Light clothes and footwear (for evening wear in the Hostel)
Sheet sleeping bag (these may be hired at Hostels or two sheets and a pillow case
Nightwear
Towel, soap and other toiletries
Spare underclothes, shirt(s) and socks
Spare handkerchiefs
High energy emergency food (for emergencies and not to be eaten on the first day!)
First aid kit
A bivi-bag (for mountainous country)
Spare bootlaces and some repair materials

YHA membership card (there is a special membership concession scheme for groups)

Pen and paper (for those vital notes/addresses and postcards home!)

Camera (for those memorable moments!)

Rucksack (a backpacking type with padded shoulder straps and wide hip belt; obtain advice from a reputable supplier)

Choose your clothing and equipment carefully, keeping the overall weight as low as possible. You will not need, for example, to carry spare underclothes, shirts/blouses, socks and handkerchiefs for the whole trip as facilities are available in Hostels for washing them.

• PACKING THE RUCKSACK •

Remember that rucksacks are rarely waterproof and a large thick plastic bag should be used as an inner liner. When packing the contents bear in mind two rules: **1.** Put the heaviest articles to the top and close to the back, and **2.** arrange them so that you can reach articles quickly and easily when you need them. (For group equipment see the section 'Leading a party'.)

• SAFETY ON THE HILLS •

Although the altitude of British mountains is fairly low, they should never be underestimated. It is an unfortunate fact that some deaths occur each year on mountains and moorlands in Britain, a proportion of which are certainly due to carelessness and lack of preparation. Care is necessary at all times of the year, although the dangers which arise from the shorter days, lower temperatures and snow or ice conditions of winter are obviously much greater. The price paid for ignoring this can be a great deal of hardship – even, possibly, the loss of life – to yourself, and to others, such as Mountain Rescue teams, who may become involved.

It cannot be emphasised too strongly that weather conditions can change very rapidly in mountain areas; during the day, for example, or from one part of a mountain to another or as you climb to higher ground. Always bear this in mind when you are selecting your clothing and equipment before you start out at the beginning of a day.

Some golden rules for safety in mountain and moorland areas are:

DO:

Carry appropriate clothing and equipment, all of which should be in a sound condition.

Carry an appropriate map and a compass and be competent in their use.

Plan your route carefully in advance, allowing a wide safety margin for time. Take care not to overestimate your own capabilities.

Leave a note of your intended route with a responsible person (and keep to it – unless you need to use an escape route in an emergency if, for example, weather conditions deteriorate suddenly and severely).

Report your return as soon as possible.

Keep warm – but not too hot – at all times.

Eat nourishing foods and rest at regular intervals. Avoid becoming exhausted.

Know First Aid and the correct procedure in case of accidents, illness and emergency bivouacs.

Obtain a weather forecast before you start out. This can be obtained by telephone from Weathercall – obtain the number from Directory Enquiries.

DO NOT:

Go out on your own unless you are very experienced; four is a good number for a party.

Leave any member of the party behind unless help has to be obtained.

Explore old mine workings or caves, or climb cliffs (except scrambling ridges).

Attempt routes which are beyond your skill and experience.

Be afraid to turn back if weather conditions worsen.

It is possible, however, that despite these rules you or a member of your party will meet with an accident or you may find someone who has had an accident. In such cases the procedure to be followed will depend to some extent upon the circumstances of the particular incident, but briefly and in general it is as follows: Ensure that the patient is safe and then apply whatever First Aid you are able to give. If the injured person is capable of walking without making the injury worse and of reaching the destination before night draws in, then proceed slowly and carefully down to a house or village where further attention can be given. If the person cannot walk then ensure that he or she is safe, warm and protected.

Give the International Distress Signal. This is six blasts on a whistle (or six shouts or flashes of a torch) repeated after an interval of one minute. Keep giving this signal. The reply is three blasts and a pause of one minute before repeating.

If no help arrives then ideally two people should go for help leaving one behind with the patient, but this will obviously depend upon the size of the party. Whoever goes for help should take a written note of the exact position of the patient(s), the details of the accident, the number of people who will need attention and the extent of the injuries and proceed down to the nearest telephone (*i.e.* nearest in terms of time and not distance) where the police should be contacted by dialling 999. They will then take charge of the rescue operations.

A recommended booklet, which gives more detailed information, is *Safety on Mountains* by the British Mountaineering Council.

• LEADING A PARTY •

Group leaders should be adult, adequately clothed and equipped and capable of leading the party safely over the route by virtue of their personal qualities, skill and experience. In particular, in the case of those intending to take parties into mountainous areas, *i.e.* wild country where walkers are dependent on themselves and remote from any immediate help, they should have satisfactorily completed the full requirements of the Mountainwalking Leader Training Scheme (Summer) (Crawford House, Precinct Centre, Booth Street East, Manchester M13 9RZ) or be conversant with and competent in all aspects of the syllabus for the Scheme. It should be noted that this Scheme is not applicable to walking in the United Kingdom in winter conditions. Those interested in leading parties on the high ground under winter conditions should contact the Scottish Mountain Leader Training Board (The Scottish Sports Council, Caledonia House, South Gyle, Edinburgh EH12 9DQ) for information on their Winter Mountain Leader Scheme. The information given below is also only applicable to summer conditions.

Group leaders should have followed the route already on a previous occasion so that they are familiar with it and capable of leading a party along it. In mountainous country, in addition to the route itself, they should also have a good knowledge of the local terrain with the location of assistance facilities and possible bad weather alternatives/escape routes.

Equipment. Apart from their own personal equipment, all leaders should carry:
A First Aid kit (A more comprehensive kit is required for routes in mountainous country than for other walks)
Money for telephones and a list of appropriate contact numbers in case of difficulty
The relevant map and a compass
Suitable pen or pencil and paper
Bivi-bag
Spare warm clothing
Hot drink or a method of making one
Knife
Watch
In addition to these, in mountainous areas a leader should also carry:
A whistle and torch (with spare bulb and battery)
High energy foods for use in emergencies
45m length of 9mm kernmantel climbing rope
The leader should, of course, be fully conversant with the use of all equipment, and in particular with the First Aid kit, map, compass and rope.

Size of party. Even for low level routes the party should be no larger than 15 people for each leader. For routes in mountainous areas this should be reduced to six people per leader. With groups of children there should always be at least two adults in the party.

For all walks the leader must:
Leave a route plan with the Youth Hostel Warden to facilitate action if the party is overdue.
Obtain a local weather forecast and take it into account before the party sets out.
Ensure that the walk is well within the capabilities of each member of the party. In particular, a leader taking a party into mountainous country should ensure that all members have previous walking experience. It is emphasised that the route chosen should not require the pre-planned

use of the rope, which is for emergency use only, *e.g.* where someone is having difficulties with the terrain.

Know about any relevant medical problems and disabilities of the party members and take them into account.

Ensure that all members of the party have adequate clothing and equipment.

Ensure that all members of the party are familiar with the Country Code, Mountain Code and as appropriate, 'The road user on foot' section of the current edition of the Highway Code.

Ensure that all members are aware of the procedures to be followed in the event of emergencies.

Before starting brief all members of the party on the plan for the day and the route to be followed.

Ensure that the speed of the party is kept at all times within the capabilities of the slowest member.

Make sure that the party always stays together and that on no account does any member ever become detached from it.

Ensure that the members of the party behave correctly on all types of terrain.

Watch for signs of distress, such as caused by illness, over-tiredness, heat disorders or Mountain Hypothermia (exposure), and take prompt and correct action if any are observed.

Respond to changing weather conditions.

If possible, contact the Youth Hostel Warden if there is any change in the route or the expected time of arrival.

A highly recommended book is *Mountaincraft and Leadership* by Eric Langmuir, which is the official handbook of the Mountain Leader Training Boards of Great Britain and Northern Ireland.

• MAP READING •

The most valuable maps for walkers are: **1.** Landranger, **2.** Pathfinder and **3.** Outdoor Leisure, all produced by the Ordnance Survey. The first of these has a scale of 1:50,000 (one centimetre on the map represents 50,000 centimetres on the ground), while the others have a scale of 1:25,000. Landranger maps, which cover the whole of England, Scotland and Wales, are readily available and widely used. Pathfinder maps have been published for most of that area, but Outdoor Leisure maps are restricted to popular areas such as Snowdonia. Pathfinder and Outdoor Leisure maps, although much more expensive on an area basis, give greater detail – in particular, field boundaries – than the Landranger.

Setting a map. When using a map to follow a route the best method is to hold it so that the features on it are in the same direction to each other as are the features on the ground. This is known as 'setting the map' (*see* figure 1, overleaf). It is much easier to follow a route this way than if the map is held in the normal reading position. The map has to be held in a different position, however, each time a change of direction is made.

Taking a compass bearing. This is an essential skill in map reading when large areas of featureless country, such as moorlands, have to be crossed. The method using a typical compass is shown in figure 2 (overleaf). **1.** The compass is placed so that one of the long edges of the base plate joins your position to the point that you want to reach, with the large arrow pointing in the direction that you want to travel. **2.** The compass housing is then rotated until the orienting lines are parallel with the grid lines on the map and the orienting arrow (*i.e.* N on the housing) points to the top of the map (see **a**). **3.** For accuracy a small correction, known as the Grid-magnetic Variation, has to be added; the value of this is given on each map. For example, if the variation is 6° West then the housing is rotated anti-clockwise to increase the angle given on the housing by 6°. **4.** The compass is now held with the needle pointing to N on the housing; the large arrow then points in the direction that should be followed (see **b**). The reading on the housing is called a magnetic bearing.

Maps can be used for many other purposes, however. For example, distances can be measured by 'working' a length of string along the route, with a strip of paper by marking off the route along the edge, or with a special instrument called a map measurer. The amount of climbing involved on a route or the steepness of slopes can be estimated. They can even be used to determine if you can see particular features from a hilltop! The ability to 'read a map' is undoubtedly the most valuable skill that a walker can possess.

FIGURE 1 Setting a map

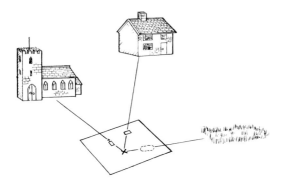

FIGURE 2 Taking a compass bearing

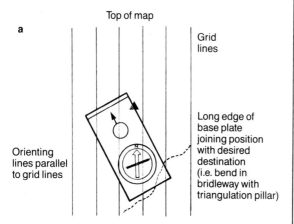

a

Top of map

Grid
lines

Orienting
lines parallel
to grid lines

Long edge of
base plate
joining position
with desired
destination
(i.e. bend in
bridleway with
triangulation pillar)

b

Direction
of travel

Compass needle
now points to
N on housing

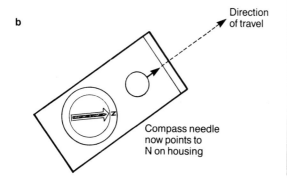

• GIVING A GRID REFERENCE •

Giving a grid reference is an excellent way of 'pin-pointing' a feature, such as a church or mountain summit, on an Ordnance Survey map.

Grid lines, which are used for this purpose, are shown on the 1:25,000 Pathfinder, 1:25,000 Outdoor Leisure and 1:50,000 Landranger maps produced by the Ordnance Survey; these are the maps most commonly used by walkers. On these maps the grid lines are the thin blue lines one kilometre apart going horizontally and vertically across the map producing a network of small squares. Each line, whether vertical or horizontal, is given a number from 00 to 99, with the sequence repeating itself every 100 lines. The 00 lines are slightly thicker than the others, thus producing large squares with sides made up of 100 small squares and thus representing 100 kilometres. Each of these large squares is identified by two letters. The entire network of lines covering the British Isles, excluding Ireland, is called the National Grid.

FIGURE 3 Giving a grid reference

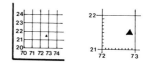

The diagram above shows a corner of an Ordnance Survey 1:50,000 Landranger map which contains a Youth Hostel. Using this map the method of determining a grid reference is as follows:

Step 1.
Holding the map in the normal upright position, note the number of the 'vertical' grid line to the left of the Hostel. This is 72..
Step 2.
Now imagine that the space between this grid line and the adjacent one to the right of the Hostel is divided into ten equal divisions (the diagram on the right does this for you). Estimate the number of these 'tenths' that the Hostel lies to the right of the left-hand grid line. This is 8. Add this to the number found in Step 1 to make 728.

Step 3.
Note the number of the grid line below the Hostel and add it to the number obtained above. This is 21, so that the number becomes 72821.
Step 4.
Repeat Step 2 for the space containing the hostel, but now in a vertical direction. The final number to be added is 5, making 728215. This is called a six figure grid reference. This, coupled with the number or name of the appropriate Landranger or Outdoor Leisure map, will enable the Youth Hostel to be found.

A full grid reference will include the identification of the appropriate 100 kilometre square of the National Grid; for example SD 728215. The identification letters of the 100 kilometre square or squares on the map is given in the margin.

• COUNTRYSIDE ACCESS CHARTER •

Your rights of way are
Public footpaths – on foot only. Sometimes way-marked in yellow.
Bridleways – on foot, horseback and pedal cycle. Sometimes waymarked in blue.
Byways (usually old roads), most 'Roads Used as Public Paths' and, of course, public roads – all traffic.
Use maps, signs and waymark. Ordnance Survey Pathfinder and Landranger maps show most public rights-of-way.

On rights of way you can
Take a pram, pushchair or wheelchair if practicable.
Take a dog (on a lead or under close control).
Take a short route round an illegal obstruction or remove it sufficiently to get past.

You have a right to go for recreation to
Public parks and open spaces – on foot.
Most commons near older towns and cities – on foot and sometimes on horseback.
Private land where the owner has a formal agreement with the local authority.

In addition you can use by local or established custom or consent, but ask for advice if you are unsure
Many areas of open country like moorland, fell and coastal areas, especially those of the National Trust, and some commons.
Some woods and forests, especially those owned by the Forestry Commission.
Country Parks and picnic sites.
Most beaches.
Canal towpaths
Some private paths and tracks. Consent sometimes extends to riding horses and pedal cycles.

For your information
County councils and London boroughs maintain and record rights-of-way and register commons. Obstructions, dangerous animals, harassment and misleading signs on rights-of-way are illegal and you should report them to the county council. Paths across fields can be ploughed, but must normally be reinstated within two weeks.
Landowners can require you to leave land to which you have no right of access.
Motor vehicles are normally permitted only on roads, byways and some 'Roads used as Public Paths'.
Follow any local by-laws.

And, wherever you go, follow the Country Code
Enjoy the countryside and respect its life and work.
Guard against all risk of fire.
Fasten all gates.
Keep your dog under close control.
Keep to public paths across farmland.
Use gates and stiles to cross fences, hedges and walls.
Leave livestock, crops and machinery alone.
Take your litter home.
Help to keep all water clean.
Protect wildlife, plants and trees.
Take special care on country roads.
Make no unnecessary noise.

This charter is for practical guidance in England and Wales only. It was prepared by the Countryside Commission.

INDEX

Page numbers in italics refer to illustrations